Belligerants

Belliger*ants*

Things You Never Knew You Need to Know

by Peter Brinday &
Ray Walker

Contents

Don't Read This Introduction

Introductions are boring and they suck. Why should this be different? Sorry.

Flip right past. There's nothing in advance you need to know.

Just that you'll notice a mix of British and Canadian spellings, idioms and references, because Peter lives in England and Ray in Canada. So?

And that Ray grew up in Sudbury, a bleak, northern Ontario mining town unfairly maligned herein, whilst Tuvalu, another real place, is as delightful as we imagine. Who cares?

And that Peter has a peculiar obsession with scorpions and dolphins and septic tanks, Ray with dung beetles and kidney stones. Some things have no explanation, like Yoko 'music', or presidential hair, or hipsters, or hummus, or meetings, with no real pertinence here or anywhere other than that they appear to animate the authors to a disturbing degree. What's the point?

Maybe it's that, in an anxious world fraught with woe, a little mockery is the best balm, as long as it starts with ourselves. If the one thing we know for sure is that we're all ridiculous, at least then we can be laughable together. Right?

And if in any way you made the road even rougher for the rest of us because you never got the joke, now it's you.

Sorry, not sorry.

But you get that, so you don't need to read this.

Too late?

Sorry.

We did say skip it.

Peter & Ray

1. Signs Your Doctor Is Really A Vet

You must be dragged scrambling and whimpering into his office.

You always leave wearing a plastic neck cone.

You are offended that he has to peer between your legs to determine your gender.

His latex gloves extend to his shoulders.

When you put your shoes back on, he nails them in place.

If you don't squirm while he examines your prostate, he rewards you with a belly rub.

His diagnosis is invariably mange.

He offers you a free spaying.

When you have the sniffles, he recommends that he end your suffering.

Muzzles you before starting the examination.

You are unnerved by the sound of the other patients howling.

Your flea problem clears up quicker than ever before.

He seems less alarmed than you that you're molting.

Says you're a good boy more than other doctors.

The consultation rooms have straw on the floor.

The nurse is an old man with a grubby hat and a border collie.

The pills he prescribes are the size of muffins.

More than the usual volume of pee in the waiting room.

Completely freaks out when you speak.

Asks your wife how often you use your salt lick.

Assumes your infection is from eating your own poo.

Inquires if you're an indoor or an outdoor human.

Stuffs you into a plastic crate before you're hauled out to your car.

2. Complaints Of Gladiators' Wives

Blames inability to remember anniversary on brutal broadsword injury to head.

It takes ages to wash dried lion shit off his sandals.

Always conveniently can't visit the in-laws because he's impaled on something.

Bitches incessantly when scheduled to battle an ostrich.

For not cleaning their rooms, the children are crucified.

Would just once love a rug that isn't the pelts of Gauls.

The more of him that's lopped off, the crankier he gets.

Disembowelment practice always seems to take priority over snuggle time.

There are more romantic gifts than Valentine aortas.

The only food he brings home for dinner is dead Christians.

Flies into wild rages at the merest passing mention of Russell Crowe.

Is a sensitive lover in the same way that a claw hammer is a sensitive kitten tickler.

Claims his missing chin makes it easier to shave.

Salts his wounds for luck at the table.

Sleeps with (his) one eye open.

Other sports champions have trophies of gold. His run more to a necklace of noses.

At the beach, remarks that the sand would be good for soaking up Sumerians.

Always bleeding out on the good quilt.

3. Unmotivational Sayings

Just when the caterpillar thought his world was ending, he turned into a butterfly and was munched by wrens.

Life is what happens to you while you're busy making other plans, but not if you plan to take a fatal overdose of pills.

Don't count your chickens with a mallet.

If you can't explain it simply, you don't understand it well enough, unless it's advanced trigonometry.

Be true to yourself; lie to your spouse like a motherfucker.

Laugh and the world laughs with you. Cry and it's the last party you'll be invited to.

Don't throw out the baby with the bath water, they'll find it in no time. Bury it in the woods.

Give a man a fish and he'll eat for a day, teach a man to fish and he'll never get any work done.

If you think you can, or you think you can't, make up your mind.

We become what we think about, unless we think about giraffes.

If you're not part of the solution, you're the one we'll blame.

Life is ten percent what happens to us, ten percent how we react to it and eighty percent waiting for websites to load.

It is better to fail in originality than to succeed in imitation, unless you're cloning sheep.

Easy come, the first time.

Power corrupts and absolute power makes you exponentially more attractive than otherwise possible with that face.

A journey of a thousand miles begins with a single trip to the bathroom.

If you love life, life will love you back, or at least grind on you.

4. Pointless Warning Labels

Cheese grater has no scrotal utility.

Boomerang chiefly for outdoor use.

Removal of Pontiff renders Popemobile merely a car.

Filing cabinet not to be rented to Japanese tourists as Airbnb hotel suite.

Caution: Yoko album audible when played.

Point hot end of flamethrower away from groin.

Do not insert glass eye elsewhere.

Pest repellent ineffective on mimes, alas.

Flyswatter not for trouser fly.

Cat-o-nine-tails ideally suited for cat.

Do not believe that 'I Can't Believe It's Not Butter' is not butter.

Fannypack sold separately from douchebag.

Do not worship frozen shrimp as gods.

Consult physician before using bone saw.

Emu flightless - do not attempt transatlantic crossing.

Scorpion inappropriate for petting zoo.

Milkshake may contain bovine mammary secretions.

5. Ironic Mysteries Of Life

Why are beauty marks so ugly?

Why is a sausage party generally seen as undesirable and yet Oktoberfest remains immensely popular?

Why do parents insist you go to school and then say, 'Don't get smart'?

Why is it wrong to use hand tools for a handjob?

Why do so many hot women give you the cold shoulder?

When it takes forever for your food to come, why is HE the waiter?

Why is it bad for something to be pungent except Thai food?

Why is saying 'Nice face!' so rude?

How come it's a virtue to be a stand-up guy until you stand up your date?

Why does licking your lips mean something is appealing but lick others' and they lose their minds?

Why do lovers ask if the earth moved for each other and then fly into wild panic over the least little earthquake?

If you must set something free if you love it, does that mean that everyone adores garbage?

Was the Wicked Witch Of The West really great?

How can removing just one little 'l' from the word 'public' make something the opposite?

Why do you count down to retirement and save up for it?

Why do people complain about 'lips and assholes' in hotdogs but love nothing more in intimate moments?

Why can't banks, food banks, blood banks and sperm banks all be in the same place?

Why do we give someone a hand up with hand-me-downs?

Surely calling someone a son of a bitch is an insult to their mother and not him?

Why is it that the lighter running shoes become, the more expensive they are?

Why is a take-off on something your take on it?

How come nobody can really conceive of how much a trillion is but 'shitload' makes sense to everyone?

Why crash a party then party till you crash?

How can a nap be forty winks when your eyes will be closed the whole time?

6. Secrets Of The Zoo

Recent legislation requires zoos to provide the animals with a break every four hours and two weeks' annual paid vacation.

Lions seldom eat zoo visitors, but a penguin will peck your eyes out just to impress his buddies.

Zooscamophobia is the fear of spending thirty-five dollars to stare at some trees where a wolf might be.

In an effort to make the animals feel more at home, zoo environs are designed to feel more African by employing scores of local poachers.

You are discouraged from feeding the animals, but owing to their lamentably low salaries, workers will always gratefully take a snack.

There are many escapes yearly, but the net population is balanced by the number of children abandoned there.

The most timid animal in the zoo is the lion with its mortal fear of gift shops.

Pandas would happily breed in captivity, but the stench of humans makes them too queasy.

Zoo is the short form of the word 'zoolag'.

Matt Damon did legit buy a zoo. No-one knows what he does in there.

Snakes are legless only after centuries of selective breeding in zoos, because the human mind cannot cope with the intense fear of a six-metre-long, fifty-legged, poisonous reptile that can move faster than a cheetah even with a whole slowly-digesting zookeeper in it.

Peacocks are disparagingly known by the other zoo inhabitants as the Liberaces of the animal kingdom.

Those hyenas aren't laughing; they're barking Yoko tunes.

The real money-maker at the zoo is selling the meat of people that tumble into the panther enclosure.

Zebras' camouflage works so well that zoo workers have never seen them, even while feeding them.

The total tonnage of feces produced in the average zoo daily is staggering, if you try to carry it all at once.

Male hippos will breed only in captivity, and only with zookeepers' wives; their husbands' resultant chronic sense of inadequacy is a well-known occupational hazard.

Animals get moody in zoos, especially the bipolar bears.

It's not just safari parks where the monkeys climb on your car. While you're enjoying the meerkats at most zoos, the chimps are busy stealing your alloys.

Zoo animals are as curious as those who come to see them, keeping up on current events by watching the gnus.

Despite their intimidatingly vast size, elephants are gentle creatures whose chief activity in zoos is interpretive folk dance.

Employees greet each other with 'Hay!', a joke that never seems to get old.

7. Horror Movies For Kids

Intensive Care Bears

The Cat In The Hatchet

Snow White And Seven

Willy Wonka And The Exorcist

A Charlie Manson Christmas

Beauty And The Beast Of Jersey

Beelzebubjuice

Bloody Mary Poppins

Honey, I Possessed The Kids

Jack Frost The Ripper

Lady And The Crazed Killer Tramp

Shr(i)ek

Texas Chainsaw Panda

The Garrotte Kid

The Little Weremaid

8. Things Said By No-One Ever

I think I'll ask my special forces colleagues for advice about my sexual confusion.

There's no business like the septic tank business.

The appropriate response to 'How was work?' is not 'Fine, dear', it's an epic, angst-filled yarn that lasts the gestation period of an elk.

What the beach needs is more Asian people in business attire taking pictures of the water.

Due Date was robbed of its Oscar.

What? The bass solo is over already? Noooo! More! MORE!

Stop panicking, I spent your insulin money on lottery tickets.

No blowjob for me, thanks, I have taxes to do.

Sure wish bacon tasted more like cinnamon.

I miss dial-up Internet.

There's nothing I like better after a double shift at the rock-smashing plant than a big plate of steamed asparagus.

Moron with a gavel says 'what'.

I'm just going to sit right here and hold my breath until they make another Transformers movie.

Those guys at the gym really opened my eyes to haiku.

I'm opening an alcohol-free, vegetarian biker bar.

I just ask my barber for The Trump.

More Jar Jar Binks, please.

9. How To Live It Up In Grandma's Living Room

Crank the Patsy Cline.

Full-contact knitboxing.

Switch the pile of Reader's Digest to Penthouse Forum.

Crackpipe windchimes and teapot bong.

All-prune food fight.

Doily Frisbee.

Hunt for a part of the room where the picture of Jesus isn't staring at you and judging.

Become a contortionist trying to find a comfy position on the 19th-century stiff Spanish Inquisition chesterfield.

Take photos of actual wallpaper to show your friends.

Indulge in a little thrill-seeking by putting down a cup without a coaster.

Massive Werther's Original high.

Crowd-surf on the cats.

Set the temperature on the heating pad to supersolar.

Get high and hallucinate that it's the good old days again.

Add rude words to her embroidery of the Ten Commandments.

Sneak the odd dick pic into the family photo albums.

Rant about the deterioration of good manners and make horrific racial slurs in the same sentence.

Get an intense upper-body workout trying to turn the TV dial to something other than PBS.

Say gobble-gobble and jiggle her turkey elbows.

10. Kevin Spacey's Christmas Plans

Go a-groping door to door.

Break into the Macy's storage room and have a go at the giant balloons.

Make snowmen whose carrots ain't noses.

Perform a play in one indecent act.

Host a tearful press conference where he reveals that as a child he was groped by himself.

Stuff a turkey so thoroughly it comes back to life.

Deploy a million mistletoe-carrying drones to encircle the Earth.

Ogle the well-hung tinsel.

Give to the kneady.

Go to the mall and sit on Santa's knee until you get off.

Increase efficiency by devising a radical new high-speed drive-by groping technique.

Lay a wreath.

Make the rounds on cold nights to spoon the homeless.

Ride in a one-horse open-fly sleigh.

Start spreading a rumour that he's why Benicio Del Toro speaks like that.

Listen to the soothing crickets that used to be ringing phones.

11. Clues Your Kid Will Be A Washroom Attendant

Shuns birthday cake in favour of urinal cake.

Lacks friends, grades, skills and goals, but never a hot towel.

Is utterly inconsolable when he loses his favourite plunger.

Don't get him started on 'the misting radius'.

His bedtime prayers are for more ply.

A parent-teacher conference reveals that, as they have never seen him outside the school washrooms, he is not technically enrolled.

His motto is Another Dump, Another Dollar.

Stands so unobtrusively in the corner of the family bathroom that you don't notice him until he hands you paper.

Cannot count past ten but offers insightful advice about the best hand soap for your skin type.

Most families commune at the dinner table or the TV. Yours gathers 'round the toilet.

Insists his allowance be paid in small change tossed into a basket by the sink.

Courteously pre-warms the commode seat for guests.

Somehow, in cramped loo quarters, performs encouraging cheer routines.

12. Brutally Truthful Ads

Burger King Whopper: A McDonald's Quarter Pounder With Lettuce.

Maybelline: Maybe She's Born With It, But No.

Ice Capades: The Never-Ending Hellish Torment You Were Promised For Your Sins, Only Longer, And With Somewhat More Leaping.

Pizza Pizza: Betcha Can't Tell Which Is The Box.

Audi: Bellends Gotta Get Places Too.

Kevin Spacey Fan Club: Enter To Win A Private Meet-And-Grope!

Tesla: So Cool You Won't Mind The Fireballs.

Apple: Ha Ha Ha! Sorry, But Ha Ha HA HA!

KFC: Bowel-Evacuatin' Good.

Pringles: Now With Alleged Potato.

Slinky: They Wouldn't Let Us Call It 'Only Three Stairs, Fuck'.

Monsanto: You Really, REALLY Don't Wanna Know.

Ferrari: So Cool You'll Believe She's With You For Your Personality.

Starbucks: For The Douche On The Go.

Dr. Pepper: Like Nothing Your Tastebuds Can Fathom.

Disney: Magically Brainwashing You With Cuteness.

NASCAR: Because Vroom.

Kraft Cheese Singles: You Know It Ain't Food But You're Eating It Anyway.

Del Monte: Sticking It To Poor Farmers So You Can Save A Dime On Pineapple Chunks.

Oreos: Now Offensive To All.

IBM: We're Still Here.

Tim Horton's: A Lineup Stretching To The Very Horizon Of Your Dreams, Although, Let's Be Frank, If Your Dreams Are Made Of Coffee And Donuts, Chances Are You Have Nowhere Else To Be.

Fly United Nearly The Whole Way There!

13. Wilderness Survival Tips

Walk a hundred yards in any direction and you'll find a Starbucks.

Your greatest survival tool is a sturdy knife or helicopter.

Holding a wolf cub hostage is a surefire way of stopping the pack killing you.

Follow a game trail to a pond or creek, or ask your guide.

Birchbark will insulate you from the cold if you're a tree, but then you're far less liable to be lost, so never mind.

Lichens make dandy pizza.

When you're lonely, porcupines are sensitive lovers if you're extremely careful.

Navigate via Nature's signs. For instance, moss always grows on the north side of tree trunks, and the south.

Mudslides are a surprisingly nutritious snack.

Remember, panic is the woodsman's friend, so lose your shit early and often.

Rainwater filtered through soil is a good source of soil-filtered rainwater.

On cold nights, keep warm in the hollowed-out carcass of a hiker.

When swept away by a flash flood, try to head downstream, as this takes much less effort and you can collide with tasty salmon going the other way.

Focus on the positive, such as how no-one will hassle you about your gingivitis while you're being sodomized by a pack of raccoons.

14. Classic Male Logic

A wagon wheel is far less useful as a transportation device than as furniture.

Fishing is to beer as ice fishing is to cold beer.

We check the drawer for the pliers again despite having already looked because sometimes things magically materialize, like clean, folded laundry.

We look good. It's not fair, it makes no sense, but it cannot be denied.

If a towel is dry, then it must also ergo be clean.

Favourite old t-shirts are now garishly tight because over the decades they shrank, and that's just elementary science.

If it cannot be fried or barbecued, then it probably isn't food.

How are we supposed to know we can't fix it if we don't try?

I have only two feet and so require only two shoes.

Existence is arid indeed bereft of hope. It is this simple faith that tells us that the letters in Penthouse are not made up.

A TV is only ever too large for a room if part of it hangs out the window.

A billion years of evolution have yet to produce an illness that cannot be treated with a bacon sandwich.

The phone is for conveying information, such as the information that I require a pizza.

Miscellaneous cables, chargers and leftover screws must be retained in perpetuity lest a terrible fate befall mankind.

Humans have neither ankle-mounted genitals nor stubby T-Rex arms, and thus evolution demands that we masturbate.

One would think that the towels that must not be used on pain of death would be kept in a locked cabinet, like a gun, instead of on the towel rack, like bait.

15. Classic Female Logic

Give a man a fish and he'll probably fry it; teach a man to fish and he'll disappear for fourteen hours, come home stinking even worse than before and probably have no fish.

Other attractive women most certainly exist, but they are vile whores.

Secrets are best safeguarded by telling only your three closest friends, each of whom can be absolutely trusted to tell only her three closest.

If men were more emotionally attuned to the world of feelings around them, they would perceive that the workplace is a seething hornet's nest of treachery and slander and intrigue, and be keen to hear about the bitch in Accounts Receivable who owes her career to nymphomania.

Men will learn only through constant correction and reminder, acts of sheer selfless educational altruism.

A scrotum is gross. The word itself is gross. It's gross that your main hobby is scratching it. Just ew, all of you.

Look. Let's make a deal. You can have your puerile men's magazines and your arrested-development rock-band keychains and your hockey-team beer mugs and your six remotes if we can play quietly with our potpourri.

Farts and toilet activities are shameful and reside in the same comedic ballpark as tuberculosis.

Women do the duckface on Facebook because it's more attractive than the male fuckface.

Men drag around a crushing load of responsibility all the time, so when you drag them somewhere, like a crafts fair, it's a big relief.

The greatest threat to the survival of the human race is the extreme ickiness of perpetuating it.

16. How To Be Finnish

Give your children names not at all similar to the more peculiar Star Wars characters.

Show great pride in your nation's many and varied inventions, such as fish-pickling stills, pickled fish churns and pickling barrels for fish.

Put two dots over most words, and under, and between, and in lieu of.

Refuse to shop at Ikea on account of the weird product names, even though folks called Jäätteenmäki are very common in your town.

Get heat stroke in strenuous snowball fights.

Enjoy the world's greatest variety of salty desserts.

Fly into a wild rage at the merest suggestion that you are in any way like Swedes, Norwegians or cuttlefish.

Boil yourself in a sauna and then roll naked in the snow to model optimal mental health in a climate more relentlessly hostile to human life than Pluto.

Extol your 1990's Nokia as the absolutely pinnacle of mobile phone technology.

Chill out, after a hard day of being open-minded, with the sort of ear-ruining heavy metal that the CIA uses to torture terror suspects.

Enhance any meal with the liberal addition of pickled fish from a crusty jar.

Demonstrate that no sport is a real challenge unless done on skis, and likewise seduction.

Be simultaneously mind-mindbogglingly gorgeous and stomach-churningly androgynous.

Never be able to remember if your capital city is Oslo or Stockholm.

Proclaim the accomplishments of world-famous Finnish celebrities, such as those that are famed worldwide, the really well-known ones, for instance.

Enjoy a regularly-scheduled masturbation break at work over Mika Häkkinen and Kimi Räikkönen.

Grow so used to gender-neutral terms of address that you forget whether you or your spouse are the boy.

Smile annually in a manner indistinguishable from gas pains.

Disdain all other international honours but proudly tout being number one for milk consumption and thus rancid breath.

Get the neighbours together for orgies of depression.

Shun freaks that sauna only five times per day or, horrifyingly, alone.

Keep a scrapbook of things that fell off due to frostbite.

Make cabinets, whether folks want another one or not.

Compete with your neighbours over who has the largest shrine to Linus Torvalds, or the one with the most pickled fish on it.

Dream of one day staying in the Ice Hotel, or just sleep in your bedroom.

Enjoy your 165-year life expectancy, but die at 81 anyway to be polite.

Be sure to include a wide variety of nutritious foods in your diet besides pickled fish, such as pickled fish sticks.

Learn to text the word epäjärjestelmällistyttämättömyy-dellänsäkään in the dark.

Know a thousand words for snow and none for fun.

17. Love Songs For Hermits

I Don't Want To Know What Love Is

Ain't No Mountain Far Enough

My Song

You've Lost That Leavin' Feeling

Easy Habit To Break

I Think I Loathe You

How Deep Is Your Moat?

Less Than A Feeling

I Want You Not To Want Me

I Just Want To Be My Everything

Just The One Of Me

You And Not Me

I Got Me Babe

(Everything I Do) I Do It For Me

18. Wrong Stuff We Were Taught In School

In all of recorded history, no-one has ever had occasion to calculate the cosecant of thirty-six degrees.

The Newton is not a unit of force but of figginess.

There is no explanation for the word 'economics' in Home Ec.

You can in fact put apostrophes wherever you like, including in a casserole.

There's no such thing as a negative number, unless you believe in voodoo.

Hitler's followers raised their hands and look where that got them.

An isthmus is just a pitiful wannabe peninsula.

Anything on a plate with good food is thus 'part of a nutritious breakfast', including gravel.

He never rose to greatness who waited his turn.

It's legitimate to blatantly make up words like 'foolscap'.

Lightning doesn't go up or down. It hangs around in one spot for an instant.

Photosynthesis is bullshit - plants eat snails and small rodents.

Science has proven that the human mind is actually fifty times more efficient when studying ten minutes before the test.

The chief skill graduates have absorbed is how to carve rude things on desks.

The War Of 1812 was fought in 1604. No-one knows why they called it that.

Whales aren't mammals but, obviously, massive fish.

Schools have fountains only because it would be too blatant to just hand out lead crackers.

Two wrongs absolutely, without exception, make a right.

The staff room is NOT a non-stop, coffee-fuelled orgy of depravity.

19. How Your Life Changes Once You've Gone Over Niagara Falls In A Barrel

The sound of rushing water causes not just a need to pee but spontaneous evacuation of your bowels.

Get used to being asked for donations to the International Brotherhood Of Fuckwits.

Despite the fame and adoration, you cannot escape the nagging sense that you simply obeyed the law of gravity and neglected to drown.

Folks in bars always want to tell you about daring things THEY did, and it's always SO not the same, but you still somehow end up buying THEM a beer.

You grow depressed as it slowly sinks in that you're useless, that there will never be a circumstance in which someone shouts, "THIS IS AN EMERGENCY! HAS ANYONE HERE EVER GONE OVER THE FALLS IN A BARREL?"

To spare herself the embarrassment, your mother tells her church group you're a fluffer in bestiality porn.

When your kids start telling you about getting a prize for fingerpainting, all you have to say is 'barrel' and they shut up.

In the eyes of your mother-in-law, you become even more not good enough for her daughter.

You routinely doze off on roller coasters or the NASA G-Force Simulator.

You look at other containers, such as oil drums, paint cans and Kinder Eggs, and wonder.

Your hilarious pals will gift you Barrel Of Monkeys each birthday and Christmas until you die.

It's a blow to realize that the total number of women who want to have sex with you for what you did turns out to be zero and that, sadly, your love life will thus forever consist merely of the faint hope that Kevin Spacey will still grope you.

You spend a lot of time alone, because everyone's thinking is, if you'll go over the Falls in a barrel, what the hell else will you do, and whatever it is, they don't want you doing it around them.

Jokes at work about how you're starting to look barrel-chested are so stale they should be studied by comedy archaeologists.

When you defend a speeding ticket, the cop always says you were barrelling along past the speed limit and then everyone in court laughs for a really long time, including the judge, before ruling you a two-time loser.

Your kid's school mysteriously stops inviting parents on Career Day.

No-one cheers when you tell your story. At best, there's a polite splattering of applause.

People keep asking if the birthmark on your forehead was caused by the Maid Of The Mist hitting you.

The sad truth is that, okay, people bursting into mirthful choruses of Roll Out The Barrel is mildly amusing the first time.

When you ask where people want to eat, they always say The Keg and nudge each other.

You can never again sit comfortably due to the agony of four-inch oak splinters in your butt.

When you order a drink, you hasten to add, before they can ask, no, not on the rocks.

Notwithstanding your attempts to refer to your courage as Niagara Balls, you mostly hear the term Niagara Fails.

20. Signs You're Being Cheated On

To save shipping costs, Durex opened a warehouse in your basement.

She says not tonight, she has a headache from bashing it against the headboard in her sleep, and those whip marks are from falling backward onto the hose a lot.

When she asks how you'd feel about a threesome, you aren't involved.

Your trust issues are so intense that you ask your mom for ID before you let her in the house.

She calls out names in her sleep alphabetically.

You supplement your income by selling late-night post-coital burritos.

Your dog is so hoarse from barking at strangers it has to howl at the moon via email.

In order to avoid running into other boyfriends, a team of whore traffic controllers work 'round the clock to track her movements.

Your Dear John letter begins, 'To Whom It May Concern…'

The coyote noises at construction sites come from her.

Her phone is locked, password-protected, encrypted and at some guy's house.

You have to wait in line to use your bathroom.

Local sperm banks surrender and close.

A Google check of her name reveals that the horndog demographic see her as their queen.

You're forced to wear a Hello, My Name Is tag.

Your bedpost is so notched it crumbled.

The 'ding' notifications of chat-room messages are so continuous you chalk it up at first to tinnitus.

She holds daily yard sales but she's the only item.

21. How Real Police Work Is Just Like The Movies

There is nothing softer and safer to land on from a great height than the contents of a dumpster.

A car speeding down an alley will always launch flying boxes of produce and fruit.

In spite of their allegedly special tactics and weaponry, the SWAT team is appallingly ineffective and risk-averse.

Powerful inept or corrupt bosses can be told to go fuck themselves and a badge tossed onto their desks dramatically without consequence.

All industrial premises are chock-full of easily-breakable steam pipes at head height for the expedient dispatch of criminals without any risk of scalding oneself.

When a brilliant investigative idea comes to mind, it's best to look knowing and then race determinedly out the door whilst your partner trots cluelessly behind wondering why you don't simply tell him where the hell you're going.

Being tied up and pummelled savagely is a golden opportunity to hone one's sarcasm skills.

As long as a gunshot wound is in the leg, arm or shoulder, it is little more than a minor inconvenience to all but the flounciest of Nancy boys.

An older partner's nubile daughter will lust palpably for a young, long-haired officer who winks in tacit understanding of her frustration with her dad's repressive discipline, but never actually be subject to his, though the promise perpetually looms.

Crimes can be solved only when a critical clue is found under the furniture that teams of highly-trained forensic specialists missed repeatedly.

The best way to overtake a fleeing driver is to roar the wrong way up a crowded freeway.

Choppers whose skids are dangled from head straight over water.

Failure to have a spare weapon in an ankle holster immediately identifies one as some sort of hapless, by-the-book sissy who should be assigned perpetual desk work.

Emerging from a river makes clothes dry and hair coif itself.

Hot partners really are constantly being kidnapped.

Calling for backup under any circumstances means you might as well just blow Boy Scouts in the park.

Expensive fast food must be thrown away after only a single bite.

Out-running an explosion is not only possible but happens twice a shift.

All previous partners died in a gruesome manner for which the one who is still with us feels responsible but clearly isn't.

Sidewalk pedestrians can be counted upon to assist your hot pursuit by flinging themselves cooperatively out of the way on both sides equally.

The chief tactic all rookie cops practice in the Academy is the shoulder-roll over the hood of a car.

The detective squad gives preference to applicants who are suicidal over the death of a beloved spouse at the hands of vicious thugs.

The laws of physics do not apply to shooting a rapidly-spinning tire, which is actually super easy.

The mere flash of a badge is sufficient for any citizen to gladly relinquish his car or firetruck with no debate.

Cops easily run and dive while shooting with pinpoint accuracy from a 62-shot clip.

They insist that their partner be their polar opposite in age, race, temperament and wisecrack-proneness.

With days to retirement, a threat to civilization will present itself that wraps up neatly within ninety minutes as a result of the would-be retiree's intrepid wisdom and selflessness.

You are more likely to guess which bomb wire to clip if you sweat profusely.

22. Facts About Tumbleweeds

Seemingly aimless, tumbleweeds are in fact vicious pack hunters that can eviscerate a hiker in seconds, earning them the moniker 'piranha of the prairie'.

Young tumblecubs remain with their parents for up to seventeen years before roaming the high seas in search of adventure until it's time to settle down and start a dusty family.

You can't outrun a tumbleweed, and they are swift tree climbers, so if one is after you, your best bet is to drop suddenly to the ground and hope it tumbles right over you instead of mauling you slowly for weeks until you succumb to the humiliation like the native Indians did.

With poor night vision, tumbleweeds often become separated from their packs in the dark, their plaintive howls of distress routinely disturbing the peaceful slumber of wolves.

In many states, tumbleweeds are forced to brawl to the death by unscrupulous promoters for whom dog-fighting rings and Parliament are insufficiently savage.

A tumbleweed in your eye can be dislodged by very big blinking.

The male tumbleweed can be distinguished because of its long, flowing mane and iridescent rainbow plumage, while the female carries a purse.

Never successfully bred in captivity, tumbleweeds have ludicrously complex courtship rituals based on escalating rounds of gift-giving and square-dancing and a disinterest in mating that makes pandas look positively rampant.

Tumbleweeds live in large groups known as thickets, with a rigid social hierarchy based on tumbliness.

They aren't weeds. Originally called tumbleweaves, they're the product of careful craftsmanship by the same dry desert nomads that construct Trump's hair.

Since Kevin Spacey has a severe allergy to tumbleweeds, he must wear rubber gloves to grope them.

Despite roaming thousands of miles in the wild, tumbleweeds adjust surprisingly well to life in captivity, in zoos, say, or a box.

Conspicuously absent from the boardrooms of corporate America, tumbleweeds have nonetheless carved out a lucrative niche as movie extras.

Very small tumbleweeds can be added to ant farms for a certain lame je ne sais quoi.

Many meet their end impaled on cacti like John Wayne.

23. Headlines That Miss the Point

Best Rainbows Caused By Inland Tsunamis

Carbon Fibre Luggage Survives Packed Airliner Fireball Plummet

Drinking More Than 25 Units Of Alcohol Per Week Causes Brain Damage In Toddlers

Kinky Sex Shame For Finder Of Holy Grail

Local Firm Wins Contract To Build Tiny Chair For Duck Chess Grandmaster

New Penis Enlargement Drug Causes 5% Increase In Toenail Growth

Noise Nuisance Complaints Rise A Thousandfold Due To Exploding Toothpaste

Polar Bear Forgets Lines During Filming Of New Frozen Film

President Misses Press Conference Due To Kidnapping

RAF Fail To Conduct Safety Assessment Before Bombing Legoland

Recently-Arrived Aliens Prefer White To Brown Bread

Seawater-Powered Sports Car Not Available In Red

Tomatoes More Juicy When Grown On Grave Of Jimmy Hoffa, Say Gardeners

24. Why The Glockenspiel Is The Coolest Musical Instrument

The glockenspiel was introduced by slaves who played spirituals on it in the cotton fields in an annoying fashion.

Ain't no chick alive that won't blow a dude that rides the G-train.

You can get rich suing a surgeon who leaves one in you accidentally.

The glockmeister stands at the back of the orchestra and thus avoids being doused in spittle by the tuba section.

Any true music lover knows that a symphony without a glockenspiel lacks a certain bonky plonky something that renders it bearable.

It is vastly more manly to pass a kidney glockenspiel.

You sound all gangsta when you mention your glock.

Anything that must be operated by bashing it with hammers is automatically awesome.

Brandish your piccolo at a mugger and he'll laugh at you; wave a glockenspiel and he'll bolt.

Sir Harold Glockenspiel, the inventor, played brilliantly, though, like Beethoven, he was deaf, and, unlike Beethoven, had no arms.

It takes about seven minutes to learn how to play it, so that the rest of your weekly lessons can be spent throwing knives.

Punk glockenspiel band The Sex Pustules brought the instrument to a broader audience of, well, them.

An amplifier transforms a glockenspiel from a glockenspiel to a much louder glockenspiel.

Hitler made glockenspiel concerts mandatory for his enemies.

It was a glockenspiel that wore down the legendary Wall Of Jericho.

The Whom rose to orchestral fame by smashing their glocken-spiels to bits at the end of a symphony.

There is not a polka party on earth that wouldn't benefit from a bit more glockenspiel. Or additional anything but polka.

Any Johnny-come-lately can woo a lady outside her bedroom window with a lute or a ukulele, but only a truly committed suitor would negotiate three city buses and a tramp attack to serenade you with a romantic ditty on a glockenspiel.

The carrying case for a glockenspiel is so large that you can live in it when you get evicted for the horrible noise.

Glockenspielers think xylophonists are sad little pretenders and triangle players pesky-ass ting-a-ling fairies.

When flying with your glockenspiel, the airline is obliged to give you an entire row to yourself and the other passengers to loathe you with unbridled fury.

A band is considered a-cappella despite the inclusion of a glockenspiel.

Hamelin had a pied glockenspieler whom no-one followed.

25. Last Words Of Famous People

Hugh Hefner: I sure hope I get some cock in heaven.

Prince: Be honest. Was I just an annoyingly weird self-aggrandizing little twerp?

Garry Shandling: It's Garry Shandling's Funeral!

Jack the Ripper: I was a bit on edge.

Cleopatra: Aspirin! I asked for bloody aspirin!

Roger Moore: I liked Timothy Dalton best.

Picasso: Good thing I never sobered up.

Charles Manson: Maybe Helter Skelter was just the Beatles' usual stoned nonsense lyrics.

Chuck Berry: Johnny B. Deade.

Mikhail Gorbachev: At least decay will finally get rid of that forehead lobster tattoo.

Frank Sinatra: Shoulda done it your way.

Gandhi: I hope heaven is an endless all-you-can-eat buffet.

Mother Theresa: Finally some Me Time!

David Bowie : I really can't believe they went for that crap.

Valentino: You know how depressing it is as a global superstar to be nonetheless the second-most-famous Rudolph?

Carrie Fisher: I'm not sure why I'm famous either.

Henry Heimlich: Cough, choke, gasp, akkkk, grrr, uggghh, ffff ...

26. Lesser-Known Rights When You're Arrested

If you cannot afford an angry mob, one will be provided for you.

You have the right to be confined in a small holding cell for the lifetime of a sea tortoise with a burly, agitated individual who does not do well, to say the very least, in captivity, all of whose mental and physical ailments might aptly be described as explosive.

Notwithstanding your right to understand in your own language what the arresting officers are saying, judges have mostly upheld arrests where no Bora-Boran tribal dialecticians could with dispatch (and by Dispatch) be brought to the scene.

You have a right not to have them just root willy-nilly through your pockets unless the investigating cops have formed a legitimate suspicion, on reasonable grounds, that you might have orifices in there, or that your name is in fact Willy Nilly.

You have the right to be slapped upside your head by a random angry mother in an apron.

You have the right to drag a metal mug across your bars and to have a metal bar dragged across your mug.

You get one phone call to the Alibi Hotline.

You have the right to immediately stop bleeding on the officer's baton.

Anything you say can be used at the Annual Precinct Arrest Bloopers Gala.

You have the right to retain and instruct counsel without delay, where delay is defined as the time it takes the mountains to crumble to the sea.

You have the right to be presumed innocent even though we know you fucking did it.

You have an absolute constitutional go-nuts right to this prison food.

You won't be sent to Abu Ghraib if you can spell it.

You can read two or three books as you 'just take a seat right here for me real quick', so you are entitled to a bathroom break, but only at the end.

You have a right to the full-service VIP Rodney King Hospitality Treatment.

You have the right to soil yourself to an extent of your choosing.

Your Facebook profile picture will be Photoshopped to show you behind bars wearing an old-time comedy convict uniform.

You have the right to endure a five-fold increase in snap-judgemental condescension from Piers Morgan.

You have the right to close scrutiny by countless scary dudes while you pee.

27. How To Spot The Amish Cool Kids

Is white, but acts black(smith).

Says 'Pimp my Clydesdale'.

Keeps a button stashed under one of the floorboards.

Sins through his britches to smudged charcoal sketches of the Haymate Of The Month.

Dancin' ain't no big deal, does it whenever he feels like it.

Has an actual bucket list.

Claims to have seen ankles loads of times.

Gets invited to all the hottest sermons.

Sneaks out back to smoke hamhocks.

Doesn't get up for work until 03:35.

Has an iRod.

Sasses teachers by saying the Earth is round.

28. Other Things Tom Cruise Believes

Successful people keep their money in a healthy mix of offshore and off-planet investments.

He carried Dustin Hoffman in Rain Man.

His smile is not scary enough to trigger the primal flight impulse.

If the acting gig dries up, he can always find work as a samurai.

It will never become known that, just as he came to fame by dancing onscreen in his underwear in Risky Business, that's also what he did to get cast.

There are enough phone books in the world to make his seated height match others'.

Believing that, on planet Xenu thirteen trillion years ago, nuclear bombs were triggered in volcanoes, as taught by Scientology, does not make you, in the eyes of all sentient beings, a monumental toolshed.

Nicole didn't leave him but was summoned back to Queensland to start the mandatory forty-year kangaroo patrol duty required of every Australian citizen.

Cruise control, cruise missiles and Santa Cruz were all named after him.

Whenever someone calls and hangs up, it's the Thetans testing his faith.

His teeth are simply a result of good oral care, not harvested weekly from beggar children on the calcium-rich plains of Bhutan.

It is not for reasons of personal sensitivity that he refuses to be in a 'low' budget film.

The absence of Oscars for Cocktail is conclusive proof of corruption in the Academy.

The camera adds not only ten pounds but three feet.

His own kids would never call him an Operating Thetan Level 8 Wackjob.

Ugliness is a viral infection spread by looking directly at unattractive people.

Vanilla Sky was great, and Tropic Thunder is a dark comedy classic equal to the likes of Dr. Strangelove and Big Momma's House 2.

29. Facts About Africa

The principal difference between African and Indian elephants is that the former are flightless.

Beneath the jungle are vast arid tracts of impassable desert.

It's true that black mambas are lethally venomous, but the good news is that they are so petrified of people that they will bite themselves to death in a panic at the first sign of your approach.

In Africa, Pringles are available in popular local flavours like hyena, gazelle and Mugabe.

South Africa has the world's highest murder rate but, on the other hand, the lowest attempted murder rate.

On safari, you are very unlikely to be eaten alive by wild animals, because when you see a tarantula the size of the jeep you're in, you'll have a heart attack and die before they get to you.

They still communicate via drumbeat in parts of the Congo. Also called the Bongo.

A useful phrase when communicating with hitherto uncontacted tribes is 'Oongawa!' which means, 'I'm boiling!'

A skilled tracker, merely by sniffing urine or examining the consistency of feces, can tell the precise direction from which his next date will not come.

Trophy prey is popular among wealthy hunters. Trophy wives too. Both would rather not be mounted.

Some investors can't see the future in diamond mines, because they're dark.

All Nigerians are princes.

Anacondas can swallow their food whole, but ironically not Whole Foods.

It has oft been said that piranha can skeletonize a cow in minutes. Weeks, in the case of Rosie O'Donnell.

Kenyans are world class runners largely on account of Kenya being really scary.

Contrary to popular belief, giraffes did not evolve long necks to graze the leaves of high trees, but to drink from deep wells.

Not all animals mate to perpetuate the species. Witness the gay pride of lions.

The Swahili language has no word for 'rhinoceros', which explains why so many villagers are trampled while miming it as a warning to others.

30. How To Tell It's Time To Stop Being A Rodeo Clown

Your off-the-job fashion sense mirrors your sartorial work splendour.

It has become too embarrassing that you can stay mounted on the bull, on average, only three seconds longer than on your wife.

To avoid the embarrassment on career day, your child tells everyone you were a petty criminal who died trapped in a tampon vending machine he was trying to break into.

Bitter sons named Ferdinand.

Your rasslin' kin won't talk to you since you topped their ears with your cauliflower torso.

You frankly always root for the bull.

Your sense of superiority leads you to commit acts of clown-on-clown crime against your circus counterparts.

More bullshit than most jobs.

You can't eat pancakes because empathy.

Repeated blows to the head mean that the only thing you can remember about your wife is that she isn't the lead singer of ZZ Top.

On account of the goring, your kid brother with his job in insurance becomes less envious by the hour.

All your male ancestors died of saddle sores.

Every Father's Day, cheap plastic spurs.

Too many rows with the wife over family vacations to Pamplona again.

After a while, everything on you is cloven.

You long for the serenity of death-match cage fighting in Somalia.

Your testicles have been stomped so frequently you can only get off with the aid of a rubber mallet.

31. Translations Of Real Estate Ads

Sprawling yard (a literal yard, three feet, in which a rabid dog sprawls).

Subway nearby (and Burger King).

Warm and bright (on fire).

Finished basement (finished flooding).

Neutral colour palette (so beige you'll think you've gone blind).

Fully air-conditioned (screen door).

Eco-friendly (full of bees).

Breath-taking, panoramic view (of the parking lot).

Open-plan living space (the walls collapsed).

Close to amenities (like the sewage treatment plant).

Compact and cosy (merely sever your legs to get through the door).

Sea views (if you use the Hubble Telescope).

Low-maintenance garden (rocks, lots of rocks).

Country style kitchen (troughs).

(Guantanamo) Bay windows (none).

Cathedral ceilings (Notre Dame Cathedral, low even for a hunchback, and burned away).

Shady trees (with sketchy roots).

Raised patio (ground heaved).

Two-car garage (one in, one out).

Quirky (previously owned by a cult who joined the mothership by slaughtering themselves in the dining room).

32. Things We Tell Our Kids About How We Had It Rougher

Our Christmas present was a splat of frozen spit to suck on till the big dinner feast, a salted peanut with the salt washed off in the creek.

Our parents didn't waste money on frivolous things like tables when there were perfectly fine young backs to rest scalding pans on.

If you picked up roadside bottles throughout the county for six months, you could cash them in for a dime, with which you could see three feature films, get a popcorn the size of a grain silo and a Coke you could yacht in, take a limo home and still have enough left over for university.

We did chores every morning and then swabbed the trees, singing psalms of gratitude for the opportunity.

Our cereals' marshmallows were carpet tacks.

We didn't talk back for fear of disgracing our ancestors and everybody else's, and a cuff to the ear so hard our grandkids had Down Syndrome.

All Winter we had frostbitten shoulders from giving each other the shirts off our backs.

You didn't change jobs merrily looking for one you 'liked', you toiled at one you hated in silent misery until you died, like you hoped your son would someday.

You didn't just 'hook up', you courted a girl politely for a respectfully decent period until she moved away.

We didn't rush to the doctor for every little sniffle or sucking chest wound.

In lieu of food, our moms knit supper.

We were taught valuable life lessons from an early age, such as that kindness is its own reward, and until you're bringing home a wage, your teeth are fair game as a bottle opener.

We didn't get praised for helping out, we did it because all we ever thought about was how to pull our weight, which was that of Mount McKinley, but sometimes, as a nice pat on the back, our folks would let us dung the sewage sifter.

We had no multiple choice in our exams – two thousand questions, all ancient Sanskrit, white ink on white paper, fifteen minutes.

We had real heroes like soldiers, firefighters and that guy who swallowed his head and got to leave town with the circus.

For bringing home an A rather than A+, our fathers would thrash us for days with whittled rods and nettled thorn bushes.

We had nine hours of homework every evening and another nine in the morning, plus nine more at lunchtime.

There was no crime, so we left our doors unlocked and our windows open and our savings outside in the street.

Any kid wearing a helmet for any reason was set ablaze by his mortified friends.

33. Stormy Daniels' Most Disturbing Revelations About President Trump

Ivanka hogs the covers.

Kept shouting, 'Whoooo's your dotard?'

Had Pence sleep on the wet spot.

His advanced foreplay technique is limited to seven variations of pussy grabbing.

The word Trump is written on absolutely everything, so only industrial-grade hallucinogens and ancient Taoist meditation techniques are sufficiently potent for you to imagine you're with anyone else.

Afterward, you get an I Scaled Trump Tower t-shirt.

The creepy way Jared just hung around silently.

His second-worst combover is on his head.

His tighty whities burst.

In comparison, his hands are gigantic.

Calls out his own name, and instead of coming says, 'Believe me.'

Wouldn't help her find it.

Calls her the Secretary Of Prostate.

Tells her she was 'tremendous, that I can tell you'.

Melania sent in lawyers to enforce the Finders Keepers rule.

Barron wouldn't believe they were just wrestling, but Eric did.

Got offended when she called it Air Force One Inch.

Used the term Oval Orifice more than is appropriate.

Ivana left a book of sex tips on the bedside table. All but one was 'RUN!' The other was a map of the heating ducts.

Shrieks, 'You're fired!' at the moment of climax.

The handicapped impression is his sex face.

34. Things You Didn't Know About Belgium

Cricket was actually invented in Belgium as a prank to see if the English would be gullible enough to play it.

The town of Spa in Belgium is where the spa was invented, near the village of Nail Salon.

Antwerp is 'Prewtna' backwards.

Hip-hop was invented in Belgium, as were flip-flops.

By international treaty, a Belgian A-list celebrity is worth the same as an infomercial host in the rest of the world.

There are more llamas in Belgium than in South America, if by llamas one means Belgians.

Brussels wasn't built. One day it just sprouted.

Jean Claude Van Damme was an unpopular child known as the Ostend Bellend.

Teenage Belgian girls favour bad boys, such as those who are not always punctual or have unconditioned hair.

The Belgian royal family never appear in public because they just feel sheepish.

The Belgian army is constantly invading their neighbours' territory, but they're too homesick to stick around to hold it.

Belgian scientists invented the can opener almost two hundred years before the can.

The word 'Belgium' comes from the ancient Aramaic 'bel' and 'gium', meaning 'alarmingly bland chutney'.

A staggering 99.5% of Belgians believe that Tintin, though fictional, should be Prime Minister. The other 0.5% is Tintin himself, who was too modest to comment, but agrees.

The highest building in Belgium is known as a thighscraper.

Belgium is the world's leading producer of chocolate and diamonds and diabetic gold-diggers.

Audrey Hepburn was from Belgium, though she fought to the death rather than admit it.

Belgium has been making chocolate for over four hundred years, so you'd think it would be ready by now.

35. Poorly Translated Chinese Safety Instructions

For over age three children only scorpion.

Tealight small and hair flame plenty.

Much death from razor shards of whirling metal malfunction.

Hurl boomerang far but long then run inside.

No toss wish coin in blast smelter.

Make merry with chainsaw however not face or genital.

Insertion of bread into toaster not ever for bathtime time.

Not handle end of knife unsuitable for baby or halfwit.

Best effective rat poison make for dead rat and also husband.

Meeting of anvil and toe unwelcome for good day.

For food use only with banana.

Thrust up torch with much care in-of-doors.

Failure of cattle prod checked not by tongue but electrical man.

In case on fire, break glass wildly.

Blow flotation cushion swiftly before drowning.

Warning: Ceiling fan not lip balm.

Inflation lady for much sexual extravaganza but without flame please for avoid plastic melt over scrotum.

Unwelcome introduction of spatula to body anus.

Please for the washing of tourniquet towel before return.

Possibly toxic if shampoo for breakfast.

Sloppiness application of sealant less beneficial of submarine joy sailing.

When fire, stop, drop or roll, you choose.

Brandish only if attack.

Slippery when wet or dry otherwise.

Live wires not nasal floss.

No advance unless you steel-toe boot yourself.

Inadequate flaming render sausage botulus.

Fallen rock fine, watch for falling rock.

Don't drunk and combine harvester.

36. Ineffective Hostage Negotiation Strategies

Request a show of faith by asking that the hot women be released.

Build trust by offering your own children as additional hostages.

Send in a Kevin Spacey robot to grope him into submission.

Blast Yoko tunes and try to pick out the suspect from the crowd of those who surrender.

When food is demanded, provide vegetarian pizza.

Establish communication by hurling a phone booth through the window.

Refuse to negotiate with terrorists or big dumb losers.

Flip slowly through your collection of Pokemon cards and identify which you're willing to trade for a hostage and which are just too precious to give away.

Show the same photos of your Florida vacation that made your friends succumb.

Ensure that the kidnapper doesn't see the hostages as human beings by referring to them only by their social security numbers.

Put on a Dog Day Afternoon puppet show.

Offer the ransom money in non-sequential, unmarked nickels.

Deploy a drone, or your wife to drone.

Storm the building, or, since they'll be expecting that, send in clowns and Girl Guides, which they probably won't be anticipating.

Release a cloud of Agent Orange disguised as the president.

Designate the area an American school zone and wait for someone to shoot him.

Show a Transformer movie until he's too elderly to cause any more trouble.

37. Failed Tourist Attractions

Bland Canyon

Museum Of Air

Hanging Gardens Of Litter

Rabid Ferrets Wheel

Garage Mahal

Festival Of Maddening Fishing Line Snarls

Crusty Wonders

Vasectomy Flume

Toe Jamboree

Sheriff Harry's Radar Fun Trap

A Child's Carnival O' Carnage

Euro-urinal

Fuckface Fair

Erectile House

Debris Field Of Dreams

Tofuhenge

38. Yoko Ono Facts

If John didn't clean fast enough, she threatened to sing, so the Dakota was always so spotless you could perform neurosurgery on the floors.

Despite her diminutive stature, her ego was so massive that she tried to get her hometown renamed Tokyoko.

More computing power than the NSA can summon is required to digitally pitch-correct thirty seconds of a Plastic Ono Band track.

She inspired an end forever to the tradition of bandmates boning each other's wives.

She provided valuable constructive criticism of the Beatles' songs, such as 'Needs more shrieking' and 'Insufficiently howl-intensive'.

Sudoku puzzles are loosely named after Yoko as they too are tedious, infuriating and no fun whatsoever.

Traditionally reserved and polite, the Japanese have more than two dozen adjectives for the physical pain caused by exposure to Yoko's paintings.

By a cruel twist of genetics, Sean Lennon is only five percent less irritating than his mother.

Contrary to myth, Yoko did not wreck the Beatles, she actually ruined all music.

John gave up heroin when he realized he could still hear her.

Her real name isn't Ono. That's just what people blurt when she bursts into song, so the nickname stuck.

Yoko can light up a room, but usually it's illuminated by the occupants lighting themselves.

She's ahead of her time in the same way that a hedgehog is a head of lettuce.

She invented the bizarre screech known as yokodeling.

Yoko is a chronic bedwetter, and she forced poor John to lounge around on a foul, urine-soaked mattress while reporters looked on in pity.

39. You're So Ugly...

Amazon will only sell you a forty-metre selfie stick.

Kevin Spacey gives you a miss.

On Tinder you are matched primarily with warthogs.

You can't find employment on account of being 'over-qualified' for sideshow work.

For Halloween, you simply tie a string from ear to ear behind your head and everyone assumes you're wearing the world's most hideous mask.

You were fired from your job as a pornstar for being bukkake-repellent.

Your facecloths knot themselves together into a rope ladder and escape out the window.

Authorities deem your profile pic a terror attack.

Dentists put you under the chair.

Impromptu telethons break out wherever you go.

Legions of mathematicians work in shifts to devise a number small enough to quantify your girlfriend's self-esteem.

Mirrors crack and reflecting pools boil angrily.

No-one around you ever gets hiccups.

On the day you were born, your parents arranged for a closed casket someday.

People who meet you break their noses bolting into walls.

The neighbours circulate a cosmetic surgery petition.

The staff at Glamour Shots initiate an immediate suicide pact when you walk in.

When you were a baby, your mom was always getting into fistfights when folks said you looked just like her.

You only go on literal blind dates.

Your Christmas gifts are always turtleneck sweaters whose collars extend far above your head.

You've never seen a mosquito.

40. How Bear Grylls Would Survive In An Office Environment

Make toner cartridges out of pine cones.

Drag all the office plants over to his desk for camouflage.

Cover his face in White-Out and hide in the snow.

Lower his heartrate at will, to hibernate through meetings and 'team-building' exercises.

Use the stale coffee from the bottom of the pot to weatherproof his socks.

Insist that his annual bonus be based solely on how many scorpions he's eaten.

Lean-to cubicle.

Navigate by the moss that grows on the staff deadwood.

Porcupine phone message spindle.

When it's chilly, paper being a good insulator, make a poncho out of spreadsheets.

Coonbutt coffee mug.

Get fired by rubbing two sticks together.

Frequently call in sick with malaria and dengue fever.

When someone asks to borrow a staple remover, hand him a machete.

Open his lunchbox to reveal ten live snails and a bat.

Always struggle to find a camo tie to match his camo pants and camo shirt.

Weave a chair cover from the pelts of corporate weasels.

Face disciplinary action for overuse of the word 'bivouac' in his weekly reports.

Refuse to use the elevator, preferring to scale the exterior of the building using the plastic straps on copier paper.

Carefully straighten paper clips and shoot them at the mail guy with a pen blowpipe.

41. Failed Soft Drinks

Nurse Pepper

Lemonaids

Root Canal Beer

Papsi

Creamed Soda

7-Upchuck

Choke-A-Cola

Orange Sluice

Grape Crushed Spirit

Caesar Smoothie

Red Bullfrog

42. Clues You Hired The Wrong Magician For Your Child's Party

Your silverware also vanishes.

The kids are bummed out by tricks like The Shrinking Will To Live and The Amazing Expanding Concentric Rings Of Flopsweat.

By way of misdirection, sets fires.

'Cape' is a soiled trenchcoat.

His patter always returns to his time in a Turkish prison.

The doves are half-chewed starlings.

Tries to use magic to bring a dead hooker back to life.

When he asks for a volunteer from the audience to help him, always picks the slow-witted kid that hasn't stopped crying since he arrived.

Palms their bums.

Every trick seems to require 'borrowing' a ten-dollar bill from a member of the audience.

Asks you to pay him in shrooms.

He mostly just conjures up tales of other tricks he's turned.

His 'lovely assistant' is a surly skel from the ravine named Gus.

When you complain about the poor execution of his tricks, he directs your attention to how sparkly his jacket is.

Every time you hear Ta-Daa!, you'll be getting an angry call later from another kid's parents.

Bills himself as The Great Gangrini.

Sawing the kids in half goes so badly awry you have to call a crime scene cleaner.

His 'wand' is chiefly in his pants, his repertoire relies heavily on its levitation, and the climax of the show is his.

More than half the act is teaching the kids to pick pockets.

Proclaims, 'Nothing up my sleeve but tracks!'

Reveals the Miraculous Half-Passed Kidney Stone Of Awe.

43. New Ways For Vladimir Putin To Show How Manly He Is

Glare at an ostrich till it takes to the air in terror.

When a sturdy Russian woman asks if her butt looks big, look her in the eye and say colossal.

Taunt Kevin Spacey with claims of being ungropable.

Crush walnuts with his testicles.

Creep into the lair of hibernating wolves and awaken them with shrieking and buggery.

Run giddily about the Kremlin with scissors.

Star in a sequel to Sleepless In Seattle called Shirtless In Siberia.

Snort potatoes and press them into vodka with his nasal passages.

Snack on actual bear claws, and, metaphorically, Crimea.

Challenge Cossacks to arm-wrestle. All of them at once.

Test thumb-screws on himself to show dissidents they're wusses.

44. Unpopular Video Games

Cyst

Granny Turismo

Halo-tosis

Indifferent Birds

Lint Vs Zombies

Loom Raider

Microsoft Flight Attendant Simulator

Need For Slow Speed In A School Zone

Personal Space Invaders

Sonic The Dead Dog

Super Mario Cuomo

Wonky Kong

45. Clues Your Dentist Is A Fake

The light above the chair is a bug zapper.

Advises that your teeth will be in much better shape if you brush instead of meals.

When it's time to give you an injection, pulls a syringe out of the dartboard.

You begin to suspect that the fluoride treatment is just mint gravy.

Cups your balls and tells you to cough. (And that's just in the waiting room.)

The x-ray film he puts in your mouth is a stick of Juicy Fruit.

He misspells it 'aural' care and drills your ears.

Asks if you're comfortable, and does it hurt, and who's your Daddy.

Economizes by means of communal floss.

Proudly displays scraped plaque on a wall one.

The assistant keeps calling him Chef.

Keeps switching the spitsuck machine to blow.

Uses cut-up old socks for fillings.

Ad nauseum repeats the joke, 'Gum anybody? You will!'

Performs tooth polishing with Turtle Wax.

Can't say 'implants' without snickering.

Puts the dark glasses on himself.

There's always nipple tissue on the bib clamps.

Tells you to, 'Open wider, oh, GOD, wider!'

46. Extra-Unpleasant Parasites

Arse badger

Chesapeake phlegmworm

Puking eyelash mandrill

Ballistic boner flea

Duodenal singing slug

Left-lobe Liberace leech

Giant Spacey grope-protozoa

Transylvanian snuggling cougar

Dynamitic corneal burst fluke

Enraged rabid buzzard tapeworm shrew

Burrowing fanged urethral tortion weevil

Guatemalan spontaneous ejaculation gushmaggot

Large intestinal quilled flesh-eating high-voltage garter eel

Greater Sri Lankan duct-taped Richard-Gere-gerbilized sphincter marmot

Needlebarbed poison-ivyish megaflammable rottweiling buttockular blister boar

47. Health Benefits Of Green Tea

Cures spinal meningitis, but only for a day, and then it comes roaring back to mutate your structure in the most unspeakable fashion.

Generates peace of mind, as you will no longer have to put up with annoying people who will now avoid you because they think you're a douche who drinks green tea.

The most learned Middle Ages health practitioners knew the benefits of feeding green tea to medical leeches.

Gives additional shine, bounce and tea to the hair.

Reduces inflammation caused by impact with a city bus by as much as 0.00002%.

Gives one the power of mind control over snails and other assorted molluscs.

Can eradicate all traces of Piers Morgan when applied in a vat with a tight-fitting lid.

Very slightly reduces your fascination with hardcore underground Costa Rican weasel porn.

Improves vision when poured in the eye.

Confers immortality, but only on fruit flies.

Is a memory aid, unless you forget to drink it.

Alleviates insomnia when drunk hourly throughout the night.

Boosts the immune system, although it's called 'green' because it causes gangrene.

Snorted, it gives you a really energetic nose.

Eliminates erectile dysfunction when sipped boiling hot urethrally.

Green tea enemas will make your dog stop barking.

It's an anti-depressant, so running out of it is really sad.

You can run marathons on green tea, but it's slippery, so you'll fall and hurt yourself.

With each cup, you grow an additional gall bladder and you can never have too many of those.

Immediately changes your accent to an offensively racist version of your host's.

48. Why Grave Digger Is The Best Career

You're too creepy to be invited to meetings.

Your in-box only ever has one item.

Simply wear your work clothes and have the most disturbing Halloween costume of anyone in your trailer park.

You might not follow modern 'music', but you'll know all the hippest dirges.

You're allowed to have all the sex you want on the graves.

Few other jobs are so forgiving when you vomit into your workspace.

Absolutely no possibility of being asked to take work home with you.

Only two health and safety rules: Don't sever your feet with the shovel and don't choke on the dirt.

Barring universal immortality, there's unending job security.

Avoid leaping out of a bush and terrifying everyone just once and you're Employee Of The Month.

Instead of making you redundant, they just tell you to stay in the hole.

You get to keep as much of the dirt as you want.

By attending the Annual Grave Diggers' Convention, you're almost sure, for once, not to be the most spine-chilling person in the room.

Unlimited access to grieving family members to hit on.

Fun work environment now that modern epitaphs are so upbeat: 'Here Lies Mom LOL!'

You are you, not your work, and a loved one will understand this, like your beau, Wilson The Volleyball.

You'll be invited to tons of gatherings and social events called 'wakes'.

You're essentially a subterranean parking lot attendant.

In no other job can you tip yourself gold teeth.

49. Potato Chip Flavours That Didn't Sell

Jehovah's Crispness

Cajun Biohazard

Fizzy Bacon

Garlic Dandruff

Mystery Secretion And Pepper

Sumo Legpit Moss

All-Undressed

Balsamic Landfill

Barbecue Tripe

Basil And Motor Oil

Bloated Roadkill

Cheesy Sneeze

Frito Good Lay

Peppy Gas Bladder

Hickory-Smoked Remains

Pringles Shingles

Blackened Cat

Salt And Budgerigar

Septic Zest

Unspecified Residuum

Spicy Scrotum

50. Superman's Pet Peeves

A scary villain name is so not Lex.

Brando's a weirdo dad.

Earth spermicides just make my guys mad.

Even Vidal Sassoon has failed to create a natural-looking gel strong enough to hold my Kryptonian curl.

If you have x-ray vision, everyone just assumes you're a perv.

It's embarrassing merely to don glasses and a building full of trained-observer reporters can't recognize you.

Liberace also wore a cape.

My parents sent me a billion light years across the galaxy not to Paris or Hong Kong but bloody Smallville.

Once word gets around that you're invulnerable, every joker thug you meet busts a cap in you. Plus, tell folks your name is Jor-El and they assume you're a rapper.

Wise guys who say, 'He's going to Krapton' whenever I visit the washroom.

Superhearing is a curse within a thousand miles of Hulk's snoring.

Superstrength sounds less impressive since the invention of maximum-strength Tylenol.

Surely I'm more super compared to a man than a supermarket to a market.

Try to convince a cop your red eyes are from heat vision.

Now that there are no more phone booths, you have to change via Uber.

51. How Sloths Are The Heart-Throbs Of The Animal Kingdom

He's full of fun little surprises like not being dead.

Loves to Netflix and chill, without the Netflix.

Doesn't bother acting sneaky, because in the time it takes him hurriedly to close his phone, you can read everything on it, plus War and Peace.

Will protect your honour by slumping lifelessly onto any dude who insults you.

Can always whip up a romantic meal of leaves, if by 'whip up' you mean 'not complaining when you go and find yourself some leaves'.

Slow hands.

Takes a week to ejaculate prematurely.

Far too slow to check out a jogging chick in Lycra.

On a date, never complains that the food is taking forever to arrive.

A nice extended holiday is a walk to the corner.

Will never destroy a relationship by sleeping around, though regular sleeping might be problematic.

Has no fear of longterm courtship. Everything is longterm, even winking.

Sex is varied and creative and tender, though saying, 'I love you' takes a season.

His fantasies run to three females, for warmth while napping.

Will attempt to bring you flowers, so be polite and thank him earnestly for the dried stalks he hands you.

52. Funeral Home Secrets

Autopsies are referred to in the business as pumpkin carving.

A disturbing percentage of funeral home workers are paid only in the underwear of the deceased.

Funeral directors see many benefits of death, not the least of which is that it's a surefire cure for restless leg syndrome.

The guys who apply the cosmetics to the corpses unwittingly start fights simply by telling their wives that their makeup looks good.

The term 'deadbeat' means something quite different in the funeral industry.

Scientologists' funerals are largely the same as others, except that the coffins are shaped like rocket ships.

It's a standard prank to send the new guy to a McDonald's drive-thru in a hearse to get Happy Meals.

For a fee, you can be buried with a mobile phone in case you're not really dead. For a smaller fee, you can be beaten with one to ensure that you are.

Funeral directors study for three years, though most of that is learning to steal jewellery surreptitiously from the stiffs.

If you weigh over 150 pounds, you'll be hollowed out with spoons to make you easier to carry.

It's a slanderous rumour that most funeral directors are necrophiliacs. In fact, they primarily prey on grieving relatives.

A Mortician is a cocktail served at funeral director conventions which is one part vodka, two parts gin, a splash of tomato juice and a load of formaldehyde.

Hidden from the view of distraught families is a metal rack above the crematorium for grilling sausages and steaks.

If your family fails to pay for your funeral, management can lawfully dig you up and recover their costs by selling your corpse for use in a very specific genre of motion picture.

Your time of death is no longer determined by a doctor, it's when your Facebook profile goes inactive.

A standard joke is to 'grab a cold one' during work, not after.

The most common things people want buried with them are their wedding ring and browser history.

Staff amuse themselves by betting on which of the bereaved will wail the loudest.

The most common funeral service song request is Bob Marley's Get Up Stand Up.

Judging of the annual funeral director costume competition requires an eye so discerning it can select a winner from hundreds of identical reapers.

An Uber sign in the back of a hearse is an indication that the deceased was not a person of means.

A standard joke among Mafia mourners is that the deceased was a good urner.

53. Signs You Need A Better Deodorant

Even teenage boys think you're disgusting.

If you get within ten feet of a cow, it makes yoghurt.

You sustain frequent concussions when birds plummet from the sky onto your head.

Your pheromones attract wildebeest.

Your soap curdles.

You've always thought buses and trains were just for you.

Phonesex partners gag.

Speedstick invents a new garlic-and-Limburger variant just to take the edge off.

The Geneva Convention deems you a chemical weapon.

The neighbours check The Weather Channel for the wind direction.

The only comment any teacher ever made on your report card was, 'Reeks'.

When you go for a walk in the park, folks push you into the sprinklers.

You are responsible for many more holes in the ozone layer.

Your family buys air fresheners by the silo.

You learn that your mother isn't shedding tears of joy when you visit.

You make airport sniffer dogs have seizures.

You sashay through bad neighbourhoods counting large sums of cash without a care in the world.

Your car has tinted windows now.

Your immune system has attacked and destroyed your olfactory glands.

Your nickname at the manure plant is Stinky.

54. How To Lose Your Job As A Bull Semen Collector

Insist the bulls take you to dinner and a movie first.

Fail to provide a plausible excuse when thirty cows are born that have your eyes.

Wear a cologne called Eau de Ferdinand.

Try to make them jealous by blowing kisses at the oxen.

Ask more than one to the Pasture Prom.

Sell your collection at night in the park.

Dress in a manner you think the bulls find foxy.

Be seen wiping your mouth after each procedure.

Drain the canteen ketchup dispenser in a single motion.

Let slip that you're also Donor Of The Month at the sperm bank.

Get caught selling unopened boxes of rubber gloves on eBay.

Reveal that the bulls are carving notches on their stalls with their horns.

Take job applications from Kevin Spacey.

Keep phoning the bulls in the middle of the night and hanging up.

Make them sleep on the wet patch of hay.

Call them matadorable.

Start wearing silk pyjamas and a velvet smoking jacket.

55. Nazi Versions Of Great Literature

Crime And Swift, Brutal Punishment

The Sound Of The Fuhrer

A Kristallnacht Carol

Of Mice And Mengele

Pride In Prejudice

Great Executions

Himmlet

The Great Gatsenubernschlossery

The Divine Seriousness

The Catcher In The Rhine

Anne Frank Of Green Gables

Panzer's Progress

Fuhrerheil 451

Three Men In A U-Boat

56. Why The Sombrero Is Cool

The ten-gallon hat cowboys think is so impressive is known south of the border as a thimble.

If you have a sombrero and a douchy beard, shallow senoritas will stalk you wherever you go.

They used to be worn by rustlers so they wouldn't be recognized in the moonlight by cows.

Rob a bank wearing high heels, a Kim Jong Un t-shirt, no pants and a sombrero and everyone will describe the assailant as a guy in a sombrero.

Evade capture by blending in with any of the dozens of mariachi bands that roam every place on Earth hourly.

The sombrero has a uniquely-designed, physics-defying shape that causes tornados to bounce right off it and yet the merest hint of drizzle will shatter your skull.

You can hide a Pope hat under it.

Sleeps four if they happen to be lizards or a quartet of Tom Cruises.

A sombrero in an emergency is a flotation device, an igloo and a spittoon.

There is evidence that sombreros were worn much earlier than we think, by napping cavemen.

Like snowflakes, no two sombreros are the same, but unlike snowflakes, it's fine to eat the yellow ones.

Nobody messes with a dude that walks into a biker bar wearing a sombrero because he's either tougher than Chuck Norris' tooth enamel or delivering nachos.

57. Secrets Of The Barbershop

There is famously only one barbershop in the northern hemisphere that isn't a front for organized crime and it's a Mossad safehouse.

Aftershave is actually more effective when used at least thirty-six hours before shaving.

When barber poles are set to spin in reverse, it's an indication that the barber is available for gay sex.

Hairspray's hold is because it's largely aerosol snot.

Barbed wire was originally designed to let you pass, but scalp you.

You can still get a mullet, if you haven't been vaccinated.

That liquid they soak the combs in is snake urine.

If you actually have a short back and sides, no haircut can make you attractive.

'Just a trim' was a popular guillotine joke of French executioners.

Though it's seldom advertised, all barbers are trained to sculpt pubic hair into jolly animal shapes.

In some countries, the little hairs that go down the back of your neck are foreplay.

Each year, improper scissor grip causes thousands to have their their lips sliced off, doomed to cruel, bitter lives of kissless isolation, unable even to whistle in a brave effort to be cheerful anyway.

The sacred oath taken by all barbers compels them to provide a free haircut to feral children and wayward hounds.

All nations have a secret law that permits the enlistment of barbers to quell small-to-medium uprisings.

The storied barbershop quartet started as one nerd coughing.

Crows are so clever some have been known to graduate barber college, but swans drop out.

Shaving foam enables you to be geotracked by passing satellites.

The only natural predator of the barber is the polecat.

They are the only other people who take your dandruff as a shameful personal defeat.

58. Exam Tips

The first question is usually a trap. You are well advised to skip it, and the fourth through ninth.

The best tactic is a good night's sleep, preceded by eleven months of nineteen-hour study days.

A small diagram of your inflamed duodenum and a pouty face will get you sympathy marks.

In case your pen runs dry, they say you should bring another, though two dry pens seem about as useful as one.

Prepare your supplies the night before: pens, pencils, ruler, Encyclopaedia Britannica, Noam Chomsky.

You will not be pushed on the matter if you calmly explain that this is your comfort bong and these are service hookers.

The positive messages we tell ourselves gain effectiveness when shared, so, as a motivator, say audibly to those around you, with genuine confidence, 'I am going to excel, and you are all gonna suck like your moms.'

Trigonometry is sorcery, so you'll never be asked about it.

You can never go wrong with the phrases 'triumph of the human spirit', 'lowest common denominator' or 'bottlenose dolphin'.

If you're doing badly, write someone else's name on the front.

Brainpower is boosted by a healthy breakfast of protein bars and fresh fruit, along with whole grains, a dairy food and sixteen steaming cups of thick Turkish coffee.

Cheaters never win, but winners often cheat.

Even sleep-deprived, the body can generate a second, third and fourth wind, as it has been equipped to do by Nature and meth.

To soothe yourself under pressure, breathe evenly and deeply, and polka.

The word essay means simply to try, so on the big essay question, try to make sense this time.

59. Australian Tourism Slogans

Stay on your toes with our Gargantuan Toilet Snake Of Horror.

Exciting new ways to contract chlamydia without going anywhere near a hooker.

You'd be surprised how much of this place is potentially habitable.

Even piss beer goes down smooth when it's nine thousand degrees in a bush inferno.

Gape in disbelief to see Men At Work still touring.

When you're tired of Australia, it means you've left the airport.

Enjoy the endless beaches, sprawling plains and vast spiders.

See for yourself why we're Earth's penal colony.

Enjoy every sentence sounding like a question?

More than five channels devoted to showings of Crocodile Dundee.

So many weird creatures collected in one place. And the animals are strange too.

Expand your horizons with more new horrific ways to die than you ever thought possible.

Progressive liberal thought-leadership inspires the world in a land where the national sport is dwarf-tossing.

Experience true freedom in tens of thousands of acres of nothing but an infinite array of things that are desperate to kill you.

Join the locals in their weekly elections.

You walk out back to smoke. We walk the outback on fire. Be a man. Come to Australia.

Get run over by a mile-long truck driven by a cross-eyed drunk.

Scorpions, scorpions everywhere and nary a serum to drink.

Learn the many differences between crocodiles and alligators by inserting your torso into one.

Help sneak in his dogs and be given a lake of wine by Johnny Depp.

Make up nonsensical phrases and watch the world copy them like idiots.

Join us on sleazeabout!

Flee into the water to escape the venomous predators and be devoured by a shark.

Delight in a wide variety of tasty snack food if you're a tarantula.

Ain't nothin' funnier than a bloke dressed as a woman.

Marvel at advanced population control by dingo.

This is one country where women are empowered, mostly by the fact that they can thrash you at arm wrestling.

60. Pet Peeves Of New Zealanders

We're forever being confused with Australia, a big hot prison nation chockfull of the descendants of arsonists and dogfuckers nobody else wanted around.

People overlook the many key contributions to the world that New Zealanders have made over the course of history, such as those that are so often overlooked.

The one celebrity Australia has had, let's face it, is Paul Somehow-Shorter-Than-Cruise Hogan, who was famous for about eight minutes in the Eighties, and Men At Work On Sapping Your Will To Live, where New Zealand could have had so many more but we didn't want to, all right?

The Kiwi can be trained to perform a wide variety of helpful tasks, most likely.

I mean, ohhhh, a bloody kangaroo, boing boing, big whoop, any mangy outback critter can bound. Kiwis can FLY!

Also, what is it with Aussies that they have to give everything a cutesie name? It's just a barbecue, you oddballs. The only 'barbies' in your godforsaken land are the ones the boys play with.

But anyway, back to New Zealand, another great thing is that there are no tarantulas here, unlike Australia, where you are quite literally knee-deep in them everywhere you go, are you kidding me?

Plus we won't mention that Australia has snakes even longer than the lines at the drag queen shows.

The truth is that we frankly don't even think about Australia very much.

But if we did, we would point out that no guy has ever faked an Australian accent to get laid, and, I mean, look, fair enough, people don't put on a New Zealand one either, except in Inver-cargill, where they're too dim to realize they already have one.

Kiwis mate for life. With you. Non-stop.

Whereas Australians can't mate until the beer wears off.

Which is warm. You call yourself a civilization and you can't chill beer?

Hey! Wait! I have it! The entire Lord Of The Rings trilogy was filmed in New Zealand! YES! That's IT! It was filmed RIGHT HERE, and guess where, nearby, not?

61. When Rednecks Win The Lottery

Rolls Royce on blocks in the front yard.

All the young-uns get to go to air-conditioning college.

Marginal decrease in shoplifting.

Velvet Elvis artwork framed.

I'm With Stupid shirts now have collars.

Brand new radial tire swing.

Crawfish caviar at every meal.

Now steal HBO in HD.

Take the kids into the Old Town Buffet instead of leaving them in the truck and sneaking out a bag you've filled for them.

A dozen clones of Garth Brooks for bedroom duties.

Wagon wheel coffee table spray-painted gold.

Subscribe to National Enquirer rather than just leafing through it in line at the supermarket.

Vittles chef.

Move the Richard Petty memorabilia out of the barn and into a purpose-built, climate-controlled, 200,000-square-foot shrine.

Fourteen-year-old daughter now good enough to marry the son of the local repo man.

Bait valet at the ol' fishin' crick.

The kids get their own spittoon.

Fancy chrome kitchen sink to pee in.

Actually try European beer to proclaim with authority that Old Milwaukee is superior.

Stained-glass 'Incest Is Best' wall art.

Ralph Lauren wifebeaters.

62. Bad Names For Your Penis

Moby

Boner Lisa

Barnacle Bill

ScruTube

The Toxic Avenger

The Lurker In The Bush

The Brittle Mermaid

The Cheese Factory

Tiny Tim

Ol' Woebegone

The Flash

Lady Gag-On

The Little Engine That Won't

63. You Know You're The Doomed Movie Character When...

You see the evacuation of the town as a very clear sign that you absolutely must stay put.

You reassure the others that if they're too chicken, you'll go see what's whispering their names in the crawlspace.

You're the beady-eyed mayor of a seaside tourist community who merely wishes to remind the bleeding-heart snowflakes how much money will be lost if they close the beach over one measly giant death squid.

You're lovable, funny and have a joyful, grateful, carefree attitude toward life.

When the rustling in the bushes turns out to be a raptor, you coo something like, 'Easy, boy. Eeeeeasy does it...'

There's a number after your name in the credits.

You explain how you're travelling to visit your pregnant wife and/or dying mother that you haven't seen for six months an account of your volunteer work with one-legged blind autistic leper children in war-torn Madeupistan.

You're camping at Grisly Lake and you say, 'Let's smoke a joint and go skinny-dipping!'

You have a weasly idea how to profit from depriving some gigantic roaring behemoth of its freedom.

Whilst fleeing a supernatural terror beast of some kind, you figure it's fine to scoop up some of the sacred diamonds in spite of that silly prophecy.

You're the obnoxious, body-building older brother who taunts his younger sibling mercilessly over his fascination with nebbish science stuff.

64. What You Wish You Didn't Know About Fast Food

The salads are a healthy choice, sure, but if you get the dressing, you might as well have a side of hemlock.

More teenagers die in grease traps each year than in any other type of trap.

Generally speaking, in Nature, nuggets of something are not food.

The ketchup packets are so small you can squirt some in your eye without noticing.

The milk used in the shakes is not from cows, nor any farm animal nor female creature.

The fries contain the same amount of actual potato as a tuba.

It's called fast for how swiftly it thunders through you.

Slushies have changed only in name, from Flushies.

Fast-food scientists are working day and night to find a way to deep-fry a patty made only of butter and lard.

It was first called Windy's for obvious reasons.

An immigration investigation revealed that Burger King is more of an honorary rank, along the lines of Colonel Tom, though his attire is more reminiscent of Elvis.

"Will that be all?" is the question fast-food workers lie awake at night and ask the universe.

For the greatest nutritional value, skip the meal and eat the free toy.

Employee bonuses are based entirely on the napkins they don't give you.

'Secret recipe' is industry-speak for 'woodchip'.

If you spill a vat of drink syrup, that's fine, as it soon hardens into another layer of heavy-duty industrial flooring.

You get a free fry if you can guess how many times a day the staff hear, 'Supersize THIS!'

Pressure-washing the ketchup dispenser is a more potent cause of PTSD than five tours of duty in Kandahar.

Vultures can eat a bucket of anthrax with barely a belch, though dead buzzards account for more than half the garbage volume at fried-chicken joints.

65. Google's Plans For Humanity

In addition to Google glasses and watches, consumers will proudly sport Google belts, trusses, cock rings and kidney stones.

Searching the letter 'k' will immerse you in Kardashians and kittens.

Google 'Yahoo' and that is exactly what will be laser-etched onto your smouldering corpse by a Google marketing drone.

Google's updated Form Wizard will automatically enter the correct answers on online documents, surveys, credit applications, organ donations and legally-binding undertakings without the tedium of human intervention.

Google family members and a massive push-pin will drop onto them from the sky.

All verbs, not just the act of Internet searching, to be replaced with 'to Google'.

Google Map Street View will include Nudist Colony Scenic View, Rose-Coloured Nostalgic View and View Up Your Nose.

Google Sheets will make known to the world what takes place between yours.

A complex new predictive logarithm will determine in advance any intended unsavoury online activity and activate your wife's cold shoulder.

Google will proactively search former romantic partners and update your social media feeds with details of how foolish you were to let them go.

A search of Qatari posthumous dromedary lactation porn will be reported in your hometown newspaper.

Any effort to seek information by any other means will result in Google sending actual trolls to infest your place of dwelling.

Next-generation A.I. will detect when you accidentally enter a search for the wrong political candidate and helpfully redirect you to pages about the one you should be voting for.

In addition to, 'OK, Google', you will also be able to say, 'Hey, Google', 'Yo, Google' and 'Hosannah unto Google in the highest!'

66. Behind The Scenes At The Fair

Should trouble arise, the universal fairground distress code is to yell, 'Hey, rube!' Staff will immediately drop everything, race to you and pick your pocket.

There's no whittler's pride in a shiv these days.

Note that, when there's an announcement of a lost child, they don't suggest looking in the van.

Allowing your teenage daughter and her friends to ride the ghost train is basically putting them on carnival Tinder.

It's unfair to think all ride operators are drunk, since some are also high.

If you don't get felt up on the Dodgems, you can be proud that you're an extremely rare and special kind of ugly.

There's a dude behind the Tilt-A-Whirl who will really give you a whirl.

In more innocent, romantic times, there was just kissing in the Fisting Booth.

Guess Your Weight Without Your Dope And Blades is always the most popular draw on the circuit.

Turns out the Bearded Lady was just Ralph all along.

Probation officers ride free.

Try your luck at Smoke Yourself Unwell.

It's fun to tell the locals there's a ferris-wheel mile-high club.

Ninety percent of the 'arts and crafts' are little stash boxes.

Nothing smaller than a naval frigate has the ballistic power to dislodge one of those coconuts.

'May I see the safety certificate?' is fairground slang for, 'My ribs yearn to be pounded into dust.'

The process servers are in the dunk tank.

When the fortune teller predicts you'll meet a tall, dark stranger, it'll be Dirk, and you won't swoon.

67. What To Get Someone Who Has Everything

Narwhalquarium

Helicopter cosy

Rhesus monkey Cirque Du Soleil shower dance troupe

Fridge with an actual little man to control the light

Giant steam-powered kiss-my-ass machine

Faberge egg cups

Another private jet to keep the first one company

Panda-teste cufflinks

Assless chaps and a ten-foot room to wear them in, plus Kevin Spacey and a nine-foot chain

The unmodified square inch of Cher

Gillette Mach-Ultimate million-blade razor

68. Lies We Tell Ourselves

I look hot in these crocs.

This stripper thinks I'm special.

I'm a great driver and everyone else is an obstacle or a maniac.

I dance nothing like a sack of frying eels.

My sex face doesn't give the impression I'm chewing wasps and being savaged by badgers.

These trousers aren't too small, just an incompatible shape.

What's-her-name is my soulmate.

This hipster beard is a statement of my individuality.

Karaoke will be the means by which I am discovered.

I can differentiate between Coke and Pepsi and shellac.

Fifty is the new anything.

Dudes with massive penises drive this sports car.

I'm the only competent one in my office. At the nuclear launch facility.

I sing great at concerts.

No woman has ever faked it with me. Believe me, I'd know.

Mmm, kale.

This year I'm keeping whatever my resolutions were.

My dog's adoration of me has nothing to do with the treats in my pockets.

I am fully prepared for the mild discomfort this might cause.

The president will grow into the majesty of the office.

A can of Pringles is a single serving and in no way related to my weight problem.

I'm really going to get my money's worth from this gym membership.

I'm in no danger of shredding my fingers while grating cheese.

I'm classy because I eat hummus.

No-one else can smell that.

69. Bands For The Elderly

Bedpantera

AC/BC

The Fracturedly Hip

Arrhythmics

Jaundice Priest

The Rolling Kidney Stones

Iron Deficient Maiden

Diseased Gums & Roses

Gerryatric And The Pacemakers

Grateful Not To Be Dead

Gray Sabbath

DNR Kelly

Counting Crows' Feet

The Stray Cataracts

Creedence Clearwater Attempted Revival

The B-92s

Dexy's Mall-Light Walkers

Wheezer

Flu Fighters

Rage Against The Television

Wheelchair Van Halen

70. You Know It's Cold When...

You have to scrape ice off not only your windshield but your corneas.

Your manhood becomes so shrivelled you're technically female.

You hire sherpas to walk your dog.

You dream of gold at the shivering Olympics.

You buy six documentaries on volcanos.

The aurora borealis flies south.

Squirrels keep their nuts in their cheeks.

You warm your home by cranking the AC.

You long for the warm glow of your ex's black-ice heart.

You have to chase away the snowmen seeking shelter on your porch.

The staff at Baskin Robbins swap their scoops for jackhammers.

Your sneezes come out in cubes.

You can't be seen behind the goosebumps.

Dogs bond fast to hydrants.

There are slightly fewer Canadians grilling.

The queues at Tim Horton's circumnavigate the globe only twice.

71. Inspirational Gym Posters

If it hurts, it's working. If it bleeds, it's REALLY working.

Winners never quit pounding on quitters.

This is a 'roid-free gym. Yes! They're complimentary!

Would you rather be fat and ugly or fit and ugly?

Don't stop attendin' till you pop a tendon bendin'.

Pump more iron, pump more chicks!

You can never have too much money or too many abs.

Give a hundred and ten percent, because if your brainpower is such that you're that bad at math, you're gonna need brawn.

Similarly, if you know squat, do squats.

If you love something, don't set it free, press it.

The bigger the man, the tinier the t-shirt.

72. Benefits Of The Coronavirus

Less worry about gingivitis.

Reduced population makes it possible for Kevin Spacey to grope everyone twice.

Might curtail the Red Hot Chili Peppers.

Something to make small talk about other than the weather.

The End Is Nigh sign-carriers experience a renewed sense of job satisfaction.

Annoying coworkers soon suffer gratifyingly agonizing, lonely death.

Conservative media barely able to blame it on immigrants and welfare recipients.

Convenient excuse to cancel party plans except in Sudbury.

Sharp decline in the twitish hipster dipshit population.

Nice to see something go old-school viral.

Opportunity for leadership to take charge by sending thoughts and prayers.

Significantly shorter Christmas card list.

Those lovely decorative last-rites dream-catchers really perk up the decor.

With fewer people, individual intensity of loathing for Piers Morgan must be increased to maintain acceptable level.

Finally an end to the zombie craze.

73. Clues You're Being Murdered By A Gay Serial Killer

Sews your skin into a lovely tiffany sunsmock.

Remarks that you tremble adorably with the engaging allure of a newborn fawn.

Will eat your liver only when you confirm in writing that you're gluten-free and organic.

Complains ceaselessly about the cancellation of Will And Grace as you bleed out.

Plays showtunes to drown your screams.

The lotion in the basket is scented.

Tries to get the press to start calling him The Fabulous Fiend.

Giggles gleefully as he hacks a likeness of Liberace into your chest.

Calls it his Fraidy-Cat-O'-Nine-Tails.

His multiple personalities are psychotic cowboy, murderous cop, death Indian, homicidal construction worker, stabby sailor and submissive leather man.

Sees chasing you through the woods as cardio.

74. Tabloid Headlines From History

Crafty Pharaoh Solves Problem Of Not Much To Do In Egypt

Sir Hillary First To Climax In Nepal

Crazy Apple-Loving Bitch Invents Fashion

Jocks Joyride On Moon

King Henry Unlucky In Love A Fifth Time

Feisty German Likes A Bit Of Pole

Spanish Sailor Probes For Passage Yet Again

Rubber Fetishist In Kinky Water Play With French Midget

Stench Of Garlic Washes Over Britons From Hastings

Orange Maniac Grabs Whitehouse By Pussy

Yankies Aim For World's Largest Cuppa Record In Boston

Japs Give Pearl A Pounding She Wasn't Expecting

London Marshmallow Toasting Gets Out Of Hand

Russian Dog Steals Spaceship

75. Why Keith Richards Is
A Great Grandfather

Lullabies given refreshing treatment sung in wheezing, whiskey-addled, phlegmy growl.

Many more strippers than at most five-year-olds' birthday parties.

Spoils the little tykes by letting them play in his stash.

Revives them from naps.

Uses baby bottles to make baby bongs.

When you pull his finger, smoke comes out his ears.

Always get to hang backstage with Barney.

Cold turkey sandwiches.

Humorous No Poofs sign to prank Uncle Mick.

For grades, A is for Autograph.

It's a bonding thing to nod off together.

No grazed knees from falling off bikes but a few splinters from smashed miniature Telecasters.

No-one else's grampa looks just like a wooden Indian.

Show & Tell is really livened up by switchblades.

Skulls crib mobile makes bedtime fun.

Shows the tykes how to drive their pedal cars into a swimming pool.

When the grandkids trash daycare, just pays the teacher to clean it up, no questions asked.

Turns out straws can also be used to drink liquids. Who knew?

76. Batman's Secrets

Alfred tries to lure kids into the Bratcave.

Catwoman litters, if you get my drift.

Growing wise to Batman's techniques, Gotham criminals have taken to dressing normally and simply robbing or murdering rather than plotting to turn everybody into housebricks or some such nonsense. Fooled by their cunning, Batman is powerless to stop them.

He is the only human on the medical books who actually passes guano.

The most successful revenue stream for Wayne Enterprises is appearing at Batman bar mitzvahs.

Never takes a bat-h.

Heath Ledger scared the living hell out of him even when he wasn't in role.

Only Vicki Vale gets to see the Batpython.

Robin wanted to be called Roberta.

If not for a mix-up at the dry cleaners, Batman would have just been a sexy transvestite nurse on his way to a party.

Prefixes the labels on things in the fridge with 'Bat' so that no-one else eats them.

The Joker actually is pretty funny at a party with a lampshade on his head.

77. Lines From Celebrities' Report Cards

Arnold Schwarzenegger - Either a world-class intellect or functionally retarded, too unintelligible to determine.

Bill Cosby - Particularly active during naptime.

The Student Who Insists Upon Being Called Prince - Chronically peculiar behaviour inspires bullying and savage beatings on a daily basis, and that's just by the staff.

Queen Elizabeth - Refuses to remove long white gloves for fingerpainting.

Tom Cruise - Hides amongst the crayons.

Amy Schumer - Confident and popular, though she does talk about her genitals rather more than most four-year-olds.

Oprah Winfrey - Evil.

Kevin Spacey - Plays well with others non-consensually.

Carrie Fisher - Inexplicably respected by the entire school in spite of being involved in practically nothing.

Yoko - In a music class by herself.

Judge Judy - Bitch. Senile.

Elvis - School nurse blames restless leg syndrome.

Roger Waters - He don't need no education.

Jeffrey Dahmer - Makes his peers nervous at lunchtime.

Ringo Starr - Not even the smartest Ringo in the school.

George W. Bush - So dumb he'll probably be president.

Madonna - A model student, other than the writhing.

Benedict Cumberbatch - Almost as pretentious as his name.

Bill Clinton - Great at sax and sex, so it's best to keep him away from the teaching assistants.

Ralph Macchio - Apparently, he's thirty-two.

Christian Bale - An intense, brooding young man who is just a little too pleased with himself for anyone's liking.

Sam Kinison - The cause of significant hearing loss among the faculty.

78. Signs You Need A New Car

It's disheartening how often you can clearly see your front wheels in the rearview mirror.

If the GPS breaks, you can always follow the trail of parts home.

Your motto of maintenance is 'Duct tape doesn't rust'.

Your girlfriend leaves you for a guy with one broken rollerskate.

You measure your speed in miles per month.

Police pull you over to give you citations for bravery.

Your blinkers aren't visible through the smoke.

The horn is an actual death rattle.

Your neighbours offer you thousands to scrap it as you're responsible for a twenty-five percent reduction in local property values.

Just as there's no dump bath, you see no point in a car wash.

Car thieves leave cash donations on your windshield.

You framed your one speeding ticket.

79. Why Harrison Ford Is Too Old For Action Movies

Where he used to run from boulders, now it's pollen.

Publicity photos are mostly snaps of him napping.

There's no room for a holster with his pants pulled up to his chest.

He can barely make out the cuebillboards.

Car chases are ruined when he tries to save gas.

Busts more hips than heads, and that cracking sound isn't his whip but his lower back.

His insurance only covers him moving from one easy chair to another.

The sound of the clapperboard gives him a heart attack.

His next movie is Raiders Of The Lost Park Pigeons.

Won't attend premieres if they conflict with cribbage night.

Demands speaking parts for every member of his mall-walking group.

In Star Wars movies now, HE's the death star.

Insists filming wrap by the early-bird menu.

Dozes during love scenes, and non-love scenes.

The director doesn't cry 'Action!' but 'Careful!'

The catering team can't meet the demand for prunes.

Removing his wrinkles by CGI takes more computing power than Google has available.

The system of winches, pulleys and scaffolding required to help him do a roundhouse kick is beyond the budget of most productions.

The fights are with bladder control.

Is early on set due to early onset Alzheimer's.

80. Chilling Secrets Of The Public Library

If a record of you doesn't appear in the microfiche, you technically don't exist and library staff are allowed to harvest your organs.

Ask at the desk for 'the collected great works of the wondrous Keats' and you'll get a free sack of opium.

If you use a library computer to access the Internet just once, your identity and those of your descendants will be used by Russian mobsters for generations.

That bar code on each book tells them when you borrowed it, when it's due, why it sparked your interest, which hard words you failed to comprehend and for what embarrassing duration you were reading it in the bathroom.

If your vision is poor, you can get large-print books, or, if you see perfectly well and have a lick of sense, no-print, for books by E.L. James.

Those who return a book past its due date seem to turn up shortly in the obituary column with 'the late' before their name.

The nastiest, filthiest, most rapidly orgasm-inducing, ultra-intense pornography is stored in the History And Culture Of Belgium section, which is why no-one knows about it.

You receive electronic notice when a book you've reserved has arrived, from a menacing dude named Vlad The E-mailer, and if you don't pick it up within five minutes, he skewers you like a human hors d'oeuvre.

The name was changed to 'study cubicle' from 're-education pod'.

Ironically, Sir Dufus 'Dewey' Decimal, who invented The System, was far less literate than everyone.

Each year, millions die of the excruciating paroxysms caused by breathing paper mildew and bookworms.

The more literate self-harming teens papercut themselves.

Every penny paid in fines is used to put hits out on people who tear pages out of encyclopedia.

81. What's Good Luck In Prison

When you get sentenced to seven years, seven months and seven days.

Finding mold in so-called solitary.

Conjugal groping visits from Kevin Spacey.

When you have tsunamic diarrhea and you get the top bunk.

Getting badly beaten in the showers on the same day the infirmary gets a delivery of fresh splints.

When a stool pigeon poops on you.

Anal four-leaf-clover tattoos.

Dreaming of your cellmate and doves.

When your array of venereal diseases finally makes you unappealing to the general population.

Whittling a Shawshank out of the 'food'.

When that dreamy guy in Cell 9 cuts you and you didn't even think he knew you were alive.

82. Most Horrifying Four-Word Phrases

Anne Frank's trombone practice

Drenched in yak urine

Hi, I'm Richard Simmons!

Rap around the clock

Albanian blobfish pornstar

Another colonic plunger incident

Bravo, Yoko, encore, encore!

Donald Trump's moral compass

Have another cinnamon smoothie

Prophet Mohammed cartoon cavalcade

Smurfs ate my baby

Dysentery ruins another picnic

Squeal, Oprah, squeal!

Sumo wrestlers' tainted mawashis

Teenage mutant hipster turtles

Call the spider whisperer

The Shriners found me

Unexpected Zach Gagglegooserapist cameo

United Airlines customer service

83. Complaints Of Tom Cruise's Personal Assistant

Having to wear lead sweaters and concrete blocks in a backpack to shed those stubborn last three inches.

Buying up all the Maps To The Demented Stars' Homes.

He never saw the humour in that trick of putting an up-ended drinking glass over him and pretending you can't hear him yelling to be set free.

Gives you 'exceedingly generous' tips but in Kolobian pygmillions.

You spend six months of the year preparing for Japanese Tom Cruise Day and then six months debriefing how fabulous it was.

Hourly errands to the cobbler to have even taller lifts installed.

Pay cuts for failing to describe his purple furies as towering.

Referring to it as the 'somewhatlessbigwave' oven.

Finding experts willing to explain at length how it's an anomaly of camera angles that Dustin Hoffman looks taller on the Rain Man DVD despite being himself a dwarf.

Inflating the driver's seat in his Ferrari so he can see over the dashboard.

Writing fake fan mail pleading for Vanilla Sky 2.

He runs screaming under the couch when he sees a moth.

Loses what's left of his mind when you teach his children nursery rhymes like Old Mother L. Ron Hubbard.

At speaking engagements, insists on a podium no taller than a floormat.

It's dangerous to bolt up trees when startled by his eerie, intense, verge-of-snapping smile.

Refers to Meryl Streep as 'that lanky hack'.

The cubes from the Planet Kolob Volcano Dressing Room Ice Dispenser are always just hot water.

You feel stupid wearing a nameplate wide enough to identify you as Personal Assistant To The Level-Eight Exulted Sky-High Shapeshifter.

Denies he's lost it but expects you to find it.

84. Other Uses For Hummus

Vampire and non-vampire repellent.

Keeps seagulls and pigeons away from landfills.

Aids weight loss; applied to even the highest-calorie foods, renders them inedible.

Can be used as a fake version of any bodily emission for hilarious practical jokery.

Anal forcefield against prison buggery.

A deodorant that doesn't make your tramp friends feel bad about themselves.

A fine appetizer before a hearty repast of rancid jockstrap.

The only thing that stands even half a chance of keeping Silvio Berlusconi away from your teenagesdaughter.

A thick layer dried in the sun for an hour provides a superior replacement for space shuttle blastoff heat tiles.

Roll it out flat, apply it to your favourite comic book and not only will it transfer the picture but it will also ruin your comic with a gross, hummusy stain.

A dab of hummus on the neck can transform you instantly from an ordinary man into an ordinary man with hummus on his neck.

85. You Might Be Pushing Your Kids Too Hard If...

You feel an A- is reasonable grounds to sell them to the gypsies.

Bred into their bones is contempt for the Japanese as slackers.

You allow them to spend their birthday money on any brand of violin strings they like.

A dreaded punishment is no striving.

They ask Santa for better bone structure.

They refer to their agent as Daddy.

They have lived in the attic ever since the great colouring-outside-the-lines calamity.

They could speak five languages before you brought them home from the hospital.

You keep a paper shredder next to the fridge for childish artwork that doesn't make the grade.

You held their teddy bear hostage until they mastered calculus.

You call them your Baby Navy Seals as a little joke, but there's still no napping during Hell Week.

They say grace in the original Latin.

The naughty step has spikes on it.

They are all named Prodigy.

They pay you allowance from their wages at the salt mine.

They make little gammaphotoproton galvinators out of plasticene.

You have a strict 'No Ph.D, no dessert' policy.

The only monster living under their beds is the fear of failure.

They'll go to sleep only if you read to them in Stephen Hawking voice.

They trained the dog to rewire the rec room.

They can name more than a hundred Popes but look bewildered and cry when asked to identify Tom's cartoon mouse pal.

You feel stage moms should be charged with abandonment.

You permit tattoos, but only of goals.

When you accidentally misuse 'affect' and 'effect', they demand a DNA test.

Teachers quit under the strain of being perpetually wrong.

You don't permit construction of any Lego structure without a full set of blueprints.

Their crib mobiles are the human genome.

86. How To Be A Loser Giraffe

Wear Trump ties that still somehow manage to be absurdly long.

Strap a webcam to your nubbies and livestream Serengeti peeping tom porn.

Nag your mom to hurry up and finish knitting you that turtleneck before she dies.

Claim the bruise on your chin is from a passing aircraft and definitely not from tripping over a hyena.

Make random clicking sounds that you pretend are great works of Masai poetry.

Sit in the front row of the movie theatre.

Steer all conversation around to whether you can really spot the trans giraffes by their Adam's apples.

Tell everyone you're a gazelle that got your head stuck in an elevator.

Try to impress girls by eating spaghetti without twirling it.

Be ridiculously whiplash-prone.

Get a python stuck in your throat.

87. Headlines That Would Cause Panic

Piers Morgan Breeds Like A Rabbit

New Law Forces Hipsters To Forge Individual Identities

Achy-Breaky Heart New National Anthem

Kevin Spacey Claims To Be On Hiatus From Groping But He Could Be Anywhere

Canada Goes Beerless As Climate Change Kills Hops Crops

Scientology Just Good Sense, To Be Taught In Schools, God Announces

Badger Uprising Claims One Millionth Life

Radioactive Drinking Water No Cause For Concern, Says Left Head Of Prime Minister

Siri Now To Point Out Physical Shortcomings

New Pizza Toppings To Include Tofu, Kale

All TV Programs To Feature Psychotic Chefs

Court Order Denies Nut Allergy Sufferers The Right To Keep Spoiling Things For Everyone Else

Pork Prices Soar As Jewish Scholars Correct Typo In Torah

Strong Winds Scatter Cher

Walmart Relaxes Dress Code

Bieber Vows To Be Worse Little Tit

Shock Papal U-Turn, Gayness Godly, Straights To Burn In Hell

Japanese Work Ethic Catches On In The West

88. Life's Injustices

It's always the folks who don't say thanks when you hold a door that beg most piteously for their lives.

No cat, no matter how considerate, has ever received a Thanks For The Mangled Sparrow card.

It never fails. You line up all day for a tourniquet only to be told they're fresh out.

The Japanese are industrious, innovative, honourable, creative, hygienic, polite, loyal and completely mental.

Eight Fast And Furious Movies and only one Howard The Duck.

Cremate your grandma the day the after she dies and everyone will be sympathetic, but just an hour before and they'll be furious.

You can be an upstanding citizen and give to charity and do good deeds your whole life, but blow one lousy goat and that's what'll be on your tombstone.

Mow people down in the welcome wagon and they'll say you meant well.

If you pee in them, the bar you over-patronized should have to buy you new shoes.

They'll criticize you for being a couch potato and then shame you for being an active shooter.

No-one gropes poor Kevin Spacey.

North Koreans are starving, but their glorious leader could be a star at Sea World.

It always rains when you wash your car and there's always a volcano when you barbecue.

Road rage is 'unfair' to the blind.

The world's finest architects, artisans and craftsmen, working tirelessly around the clock with putty and trowels, because of strict non-disclosure agreements, get no credit for Trump's hair.

We are supposed to spend more time outdoors, and yet being a hobo is frowned upon - pick a side, humanity.

Openness and honesty are fantastic, but bellends seldom wish to be called out.

99.99% of all flavour is in fat and sugar.

Airline seats are precisely two inches narrower than my arse.

Cinnamon remains at large.

89. What Makes The Pope Swear

The only gift you ever get from the guards is Toblerone.

Tiresome discussions of which is cooler, the Popemobile or the Batmobile.

Wags who shorten Heavenly Father to He-Man.

How Eminem has lost his street cred.

Only one book to read in the Vatican library.

Fools who believe his first name is The.

When he argues with a cardinal and it's referred to archly as a Pon-tiff.

Chronic depression from those joyless hymns.

Infallibility sure doesn't help with crossword puzzles.

St. Peter's square.

Hokey slogans like Yes We Vatican!

Illiterates who call it the papal concave.

God only gets in touch when He wants something.

Predecessor left nasty swastika underwear in the dresser.

Takes ages to wash spittle out of his ring.

Must always select Other from the occupation drop-down box when applying for a credit card.

Nowhere to puke in the confessional when Berlusconi seeks absolution.

90. Signs You're Not Cut Out To Be A Pirate

You're disappointed when the booty is just priceless treasure.

You're so worried about scurvy you go vegan.

You favour making wrongdoers skip the plank.

You stamp your feet until they put Diet Coke in your rum.

The 'treasure map' always seems to lead to your pants.

You've got a girl in every port, to style your hair.

You have morning wood in lieu of a wooden leg.

Try as you might, your swash remains unbuckled.

You advocate keel-hauling, but only for infractions of the dress code.

You swap your eyepatch for a nicotine one.

You embroider motivational messages about teamwork on the sails.

You thought you were just going to copy DVD's.

You giggle whenever anyone mentions the coxswain.

You keep saying, 'Avast, dear hearts!'

You submit an application to the Coast Guard every month.

You'll only swab your cheekbones.

Your cutlass is more of a featherduster.

Your interest in cabin boys begins and ends with laundry.

Your pirate name is Long John Doe.

You say, 'Errrr...'

91. How The Marines Would Be Different If They Recruited Only Strippers

They wouldn't raise the flag on conquered lands, just the pole.

Terror cells decimated as Marines burst out of cakes to shoot them.

Purple Hearts now just dollar bills stuffed into your fatigues.

General Cookie Champagne heads Joint Chiefs Of Staff.

You'd need a platoon spittoon.

Tactical training to include grabby drunk avoidance and marching in platforms.

Salutes would be largely involuntary.

It would be renamed the Marine Hard Corps.

Grunts would moan.

Full dress parade not so much.

92. Best Ways To Treat A Cold

No amount of cod liver oil is too much, except for the cod, of course, which really can't spare all that much.

Heed the old wives' tale and feed a cold, but not vegetables or tofu.

BE the mucus!

Secure an ample medicinal supply of long-lasting, fast-acting ale and bemoan the sad state of affairs when an ailing man can't get his beer refreshed by the perfectly healthy woman of the house.

You cannot catch more than one virus at a time, so take the opportunity to make out with your sickly neighbour on the ventilator.

Inhale the fumes from a sulphur spring or Piers Morgan.

If you are female, shake it off and get on with forty things to do. If you are a man, send actual butt roots down into the couch and suffer loudly and piteously, flipping through the TV channels like a strobe light with attention deficit disorder.

Go to the park and honk at the geese.

See a doctor daily - they appreciate the updates and it makes them feel useful.

93. Perks Of Dating Psycho Bitches

Their mood swings keep you so deftly on your toes you can join a ballet troupe.

Sublimated anxiety tremors let you shed flies like a horse.

The withering hate rays you glare behind her back bounce off and kill spiders.

Jolly camping vibe as you sleep on the floor because of what you did.

Finally a chance to get rid of your shitty buddies and replace them with her fabulous friends.

It's fun to secretly rub her cotton balls on yours.

You start to feel lucky as you perceive a broader range of things that are good fortune, such as dying first.

You invest in a potter's wheel to make cool batshit sculpture.

No need to bother reading your own mail or texts.

Give her pet names like Harpyheart, Snakemate and Dog On All Legs.

94. Why Dolphins Aren't As Nice As You Think

Most would cheerfully drown one of those 'dying wish' kids given half the chance.

A gentlemen's agreement between dolphins and sharks is to share the surfers fifty-fifty.

Dolphin language is complex but mostly conveys the sentiments, 'I'm gonna tap that,' and 'Fuck off!'

Dolphins dispute that humans are also mammals. They think of us as a kind of noisy mildew.

Dolphins have sex for pleasure, and money.

They find that adorable doe-eyed baby seals make the best balls for their week-long gory games of near-death volleyball.

The Bermuda Triangle is famed for aircraft disappearances and having the fattest dolphins in the ocean.

The bottlenose ones are so called because when they get their nose in the bottle, they're the surliest drunks in the world.

The little boy dolphins have the most popular blowholes.

Their longstanding bitter rivalry led dolphins to organize the Great Global Porpoise Final Solution.

They don't jump for fish at Sea World. The true incentive? Crack.

They hide in tuna nets in order to get a shot at their favourite meat, tuna fishermen.

They often save swimmers from drowning, sure, and then they tow them to their deep-sea lairs to die in vicious thrill-kill, krill-crazed gangbangs.

They think seals undignified to balance balls on their noses, so they bite their testes off and make them balance those.

They're always smiling? Yeah, so was Himmler, in the exact same way.

When they race alongside cruise ships, they're waiting for fattened buffet-besotted tipplers to topple overboard.

It's no coincidence that the sports team with the most players facing murder charges is the Miami Dolphins.

95. Surprises In Winston Churchill's Autobiography

Just when all seemed lost, in his most uplifting unreported speech, he brought Parliament to its feet with a rousing, inspiring call to surrender at once.

He dumped his then-girlfriend, Eva Braun, on Christmas Day 1938. Her rebound beau went to great pains to impress her.

In spite of everything, he always loathed the French more.

Fearless wartime leader, unwavering ally, world-class orator, barely passable at hopscotch.

The first draft read, 'We shall fight on the beaches and on the landing grounds, we shall fight in the fields and in the streets, we shall fight in the hills, we shall fight in the confectionaries and in the fish and chips shops and in the haberdasheries and in the tobacconists' and in the ludicrously ostentatious golden carriage that carts the bloody Queen around, we shall fight in the never-lifting fog and in the morning and in what appears to be the evening but is in fact the drizzly afternoon gloom, we shall fight in the quiet dead of night when the BBC at last goes off the air, but not at teatime.'

He ordered those round-the-clock air strikes just because he thought the Nazis deserved to be as bombed as he was all day.

He kept a copy of Mein Kampf, with his favourite bits under-lined, hidden in the cover of Pride And Prejudice.

He was known as Pooh at school.

Was celebrated for his dead-on impersonation of Gary Oldman.

He quite literally could not get enough sauerkraut, despite the non-stop airlifts from Berlin.

For Valentine's Day, everyone was required by law to give him brandy hearts.

What he actually said was, "This is not the end, nor even the beginning of the end, but it is, perhaps, the middle of the middle."

Ironically, as a child, his dream was to play accordion in an oompah band.

The theory that he and the Queen Mum were one and the same was largely discounted, but no-one ever saw them together.

For all his worries about the war, he was far more concerned that the Swiss were up to something.

Against the emphatic advice of his military commanders, in secret backdoor talks with high Reich officials near the end of the conflict, he came perilously close to agreeing to make it two out of three.

His initial reaction when informed about the Nazi invasion of Czechoslovakia was, 'So?'

96. Signs Of Spring In Sudbury

The robins thaw out and fly the hell outta there.

Restaurants switch from fried stews to fried salads.

The cold crunch of the snow gives way to the warm crunch of the needles.

You can go back to picking up litter instead of shovelling walks for your community service.

Police can no longer fudge the stats by recording unsolved homicides as hypothermia.

Hobos migrate back to the north side of the underpass.

The chalk outlines come back to the sidewalk.

Four-headed, glow-in-the-dark lambs frolic in the barren fields.

The hookers stop wearing shorts and winter boots.

Young men's thoughts turn to siring young, so they briefly stop begging for anal.

You don't look like such a tool anymore, leaning against the variety store, smoking an unfiltered cigarette in mittens.

The committed drunks stagger blinking out of the bars into the warm sunshine, only to dash back in.

You just openly throw rocks at store windows instead of what you pretend are snowballs.

Fraudulent lawsuits for falls on ice now trips over tulips.

Young lovers stop carving each other's names in the frostbite.

Since they no longer need to hide from the outside world, the detox centre is bereft of addicts other than the albinos.

They finally hose out the paddywagon.

You can ditch the scarf-and-wifebeater ensemble.

No more making snow angels in the blood.

97. Unpopular Baby Names

Protozoey

Urethra

Paulsy

Bully-Bob

Sphincterry

Lloser

Trumpina

Carjack

Amnesia

Dystopia

Eriction

Putrid

Peanu

Annaconda

Grandmalison

Jenocide

98. Mafia Euphemisms For Murder

Causing a queue at the Pearly Gates

Cementing our friendship

Easing the census-taker's workload

Going compostal

Keeping the coroner's kids in shoes

Making future fossils

Making the most of the bubble in the widow market

Plunked in the trunk

Pruning the family tree

Russian Roulette without the gamble

Taking harp lessons

99. Unappealing Cartoon Characters

Bedbugs Bunny

See If I Care Bears

Donald Trump Duck

Betty White Boop

Bitchy Rich

Butt Tightrear

Chronic The Hedgeho

Gnarly Brown

Peeping Tom And Jury

The Pink Pantser

Popeye The Sailors' Man

Porka Pig

The 'Roid Runner

Scabby Doo

100. Reasons To Fear Models

Armed with a cocktail of noxious hair-and-makeup substances, they can unleash chemical warfare in seconds.

Your lung can be punctured easily with a single bony finger.

How much of a bad-ass do you have to be to live a week on a sprig of parsley?

Even a relatively plain model can shrivel your heart to a prune with a single shrug.

Models living together in hotels for long periods will synchronize their mood swings.

Their extreme slenderness enables them to slide under doors or through water pipes to slaughter you where you feel most secure.

They are loved by all their personal assistants owing to Stockholm Syndrome.

They have resting bitch face even when laughing.

The intense protein rush from a single bite of hotdog triggers superhuman surges of strength.

A caviar diet is now believed to be what went wrong with Caligula.

101. Hints You Maybe Shouldn't Be A Chef

You cannot think of fish skin and vegetable peelings as anything other than garbage.

You are unable to discern the difference between pepper that has been ground freshly or by Noah.

In your home cutlery drawer, there are fewer than six whisking devices.

You can name not even a dozen grave paprika crimes.

You rarely are obliged, by principle and etiquette, to fling a cleaver.

You believe that some foods aren't improved by dowsing them in olive oil.

You once burned your house down making Cup-a-Soup.

You were stunned when someone told you fries are made from potatoes.

You can't recall the last time you braised a snack.

As an anniversary present, you have never given a Gortex non-stick heat-concentric ceramic crockpot.

You have an ethical panic attack charging someone forty bucks for an ounce of fish and an atom of broccoli.

You'd rather eat your sister's pussy than caviar or foie gras.

Your menu runs heavily to 'vittles'.

You've never signed anything in sauce.

When a diner sends something back, you don't form a bitter, seething animus toward his pets and loved ones.

You struggle to remember whether it's metal in microwaves never or always.

102. Japanese Movie Title Translations

Salaryman Inexplicably Succeeds In Spite Of Working Short Hours (Wall Street)

Super Great Perfect Hero Selflessly Tolerates Appalling Buffoon (Rain Man)

Cease Life In The Way Of The Anvil (Die Hard)

Scoundrels Without Honour, Except One (Shawshank Redemption)

Utterly Fictional Fantasy Nonsense (Pearl Harbour)

Comical Gangster Whimsy (Goodfellas)

Average Day In Tokyo (Godzilla)

I Am Aware That You Brought Shame Upon Your Family By Failing To Devote Yourself To Ceaseless Academic Study During The Recent Warm Weather (I Know What You Did Last Summer)

Office Harlot Does Not Know Her Place (Working Girl)

Cleaner Befriends Food (The Shape Of Water)

Polite Man Shares Recipes While Woman Seeks Petty Criminal (The Silence Of The Lambs)

Hilarious Malnourished Sumo With Speech Impediment Wrestles Badly (Rocky IV)

Successful Man Inexplicably Falls For Awful Geisha Who Cannot Even Play An Instrument (Pretty Woman)

Sulu-San Saves The Universe (Star Trek)

Inferior Engineering Costs Many Lives (Titanic)

Ordinary Sex Billionaire (Fifty Shades Of Grey)

Many Defy The Emperor (Star Wars)

Efficient Civil Engineering In Thailand (The Bridge On The River Kwai)

Soup Takes Revenge (Jaws)

Mismanagement At The Petting Zoo (Jurassic Park)

Vile Harlot Murders Lovely Japanese Girl (Kill Bill)

103. The Best Things About Life Without TV

With the exception of him stalking you personally, greatly reduced possibility of exposure to Piers Morgan.

The latest updates on Meghan Markle's hair will come as a delightful surprise from your buddies at the lodge.

The plight of the Ugandan lesser-pleated purple guinea squirrel will no longer haunt your dreams.

Freedom from that claustrophobic paranoid sense of being encroached upon on all sides by Kardashians.

Space in your living room for a much larger blast furnace, Hadron Collider or moonshine still.

Can now go ten minutes without anyone mentioning their mild-to-moderate colonic reflux.

No more praying to pass a rectal cactus rather than see one more instant of Trump.

Your insight and wisdom can be shared by shrieking at real people in the street rather than onscreen.

More time to read TV Guide.

Can masturbate with just as much abandon to the Preparation H commercials on the radio.

No more alarmist reporting that you're the only one who hasn't died of an opioid overdose.

The school shooting app makes sure you don't miss any.

Actual flipping around is good exercise.

104. Why Storm Chasers Make Poor Romantic Partners

He looks stupid in the lightning with a rake on his head.

No matter how well things are going, you always have the nagging sense that he'd leave you in a heartbeat for a rockslide.

Learn all the exotic sex tricks you like, you'll never leave him as satisfied as when he's ducking flying cows.

His basic survival instinct is fight-or-scamper-toward.

He's visibly disappointed when you brush your hair and no longer appear windswept.

Always wants to celebrate your anniversary in an active volcano.

His rom-com movie choice is Armageddon.

A whisper in his ear thrills him far less than a howling gale, by which he'd much rather be blown.

He'd rather date Stormy Daniels.

You want the window closed at night and he likes the roof off.

Doesn't enjoy romantic strolls in the rain as much as being swept along by a flood, and the fact that your birthday falls in typhoon season is just too bad.

When you come home unexpectedly, you catch him abusing himself ferociously to Twister.

Queued for hours to meet Rubin 'Hurricane' Carter and sulked for a week after learning he's a boxer.

Brings a bullhorn on your Alpine vacation in an effort to start an avalanche.

105. Backyard Pond Rules

No walking on the pond to prove one is the Messiah.

No using the gentle lapping sound of the pond on a breezy day to hypnotise women into agreeing to your freakish demands.

No gargling the pond and then putting it back when no-one is looking because ew.

No raw sewage in the pond. (Grilled is fine.)

No luring waterfowl to the pond for unspeakable purposes Thursdays.

No submerging oneself in the pond and breathing through a straw to launch a ninja-style blowpipe attack on remote-control mariners.

No complaining that the pond had a good time with you but then never called.

No referring to the pond as a puddle even while upset with the pond.

No removing the path in order to make the pond into a moat.

No being more putridly rancid than the pond.

No using the pond as an emergency rendezvous point when missions go south.

No secretly secreting in the pond.

No snapping and cutting a broad swath of terror through the pond unless you're a Canada goose.

No baptisms in the pond, especially of fire.

Do not add vegetables, meat and stock to the pond as some sort of giant soup art installation.

No watering your hoss in it and calling it the Ponderosa.

No gazing into the pond adoringly unless the name on your birth certificate is legitimately Narcissus.

Do not say, 'Pond. James Pond.'

All erections within 20 meters of the pond, howsoever caused, must be registered in advance with the pond ranger.

No drinking the pond in the hope of acquiring superpowers.

106. Pranks Played On Hitler

Adding bagels to the breakfast menu.

Changing the fearsome eagle on his hat to Tweetie Pie.

Giving the 'Hi, Hitler!' salute.

Hiding outside his bathroom and making a loud hissing sound when he switches on the shower.

Referring to him in memos as The Furor.

Requisitioning ten thousand cans of pink paint for new Pansy Tank Division.

Rushing frantically into his office claiming they forgot to lock Auschwitz.

Suggesting during staff meetings that left-handers should be sent to concentration camps.

Telling him his next physical is with Dr. Mengele.

Saying, 'Siege heil!'

107. Uncool Band Names

Abbatoir

The Tyrds

Crosby, Stills, Nash, Young & Schwartz, Chartered Accountants

KC And The Sunshine Chain Gang

Nirvana White

The Whom

Moron 5

A-Hem

Meagredeath

The Dung Beatles

Herman's Armpits

Piss

Queen Mum

Stone Temple Pilates

The Grammar Police

Lukewarm Bell Peppers

Rage Against The Photocopy Machine

Emerson, Lake Woebegone And Arnold Palmer

108. You Might Be A Narcissist If...

You tell folks how thrilled they are to meet you.

You charge the barber ten bucks to touch your hair.

If you sneeze on someone, you say, 'Bless you.'

You pity Trump's inferiority complex.

You smash more mirrors by over-vigorous kissing than by any other means.

You not only call out your name during sex, but propose after an elaborate self-courtship.

Your social media profile name is El Magnifico.

You say things 'unto' people.

You sprinkle rose petals in your path.

When you are a guest in someone's home, you follow up with a nice You're Welcome card.

You consider self-esteem a good start.

You slow-dance solo.

You refer to those around you as baskers.

You call yourself My Majesty.

The only hymn you know is How Great I Art.

When you break up with people, you drop them off at the hospital.

You refuse to set foot on anything that isn't a red carpet.

You failed as a portrait painter because you always improved the work by removing the subject and just painting yourself.

Your favourite pickup line is, 'You'll do.'

You can't remember your last name because you assume that everyone knows who you are and never use it.

When visiting the hall of mirrors, you simply see dozens of new ways in which you look fabulous.

109. Lesser-Known Health Benefits Of Coffee

Coffee can help even the least athletic couch potato run a half-marathon merely by supping seven or eight hundred cups.

Coffee aids the absorption of vital nutrients such as donutuline, crullerglobin and baconic acid.

Cures carpal tunnel syndrome, unless you stir it compulsively, and erectile dysfunction, unless you stir it with your penis.

Not all coffee drinkers will become hunchbacks, or at least not right at this very moment.

Coffee will not cause tooth loss, provided you do not bring the cup to your lips with undue velocity.

Sucking on the raw beans provides all the flavour, stimulation, bad breath and tooth-browning without the awful water and cream.

You are 83% less likely to be killed or injured in a traffic accident if you're standing in line for coffee.

Decaf coffee is just as good as regular coffee for staining pants.

Scalding hot coffee sipped nasally clears the sinuses.

It combats depression, although, if you drink it at Starbucks, exposure to hipsters will sap your will to live.

Colombian coffee provides fully one four-thousandth the energy boost of Colombian cocaine.

The beans grow on stalks tended by giants, affording all the cardiovascular benefits of running for your very life itself.

No-one has ever died of Eczema while drinking coffee.

Boosts cellular activity, because cells are known to medical science as the slackers of the human body.

A coffee enema has myriad health benefits too numerous to list, depending upon how thoroughly you then grind the beans.

110. Challenges Of Trump's Secret Service Detail

Snide remarks from Russian Secret Service agents about them all having the same boss.

Nowhere to sit on Air Force One because of the coffin where Ivanka sleeps.

He refers to his protective detail as The Trumpettes.

Always running out of Kevlar hairspray.

Fence jumpers now mostly staff bailing out.

Death threats vastly more numerous, and that's just from the agents.

Constant vigilance to detect dangers and instantly shove POTUS into the line of fire.

Months of tactical training and years of field experience wasted on telling prepubescent bullies to stop making fun of Barron.

Its main duty is preventing Melania from flinging herself down a well.

Perimeter constantly being expanded as he gains weight.

He insists on personally frisking the porn stars.

Convincing the public that their dark glasses are to cut glare, not because they're mortified to be seen with him.

First Lady's envious remarks about 'some lucky people who get to take a bullet'.

The main peril is tripping over absurdly long ties.

Can't rename the chopper Buffoon One.

111. How To Get Fired
From Disneyland

Argue too compellingly, with personal evidence you are only too happy to produce, that it is not a small world after all.

Distract the sniper team deployed to take out escaping dwarves.

Go around sniffling, asking who's got Snow White.

Sell the giant Mickey hands to Kevin Spacey for more efficient groping.

Appear in costume as Minnie's sewer son Moldy.

Your own World Of Slick Lesions ride is discovered.

Post big No Fairies signs.

In honour of Donald Duck, refuse to wear pants.

Extol the virtues of an attraction that functions as both a fun waterslide and a restorative enema.

Wait in line patiently to pee in the drinking fountains.

When folks ask for directions to the Magic Kingdom, point at your crotch.

Be a marauding Somali Pirate Of The Caribbean.

Sell Pluto-nium on the black-mouse market.

Call it Little Space Mountain and add a little extra splash.

Say, 'Hey, kid, wanna find Nemo?'

Stay in character at all times, but as Hannibal Lecter.

Inflict concussions with the Mickey Mouse Club.

When little kids throw up on a ride, rub their noses in it so they won't do it again.

112. Why Roller Coasters Are A Bad Choice For A First Date

It's best to reserve sobbing and soiling yourself for the second or third date.

High-pitched delighted shrieking is fine, unless you are currently not a schoolgirl Beatlemaniac in 1964.

It's hard to talk suave as your flapping tonsils pummel the inside of your face.

As you begin having more of them, you will learn that dates are generally plummetless.

It's tough to look cool on tippy-toe trying to reach the You Must Be This Tall To Ride mark.

No woman ever swooned because you can snork a plume of puke up your nose.

It's no bad thing to appear physically strong, but ideally not by crushing your handprints into the safety bar or the operator's forearm.

It's a challenge to look chill when the G-forces fling your lungs to the ionosphere.

It will diminish your machismo if a six-year-old in a wheelchair has to keep asking if you need any help.

While it sometimes will happen that things don't go well on a first date, you hate to blame centrifugal bladder stress.

113. How To Make A Visit To The In-Laws Tolerable

Count backward from a trillion and watch the time fly.

Pray for human combustion and curse the gods that foil you.

Gnaw at your leg like a trapped coyote.

When you start to take criticism for not earning enough money, reveal, as a diversion, that your wife doesn't want children.

Listen again to her mom's stories about how she said something epically witty to the Finch Society and ruminate on how you'd rather have your glottis chiseled.

Sit back and watch the sparks fly by hinting to your racist father-in-law that you're thinking of converting to Islam.

Mentally calculate the value of everything you'll inherit when these vile people croak.

See if anyone can figure out that that high-pitched whine is your teeth grinding.

Avoid, at all costs, visualizing how your spouse will one day turn into his/her parents.

Use ancient Eastern meditation techniques to slow your heart rate, ideally to a stop.

No visit fails to be cut short when you masturbate furiously over the family photo albums.

Rend your garments and lament your fate in anguished ululations, demanding to know what you have done to deserve this endless term of detention in the Guantanamo Bay of visits.

During a dissertation on the history and significance of any item within view in their house that lasts longer than the Bush administration, a convincing seizure will sell better if you secretly burn toast.

Curry favour by sharing your father-in-law's interests in fly-fishing and being an obstinate, opinionated, flatulent sack of self-importance.

114. Caveman Dating Tips

Act like you don't care when she reveals her grandparents are chimps.

Don't leave her behind when fleeing predators.

Emphasize the hunting, play down the gathering.

Remark that her brow protrudes fetchingly in the moonlight.

She'd be easier to drag around by the hair if you'd invent little luggage wheels to put under her.

Launder your hide and wear your best carcass.

Appear trendy and modern by getting rid of all the old Paleolithic stuff in your cave.

Ask politely if she'd like the last stegosaur testicle.

Bring flowers. Or flint. Chicks dig flint.

Your vestigial tail is best kept hidden until the second date.

Don't bore her with boar facts.

Even if your name is Ug, which it probably is, claim to be called Trevor.

Everyone knows seal-pup panties drop at the sight of a man making fire.

Impress her by saying how your parents both lived to their early twenties.

But it's considered rude to ask a lady her ice age.

Make cave paintings of previous girlfriends look like mammoths.

To avoid coming off like a weirdo, keep your crackpot ideas to yourself about how thunder is just a collision between air masses of different temperatures and not the snores of an angry sky goblin.

Write her a love song on femur flute.

115. Signs You're At A Bad Hospital

A guy is employed to make reassuring bleeping noises from behind equipment that hasn't worked in years.

Bedpans come conveniently pre-filled.

All anaesthetic is administered intrapenisly.

The nurses are aging strippers, recruited because they have their own uniforms.

Doctors don't make rounds so much as buy them.

'Donors' are those who fall prey to pickpockets.

Instead of a hospital gown, you get a body bag.

Signs warn you to check that you have all your limbs before leaving.

No matter your prescription, you get a bottle labelled 'placebo'.

Radiology is where they play the radio.

Spray-on rubber gloves.

Staff think you lack manners if you don't share your meds.

The Emergency Ward has been renamed the No Big Deal Department.

The gift shop stocks only condolence cards.

The gowns are open in the front.

The head nurse is aptly named.

The only place you're allowed to smoke is the burn unit.

There's a viewing gallery in Gynecology.

You are asked if you want the happy-ending spongebath.

Signs limit visitors to next of kin.

You eat in the catheteria.

Your anesthesiologist is just a guy with a mallet.

Your surgeon thinks a spleen isn't a real thing.

116. Less Impressive Top Gun Nicknames

Vertigo

The Scared Baron

Cloud Badger

Columbia

Ejector

Hindenburg

Mini-Muffin

Jettison

Plummet

The School Flattener

Sky Pixie

Splat

The Crater Creator

The Hangar Banger

The Meatier Meteor

117. Things That'll Get You Kicked Out Of The Mafia

As the others hand out swag for Christmas, give everyone a neatly-filled basket of homemade muffins.

Say it would be a shame if something happened to some guy's family out of genuine, heartfelt concern.

When a heist goes bad, encourage everyone to heal with a really good cry.

Misunderstand whacking folks.

See everything Brando did except The Godfather.

When making a guy dig his own grave in the woods, insist that he keep hydrated and bend at the knees.

Complain that the code of omerta is stifling your ability to express yourself.

If someone in the crew rats you out to the cops, write them a sharply-worded note of reprimand.

Insist on drowning people with wicker because of the carbon footprint of concrete.

Make exaggerated retching sounds whenever Sinatra is on the radio.

Even on really hot days refuse to be seen in just a white vest.

Put a seahorse's head in someone's bed.

Let it slip that the one food you can't abide is tomato sauce.

When you ask if a guy's gotta go, mean to the bathroom.

Start giving receipts for drug deals.

Not only actually file tax returns but list occupation as Perfectly Legitimate Businessman And Law-Abiding Citizen.

Give kisses on all four cheeks.

118. Life Goals Of The Unambitious

Being Employee Of The Month, as long as someone else puts up the plaque.

Making Mother proud that the sentence was non-custodial.

Genuinely understanding a New Yorker cartoon.

Learning a second language that isn't profanity.

When you want to do a little reading, buying a stamp.

When you sup from the porch jug with the X's on it, extending your pinky.

Watching Die Hard 2 without crying.

Finding a Big Mac that looks like the one on the sign.

Using a calculator for something other than writing the words 'hello' and 'boobless'.

Working out the words to that Nirvana song.

Exclaiming, "Oh, come off it!" without disrupting the sermon.

Seeing a commercial that commands you to CALL NOW! and not doing so for ten minutes.

Finishing a Rubik's-Cube-shaped cake.

Finding a job where onesies don't breach the dress code.

Advancing from couch potato to loveseat potato.

Buying art, of the non-velvet variety, featuring slightly less Elvis.

Wintering at the Riviera, or the river.

Wearing an ascot with your asshat.

Mingling with the jet-setters, or the Irish ones.

119. What This Generation Will Tell Their Kids About The Good Ol' Days

If you were offended, you could say so with great wounded pique and people would care but trained blowers weren't sent to soothe you.

The Red Hot Chili Peppers were still at large.

Boxers didn't use rabid ferrets.

A date wasn't called a Cosby.

Bisexuality was frowned upon and pentasexuality was unheard of.

The morning routine of shave, brush teeth and shower took half an hour, unlike the two-minute automated regimen of dehairification, tooth re-enamelling, laser biocleanse, liposuction, mood realignment and urgepurge.

Galactic Overlord Trump was leader of only one country.

Had to teleport ourselves from place to place on foot.

Kevin Spacey hadn't yet groped everyone.

In Formula One, they tried not to crash instead of being contractually bound to do so.

Mass shooters had to lug assault rifles around and slaughter innocents in person, droneless as they were.

The Masturbatron was your own hand.

Most people listened to music only one track at a time.

School took years, as it wasn't available in pill form.

There was a Starbucks on every corner, not a Cocainos.

Tom Cruise's level of smugness was somewhat tolerable, as he hadn't yet been proven exactly right.

Viagra wasn't added to the drinking water.

You could not yet prevent a Piers Morgan in the womb.

You had to send non-hologramic dick pics.

120. Fun Facts About Spatulas

The original Spatula-brand utensil was simply a fish slice with little white splashguards on the handle.

In the Middle Ages, wars were fought not only over spatulas but with them, though nobody ever won because both sides would end up laughing at the silliness and make friends.

'Spatula' is technically the plural. Don't put them in your recta.

Chef Mafia assassins use a razor-sharp spatula to kill and julienne their victims.

Rather than give her a microphone, 'concert' promoters give Yoko a spatula and hope she won't notice.

Michelangelo painted the Sistine Chapel with a spatula just to make it more of a challenge.

The spatula and the tarantula are closely related, though the former is generally better suited to kitchen duties.

Prehistoric spatulas had no slots or handles, and were a lot like rocks in that they were.

More spatulas are accidentally left in surgical patients than scalpels.

Historically, the job that conferred the highest social status was King's Crap Attendant, and upon retirement, you were awarded a golden spatula.

A child's greatest joy is to lick the spatula, except for Trump's kids, who were taught to prefer Daddy's boots.

Bakers' apprentices are sent to fetch a left-handed spatula as a prank, and they usually retaliate with the old icing snot trick.

You can weatherproof with a spatula, and you can swab the deck with a spoon, and you can find this funny, but why?

The Swiss are up to something with their spatulas.

There is no graver insult than soiling a gentleman's spatula - boning his favourite horse isn't great either.

The Latin name for that weird dangly thing at the back of the mouth is spatuvulus peculiarosis.

Ancient cave paintings depict something that historians believe is a rudimentary spatula, though cave-art stick people are quite spatula-like, so it could be that.

If Kevin Spacey has concerns about your personal hygiene, he gropes you with a spatula.

121. Positions That Aren't In The Kama Sutra

The Day-Old Donut

The Rigor Mortis

The Puking Spaniel

The Naughty Narwhal

The Crusty Bog

The Abject Failure

The Yawning Maw

The Wayward Waif

The Folding Lawn Chair

The Nest Of Vipers

The Rhombus

The Nagging Doubt

The Maggoty Halibut

The Humpback Whale

The Harley Kickstand

The Forest Fire

The Fetid Swamp

The Ex-Wife

The Drug Deal Gone Wrong

The Bus Shelter

122. Lame Superheroes

Black Plague Panther

Ironingman

Ciderman

The Masked Scavenger

Gnatman

Thaw

The Twitch

Spastic Man

The Thingy

Vulvarine

123. How To Boost Your Sesame Street Cred

Tell everyone you must be trippin' cuz you keep seeing a big stupid elephant thing.

Say you got gangsta spelling.

Wear a huge gold rubber duckie on a thick gold chain.

Standing in the many police line-ups in which you appear, hum One Of These Things Is Not Like The Others.

Keep the secret that Elmo's full street name is El Molesto.

Salute the buoyancy of spirit that enables one to live in the trash and still have a taste for cookies.

Gnaw on a massive fried chicken leg and casually ask if anyone has seen Big Bird.

Ignore those other even sketchier characters on the corner with desperate eyes, scratching and sniffing, pleading, 'Can you tell me how to get?'

124. Harsh One-Line Movie Reviews

Evidently the projectionist couldn't find work as a waterboarder.

It shouldn't have credits, just blames.

I have never before cursed the spirit of Thomas Edison with the venom I did tonight.

It stank so bad that gouging out my eyes and hacking off my ears would serve merely to make my nose suffer more.

Would've been better if the seats faced the other way.

Screen this in Death Row to preclude all requests for clemency.

The running time of this movie was ideally the first minute.

I spent most of it earnestly trying to conjure, in sheer self-defence, the sweet emancipation of rapid flesh-eating disease.

The cast shouldn't walk a red carpet, just the plank.

Turned the passage of a kidney stone into the highlight of my day.

I can get a refund, but who will restore my will to live?

Only German has words to describe the horror of this motion picture.

This would serve as an ideal film-school case study of how not to make a movie but for the fact that the students would immediately pursue careers in deep-sea fishing.

There are no stars in this movie, just a deep, hopeless darkness.

Nothing is more frightening than an unintentional horror flick.

125. What Bees Are Busy Doing

Making 'honey', which they know no-one would've bought a drop of under its original name, 'puke'.

Stinging Sting till he won't sing.

Saving up for a place of their own by living in their parents' hives' basements.

Thinking up cool rapper names like Buzzy-B, Stingy-B or Hepatitis-B.

Attending twelve-step meetings to free themselves from addiction to smoke.

Developing PR strategies to change their image from busy and industrious to edgy and great in the sack.

Trying to get flies to fight-or-light by calling them shit-eaters.

Shunning racist WASPs.

Forming 'swarms', a more palatable term of fellowship than 'lynch mobs'.

Forcibly pollinating everything in sight.

Hand-crafting lovely gifts for the queen, which are invariably honey.

Advocating for the rights of gay bum-blebees with their fabulous fuzzy striped booty shorts.

Trying to convince their young not to sniff RAID.

Arguing whether, in the twenty-first century, they still need the largely ceremonial anachronism of a queen.

Working to identify which humans are likely to go into anaphylactic shock so as to make wise stinging decisions.

Catching a buzz and lying around all day in sun-drenched meadows while those vain fool butterflies flutter themselves to death.

126. How Canada Has Changed With Legal Weed

Polite sex in the streets.

Board an Air Canada flight with no guarantee of where it will land, quite possibly not even at an airport.

More barbecue deaths by hypothermia.

Niagara Falls dammed by stoners in barrels.

They're high-maintenance and a pain to sell, so lakes reek of abandoned cottages rotting.

Bryan Adams at last hears the pleas to stop.

'Windchill' comes to describe the mood of the nation.

Tim's lineups longer, but more glacial.

Justin Bieber marginally less intolerable.

Celine Dion's chronic lifelong weight problem finally solved.

Poutine Earth's most popular health food.

Genius combination of Canada's two greatest commodities, weed and maple syrup, spurs GDP to exceed rest of the world combined.

Patient Vietnam draft dodgers justifiably smug.

Even more giggling at the mention of a beaver.

Now geese just crap anywhere.

The only drug law still on the books provides stiff fines for bogarting.

All scientific research funding diverted to find a way to make burritos microwave faster.

More moose being hit by pedestrians.

127. Signs You Need A New Marriage Counsellor

He shoots you withering glares whilst playing her Elizabethan courtship hymns on a lute.

You are required to stand and remove your pants while your sexual shortcomings are discussed at 'length' with the aid of a laser pointer.

You learn that the haphazard way you load the dishwasher is basically abuse.

When he sneezes, he says, 'A SHREW!'

You are required to learn the vocabulary of 'partnership', which for you means memorizing 'sorry' in thirty languages including Klingon.

Advises that you give each other little compliments, but maybe not, 'I don't care what anyone says, you're no viper.'

His former spouses constitute an entire demographic.

You catch him picking your pocket while you explain your trust issues.

Asks, "Because of your face?" too much.

Notes that, in the good ol' days, partners worked out their differences by thundering toward each other from great distances and crashing heads together like mountain sheep.

She is handed a copy of Men Are From Mars, Women Are From Venus while you are given a bar of soap, but, for good luck, you both are issued a symbolic shard of thin ice.

Recommends that you never go to bed mad, but also points out that thousands yearly die of sleep deprivation.

Suggests twin beds. In twin rooms. And houses. And countries.

To redress the power imbalance in your relationship, you are forced to sit in a tiny chair wearing an ill-fitting Boy Scout uniform as she delivers a detailed account of your character flaws through a loudhailer.

Suggests you lose the doormat that says Abandon Hope All Ye Who Enter Here.

128. Questions Whose Answer Is An Emphatic NO!

Do you get the Curling Channel?

I'm going bear tipping, coming?

Is this the Tiny Misshapen Penis Convention?

My 19-year-old, professional cheerleader, sex-addict, amnesiac sister needs a place to crash for a few nights, do you mind?

Shall I post an even bigger batch of pics of my newborn's facial expression?

Will you hold this sack of scorpions while I go to Botswana?

Can we discuss my teenage angst at length?

Coming to the Yoko singalong?

Do these pants make my...

Do you like your mother's cooking more than mine?

Don't you miss Eighties music?

Are you from Sudbury?

Another bolus of cinnamon?

Have you patronized the Camilla kissing booth?

German food tonight?

Wanna help count my pubic lice?

Hi, I'm Zach Pumpernickelfractalass, will you be my friend?

May I store this stool sample in your thermos?

Shall we dress as Harry Potter and go down to the docks to practice our spells?

There's still a bit of flavour left in this gum, want it?

Hey, are you Piers Morgan?

129. Lesser-Known Hate Crimes

Changing the name of your Wi-Fi network to reference the neighbour's skin condition.

Berating atheists for their exclamations when they hit their thumbs with hammers.

Following a driver who doesn't use blinkers to his destination, signalling that you're going to punch him, and doing so.

Forcibly shaving a hipster with a weedwhacker.

Tying up a vegan and requiring him at gunpoint to eat a dog.

Repeatedly phoning Sean Connery, telling him that Timothy Dalton was the best Bond, and hanging up.

Finding Wally but not acknowledging him.

Grasping someone who says 'At the end of the day' by the upper lip with long-nosed pliers and running him up and down, up and down, up and down the stairs.

Administering an IQ test to all Trump supporters en masse and showing them that their collective score doesn't total a halfwit.

When the passenger next to you on a flight tips his peanuts out, tasting one and putting it back.

Volunteering to do laundry for the local Klan and leaving a red sock in the wash.

Excitedly phoning the guy on the kidney donor waiting list and saying you've found him a liver.

Approaching people playing rap at the beach and rapping them sharply on the bridge of the nose like a cop demanding entry with a search warrant.

130. How To Be A Lousy Spy

When creeping around dressed like a bush, conspicuously make the sound of high piano keys.

Once they've been seen, burn all messages, correspondence, books, televisions and tourist attractions.

The newspaper with eye-holes is too obvious these days, so drill them through your Kindle.

Teach your kids to play games like I Don't Spy.

Pick your own original, signature beverage, but insist that it be made in an awkward yet meaningless way, such as 'milk, white, poured upside-down'.

Install a silencer on the stereo.

Dropping your business card into a bowl to win a free lunch, scribble out Spy and write Regular Salesman.

Wear an 'I Blend In' t-shirt.

Maintain many passports, birth certificates, driver's licenses and families.

Keep moving to the rear of any queue to avoid being followed.

Serve dinner on Matt Damon placemats.

Rather than saying hello, greet folks with, 'The yellow dog flies at midnight.'

131. Action Films For The Elderly

Alien Vs Pensioner

Drive (With Your Turn Signal On At All Times)

Full Metal Robe

Graveheart

Iron Supplement Man

Life Wish

Mall Trek

Partial Recall

Piss Piss Bang Bang

Rambotox

Slow And Cranky

Die Soon

The Bourne Atrophy

The Hurt Walker

The Terminated

132. What You Learn At Douchebag School

Attracting everyone's attention by yelling at your kids for making noise that nobody else had noticed.

Saying 'we' are pregnant without choking.

Working the word 'hydration' into more sentences than would ordinarily require it.

Purging bands from your playlists the instant they become popular.

Overcoming the abject horror of looking in a mirror and seeing yourself with a ridiculous beard that would not have looked out of place on a medieval madman.

Proper Starbucks Italian pronunciation.

Demanding to see the manager when your dressing fails to come on the side.

Parking in a disabled spot and jogging into the store.

Enjoying a nutritious lunch at a strip club while imagining the dancers are the losers.

Fannypack/trouser colour coordination.

Bringing two giant bottles of water on a five-minute bike ride.

Welding a three-foot spoiler to the back of a front-wheel-drive car that barely makes seventy horsepower.

Finding restaurants that allow you to select which of a live something you wish to consume.

Joining a socks club.

Proselytizing that the virtue of vinyl is that the sound is 'warmer'.

Taking out a Whole Foods mortgage.

133. Kevin Spacey's Romantic Sayings

"My motto is Prey It Forward."

"Behold THIS American Beauty!"

"An actor's greatest asset is a generic round face that can be easily Photoshopped out of any scene."

"Stardom is all about teamwork. It's all hands on dick."

"Keep your hopes high and your handshakes low."

"Remember to keep it in your pants until after they've answered the door."

"Bring a little movie magic to the proceedings by shouting 'You've been Keyser Sözed!' at the moment of climax."

"Always flash, as it were, a fetching smile when walking a red carpet or working a gropeline."

"A silver hip flask is a quaint stylish item but also a portable supply of Spacey's own home distilled 90 proof molestin' liquor."

"To reach the top, you must grab what you want with both hands and hang on tight."

"I love moonlit strolls groping hands."

"I hope you had fun. #MeToo."

134. How Elephants Are Just Like Ants

Both leave unwanted mounds in your window boxes.

Both are uncomfortable in your pants.

Both can carry more than a hundred times the weight of an ant.

You also wouldn't want to be staked to an elephanthill covered in jam.

Both come in varieties including African, Indian and Fire.

You can be gored by both, but you notice one more.

A bunch of either can ruin a picnic.

Elephants also provide hours of diversion in sand pressed between two panes of glass.

Equally palatable with enough garlic and cumin.

Neither takes kindly to being zapped with a magnifying glass.

As fascinating as they are, if a thousand of either were in your attic, you'd definitely call someone.

You shouldn't mess with the queen of either.

Columns of both climb trees with ease.

While differing wildly in method of execution, both have a clear vision of how they'd kill Piers Morgan.

Circus ants are also quite the spectacle, just harder to see.

Both were hunted to near extinction for their prized pelts, though rather more ants are required to make even a sleeveless vest.

Home traps get rid of both, but one is a lot more expensive.

Both lay a scent trail, just of different degrees of pungency.

The bite of both itches.

135. Gay Rock Bands

AC/AC

The Bitch Boys

Both Directions

Liar Straights

The Papas And The Papas

The All-Man Brothers Band

Queens

Metaphallica

The Monkeesters

Cumforth And Tons

Men Hard At Work

Tickleback

Nine-Inch Males

Crosby, Stills, Nash & Scandalously Young

136. Cheery-Sounding Medical Conditions

A Cute Appendicitis

Ebola Cherries

Hail Hail The Gangrene's Here

Kidme Disease

Larkolepsy

Alrightis

Cerebral Palsy-Walsy

Mygreat Headache

Peprosy

Placid Reflux

Glamydia

Playroomatic Fever

The Calmin' Cold

137. Signs Your Psychic Is A Fraud

Aftsees events.

Always on the phone to Dionne Warwick during readings.

'Aura' of fruit flies.

Calls herself The Amazing Zucchini.

'Crystal' my ass, it's a bowling ball.

Predicts nightfall within 48 hours.

'Rune stones' clearly Scrabble tiles.

Pronounces the 'p' and the 'ch' in 'psychic'.

Spirit guide is Siri .

Startled when anyone enters the room.

Uses an Etch-A-Sketch for automatic writing.

'Trance' primarily gin-induced.

Turban an obvious bath towel.

138. How To Get Kicked Out Of Starbucks

Stir your coffee clockwise then counterclockwise and completely unstir it.

Order a sprinkle of chocolate, a touch of foam and a big dollop of douche.

Just pretend to be pretentious.

Mimic the sound of the hissing machine as you pour coffee you brought from home.

Ask for directions to the No Bellends section and enjoy watching them call head office in a panic for instructions.

Accidentally let your hot rod magazine slip out from the copy of Alfalfa & Quinoa Monthly that you're hiding it in.

Have a mere conversational grasp of Italian.

Root around in your fanny. Pack.

Sit at a table intently focused on your laptop. With no computer.

Say your name's Adolf.

Insist they accommodate your service rattler.

Grow a twatty beard before their very eyes.

Use the word 'Nescafe' without following it immediately with an exaggerated gagging sound.

Fail to have an opinion on which side of some Ethiopian mountain produces the best beans.

When asked what type of coffee you want say, "I don't care. They all taste the same," and watch the place fall silent.

Show the Senior Barista no noticeably greater degree of deference than the Ordinary Barista.

Ask if there's a payment plan before committing to a biscotti.

Use foul, offensive words such as 'medium' or 'large'.

139. Signs Your Kid Will Grow Up To Be A Politician

On the first day of kindergarten, shook every hand in the school.

Is prepared to waive an increase in allowance until the midterms.

Tweets things like, "Loser teacher gives my art project a C, makes FAILING crafts herself for class display! SAD!"

In preschool, where other tykes were characterized as 'cooperative, well-behaved', etc., is described as 'slick'.

Promises to Make Juice Grape Again!

Stages cute child-like antics and summons his parents to the photo-op.

Appoints a disabled, black, pacifist, moderate, Christian, working-class, lesbian war veteran his best friend.

Kisses more babies than most tykes.

Made a megaphone out of construction paper for recess rallies.

Has bigger pre-schoolers running alongside his scooter.

Shows no discernible talent or skills other than smiling.

Trades peers' lunch money for access.

Answers the question, 'Do you want a cookie?' with seven other questions in a convoluted response that simultaneously means no, yes and no comment.

Denies he had a playdate with the Girl Guide down the road.

Asks Santa if he can count on his vote.

Fingerpaints nothing but campaign banners.

Speaks exclusively in five-second sound bites.

While the other kids play Tag, prefers Teleprompter.

Holds a daily press conference about what he did at school.

Worries about his Show & Tell 'legacy'.

Farts in tub, forms focus group to see how that'll play in the Midwest.

Wagon Force One always on standby.

The front door now mysteriously sports a magnetometer.

Still wears the Walmart shoes you provided, but has a two-hundred-dollar haircut.

Won't fulfill chore promises made, merely pledges Change!

Leaks naptime photographs of his opponents sleeping while he diligently studies.

140. Things In Kim Jong Un's Online Dating Profile

Handsome, well-built and magnificent in Approved Hairstyle Number Four.

Loves listening to Kenny G while screaming dissenters burn alive in the cool Spring air.

Naughty pics of his missile not malfunctioning.

Looking for someone to love for the rest of her life.

Never travels anywhere without a small desk and a lamp that doesn't need to be plugged in.

Can never remember the lyrics of Ode To The Terrifically Wondrous Benevolent Omnipotent Leader Of The Obsequiously Grateful And Not At All Peckish Multitudes.

Dreams of one day living in a wondrous unified Korea - specifically a glorious shining paradise in the North and a desolate corpse-strewn wasteland in the South.

Harbours a deep-seated suspicion that legions of minions sobbing with joy at the sight of him are unduly restrained.

Old-fashioned romantic who'd gleefully nerve-gas a primary school to get your attention.

Play hard to get and your corpse will be hard to find.

141. Secrets Of Human Anatomy

The small intestines try harder, so give them a break.

There are trillions of memory cells, and not one knows where your car keys are, but each will summon instantly the lyrics to the theme of The Beverly Hillbillies.

The glottis is cool, but maybe not as a name for your daughter.

The heart has four chambers and a little-known dungeon.

Awash in natural redundancy, the human body has multiple lungs, kidneys, eyes and liver lobes, but there is only a single penis, as this becomes automatically redundant once wed.

Like gerbils, humans can expand their cheeks for storing things. Likewise, the face can stretch.

No-one knows what tonsils do, or where they go at night.

Contrary to popular belief, the inner ear is actually much smaller than the inner city.

If you give yourself a big, tight hug, your lungs double as bagpipes.

There is no valid reason why we should have a funny bone and not wry aortic ventricles.

With practice, you can wink with your spleen.

A uni-brow is less conspicuous than a uni-leg.

Stretched out, the human intestines measure about twenty feet, though bad Chinese food is able to access a shortcut, reducing travel time while vastly increasing velocity.

The Achilles tendon is the most delicate part of the human body, alongside the Achilles testes.

Human knees are perfectly capable of bending in both directions, but only once.

You can live with only one kidney but you'll walk funny and cause a mysterious imbalance on aircraft.

If you break a hip, you'll never be admitted to the hottest clubs again.

142. Self-Help Books That Attract NSA Attention

Assertiveness Through Dynamite

Don't Shoot The Messenger - Get More Out Of Him First

From Vests To Virgins

How To Make Peace With Anyone You Don't Obliterate

I'm Okay, You're Evil

Standing On The Throats Of Giants

Men Are From Mars, Women Are Harlots

The Seven Habits Of Horrifically Deranged People

Underground Bunkers For Dummies

Release The Zealot Within

When Your Radical Isn't Rad Enough

143. When Tech Rage Goes Too Far

You don't have Carpal Tunnel Syndrome, but you suffer from Crushed Mouse Palm.

Your laptop computer is more like rooftop.

You can drive the roads all day in utmost serenity but get an error message and you want to drive the neighbours.

The term 'cell phone' aptly foreshadows where, as a result of your frenzies, you won't be allowed to have one.

The principal goal of tech support is to persuade you to put the bat down.

You know precisely how hard you have to press the spacebar before it ricochets off your forehead.

Bill Gates himself calls and offers to buy you a set of encyclopedia and a lifetime subscription to the pornographic magazine of your choice.

You start more than five emails a day with the words 'Dear Google Bastards'.

You download videos of people smashing computers to send a clear message to your own.

Siri has taken out a restraining order against you.

You are utterly unaware that there's a right and a wrong way to insert a USB cable, convinced that it's simply a question of force.

There's a picture of you with a line through it outside every Internet cafe in the northern hemisphere.

144. Obscure Facts About Snow

'Flurries' is a meaningless word made up by meteorologists to look knowledgeable, like 'windchill' or 'kilopascals' or 'low pressure system' or 'fog'.

If you carry a snowflake with you on a hot summer day, you will never get sunstroke.

Snowball fights were initially developed as an alternative to warfare, a notion that never caught on, especially in equatorial climes.

Wet and dry are not the only types of snow. There's also compound, low-density and ranch.

It isn't sexist that we only make snowmen. Frigid women just aren't as much fun.

Only through years of selective breeding have idiot huskies ceased pulling sleds straight into deep crevices.

All snowflakes are identical. They look different because eyesight fails in the cold. Anyway, how would we know? Think. Get a life.

Sno-Cones remain as popular with children as ever. Mind you, so is shoving things far up their noses. They should combine the two.

Snow sculpture is a legitimate art form and a cool hobby for those who can't make friends.

Snowdrifts can easily reach heights well over your head, if you sleep in wind-swept fields.

The Eskimos have 150 words for snow, but they also have a thousand for caribou crap, so...

The term 'making snow angels' is a less politically incorrect term than 'having a snow grand mal'.

Don't rub snow on frostbite. Use lava. Duh.

145. Signs You've Moved Into A Bad Neighbourhood

Kids play Toe Tag.

Folks wish each other a Merry Cripsmas.

When you hear screaming, you say, Oh, good, here comes the mailman.

New neighbours are welcomed with gifts of baking or splints.

Even on hot days, there's still a refreshing breeze from ricochets.

Lovers enjoy a romantic sprint hand-in-hand.

You root for payday in a race with life expectancy.

Any time a brick isn't thrown through your window, it means they're already in your house.

The hood is deserted on visiting day.

The guy that once wore matching socks is still called His Lordship.

The main expenditure on the municipal budget is crime-scene tape.

It's idyllic, on a pretty winter's evening, with the moonlight glinting brightly on the knives and the big, fluffy snowflakes falling gently on the slain.

Communication is chiefly in the form of last gasps.

You try to be a good crack ho-stess.

Moms stop, drop and roll their kids to school.

For Halloween, the kids go trick-or-beating.

The Fed Ex guy is more heavily armed than a Mogadishu warlord.

There are people more than a hundred and fifty years old, as the Grim Reaper can't muster the courage to visit.

The rate of muggings is so high you'll probably steal your own wallet back within an hour.

Cultural events are exclusively tramp fights.

Use of the area as a set for the latest Terminator movie resulted in significant infrastructure improvements.

Dialing 911 connects you to Earl's Discount Coffin Hypermart.

Carjacking is referred to as hailing a cab.

Parents believe that higher education means the kids take larger doses.

146. Bad Names For Football Teams

Bath Salts

Welwyn Garden City Town Villagers

Sheffield Alternate Monday Afternoons

Burnley Joke Brunts

Tottenham Hotspurts

Hartlepool Tragic Mishaps

West Ham Pessimistic

London Sex Trafficking Ring

Lumpen Cardiff

Halifax Toe Jam

Gateshead Misdemeanours

Leicester Unremarkables

Faceplant Falmouth

Argyle Arthritics

Binfield Bingekillers

Selby Hysterics

Pately Bridge Tanglefeet

Fungal Monmouth

Nosferatu Wimbledon

Leamington Wound Lickers United

Floppy Sagdroop Margate

Huddersfield Huddlelovers

Crystal Meth Palace

Taunton Teaboys

147. Rejected Children's Stories

Charlotte's Web Of Lies

Bi-Curious George

Horton Hurts A Ho

The Little Engine That Couldn't Be Bothered

Snow White And The Seven Stunted Circus Mutants

Little Red Riding Shootings In The Hood

The Three Gross Pigs

The Tiger Who Came To Tea And Devoured Baby Ronnie

Jack The Ripper And Jill

The Ugly Fucking Duckling

The Princess And The Pee

Charlie And The Bolivian Jungle Factory

The Hundred And One Damnations

Sleeping Beauty And Cos'

148. Artifacts In The Loser Museum

Collection of Star Wars action figures all unopened except Princess Leia in that bikini.

Cryogenically preserved DNA of guys who could recite Monty Python movies word for word and thus never managed to propagate future generations in the traditional way.

Anything pertaining remotely to ceramic cats.

CB radios, so tiny-todgered twerps in Toyotas talk like truckers.

Madonna's bestselling photo book Sex for sixty dollars, consisting of blurry, hirsute photos on cheap paper, I've heard.

A pile of unbearable demo CD's by wannabe rappers.

A Segway.

A selfie stick, originally called a schmuckrod.

An Apple watch.

Cease-and-desist letter from the Tinder legal department.

One of those giant Number One foam fingers sports tools wave.

Twenty-five billion pages of hand-written Harry Potter fan fiction.

Photos of women in the Eighties whose life goal was hair vastness.

Pile of worn-out Dungeons And Dragons dice.

Milli Vanilli forged autographs.

Tub of toxic blue facepaint, enthusiastically endorsed by the Avatar Fan Club, known to cause tingling, blindness and night terrors.

Enormous branded sports bags containing nothing but two festering socks, neither of which was used for sport.

149. Best Things About Meetings

Four out of five doctors say ice-cold rancid coffee is good for you.

Time to comprehend the profound compassion and devotion that led the parents of that twat from marketing not to drown him at birth.

Your daydreams drift from skipping through fields of sunflowers to beating every one of these people to pulp with the butt of a sniper rifle.

A chance to reassess your faith as, again and again, you are denied spontaneous human combustion despite the most devout supplications.

It's fun to beam mental death rays at the dweeb who, incredibly, at the long-awaited end, when the boss asks if anyone has questions, does.

For staffroom avoidance purposes, take note of those whose eyes light up at the sight of chart paper.

You can use the time to dream that the meeting has ended, but waking up from that one is a literal living nightmare.

Your threshold for happiness is adjusted so far downward that you experience sublime joy when a bird hits the window.

You can watch your blood bubbling in your veins when someone suggests that a further meeting is necessary to determine the agenda for future meetings.

You can try to start The Wave, but it comes off as The Weak Wave People Do When Slowly Drowning.

You discover previously unknown facts about yourself, such as how far you can shove a paper clip beneath your fingernail before you start to notice.

150. Clues Your Toddler Is The Reincarnation Of Elvis

One leg learns to walk before the other.

Asked what he wants to do when he grows up, says, 'Uhh, take care o' business, lil mama.'

Tells you there's a hunka-hunka something in his Pampers.

Always returns from daycare with a sack of girls' underwear.

Never says thank you, but, 'Thanga, thangaverramuch'.

You duck shots at cartoons he doesn't like.

Napoleonic onesie collars.

Will eat pablum only in pill form.

Can't always be revived from naps.

Throws a karate tantrum if his peanut-butter sandwich isn't fried.

The only kid in Sunday school with an entourage to light his cigars.

Sitters tear his clothes off.

Small sword hidden in his rattle, and Derringers in his booties.

You forget what he looks like, because he's nocturnal.

He calls you daddy, but you call him The King.

151. Facts About Nostrils

If he cannot reach any other part of you, Kevin Spacey will eagerly grope your nostrils.

If it weren't for nostrils, you'd have to snort coke with your anus.

It is physically impossible to touch your right nostril with your left eyelid without the aid of Albanian gangsters.

Census-takers have simplified their methods. They used to count the nostrils and divide by two, but tragically this yielded three Chers.

You can drink Gatorade through your nostrils, but it really doesn't improve the flavour much.

Barbara Streisand sings almost entirely with her nostrils. Michael Jackson, on the other hand, simply got rid of his.

An under-utilised storage space, nostrils will shortly become the only place you're permitted to carry luggage on a budget airline.

The evolutionary reason for nostrils is so that we don't cry eye snot.

The human nostril is sufficiently elastic to accommodate an entire banana, but at the price of brain damage and Trump support.

Those with a sexual nostril fetish are known as 'nostralians' or 'Australians'.

Ancient philosopher Nostrildamus made predictions based on the content of his hankie.

Rather than being a shameful, filthy habit, picking the nose and consuming the output is actually low-key socially-responsible cannibalism.

For a joke, Kiefer Sutherland's friends once glued his nostrils shut as he slept so he couldn't act.

If you have really huge nostrils, be glad. You are your own bus shelter!

Sarah Jessica Parker doesn't actually have freakishly large nostrils, but don't worry, there are plenty of other reasons to disdain her.

Only one in ten thousand people can snort a squid, though one in three have tried.

152. New Academy Award Categories

Longest Running Time Of A Transformer Movie Without Being Literally Interminable

Shortest Onscreen Time Of An Obnoxious Character That Claims To Be The Best Of The Best At Some Dangerous Skill But Is Rapidly Proven Wrong By A Huge Explosion, Multiple Gunshot Wounds Or A Passing Dinosaur

Highest Number Of Roles Played By Samuel L. Jackson In A Single Film

Annual Meryl Streep Whether She's In A Movie Or Not Inevitability Award

Honorary Gary Busey Massive Wackjob Nobody Wants To Work With Award

Least Worst Arnold Schwarzenegger Vehicle That Begs For Sub-Titles Although He's Been Living In This Country For Fifty Years

Least Black Actors In A Movie About Nigeria

Most Viral On-Set Christian Bale Mortifying Snitfit

Most Egregious Breach Of Fire Regulations Due To The Staggering Number Of Superheroes In A Single Film

Most Stomach-Churning Age Difference Between A Leading Actor And His Love Interest

Most Gratuitous Frosted-Glass Shower Scene

Most Obvious Product Placement Of Exceptional Apple Products Such As The Remarkable iPhone X

Most Convincing Digital Removal Of Kevin Spacey

Most Villains Opening Fire At Once Who Might Be Good At Crimes But Sure The Hell Can't Shoot

Most Straight-Talking-Maverick-Who-Plays-By-His-Own-Rulesesque Performance In Any Cop Crap

Best 'Live'-Action Technically Pre-Mortem Harrison Ford Action Film In Which A Stunt Is Something Like Getting Out Of A Car

Best Non-Kevin-Hart Buddy Picture

Best Outrunning Of A Blast In A Tunnel Or Heating Duct

Best Performance By A Heavily Blinged Rapper Who Has Decided He's Now An Actor By Virtue Of Forming A Production Company

Best Tom Cruise Unsettling Grinfest Starring Tom Cruise's Far Too Many Teeth

Best Picture That Would've Won If Harvey Weinstein Had Made It But Ew

Best Automatic Oscar For Cringingly Portraying An Affliction Of Pretty Much Any Sort

Best Bourne Chase Scene That Somehow Manages To Last Longer Than The Movie

153. More Brutally Truthful Ads

Brylcreem: A Little Dab'll Do Ya But You Should Probably Use Loads

Radio Shack: Batteries And Some Wire

Crossfit: For The Real Alpha Douche

Sea World: Whale Auschwitz

CNN: The Fastest News Isn't Always The Rightest

Ikea: Missing One Critical Screw

Google: How Sweet, You Think Amazon Is Scary

Toblerone: Just Chewing On Razors Would Be Weird

Heinz: 57 Varieties, 1 Flavour

Kraft Dinner: In Lieu Of A Life

Nike: Tiny, Starving Fingers Make You Feel Like An Athlete

Zamfir, Master Of The Pan Flute: Would He Lie?

Trump Fan Club: Come Be An Evolutionary Notch Below Lichen

Pizza Hut: Choose Your Own Kind Of Bland

Dubai: Alcohol-Free Vegas Without The Class

Aer Lingus: The Same As Every Other Airline Except That It Sounds A Bit Rude

Exxon Mobil: Don't Underestimate How Much We Hate Polar Bears

Facebook: Where Pity Whores Cry Alone

The Toronto Maple Leafs: We Saw The Cup Once

The Red Hot Chili Peppers: We're Milking This Till You Wise Up

Volkswagen: So We Lied - We WERE Founded By Nazis

African Lion Safari: A Roaring Good Yawn

154. Unsubtle Airport Security Questions

Any team jerseys in your luggage? Lakers? Leafs? ISIS?

Did you pay for your own ticket or did it arrive unexpectedly in the mail with a picture of you in bed with a donkey?

Does the foul stench of my western decadence, godlessness and treachery offend you?

If your flight is later characterized as 'ill-fated', will we have you to thank?

Just off the top of your head, how important, of all the skills a pilot learns, is landing?

Quickly list the similarities between Pablo Escobar and Robin Hood.

Any 'Allahu Akbar' tattoos at all?

Did you pack your own bag or was it loaded by a battalion of crackheads held at gunpoint by the Cali Cartel?

Ever been to Martyr Gras?

Goat snacks. Delish? Or no.

I just drew the funniest cartoon of Mohammad, wanna see?

Is that the technical schematic for a Boeing 747 in your pocket?

Can you look around the room and point out the harlots and the infidels?

Off on vacation to the caliphate, are we?

Travelling for business, pleasure or combat training?

Which do you estimate will come first, your arrival time or the afterlife?

Koran, Shmoran, that's what I say, right?

Would you like a seat in the smoldering underwear section?

Which word does not belong in this sentence? "Stow the luggage in the overhead storage bin Laden."

155. Worst Things To Write On A Cake

Sorry I Boned Your Thinner Sister

I Love You So Much I Mixed This Myself By Foot

Here's What You Apparently Expect For Helping Out Around Here

Last Night Was Great, Dad

Good Luck Living With Your Wheat Allergy

Annual Conference Of The I Hate Marie Antoinette Society

Forgive Me For Botching Your Liposuction

You're Surely A Size Six On The Inside

Not For Use In Urinal

Sorry You Got Sent Down (Ssshhh,There's A File In Here)

I Hate You, You're A Loser And You're Dumped, But Have Some Cake!

Here, You Can't Yap With Your Mouth Full

Don't Blow These Candles Out, You're So Old You Should Save Every Breath

As Always, Darling, Have This Cake And Eat It Too

This Was Made From The Stale Crumbs Of The Regard I Used To Hold You In

We'll Miss You And The Rest Of The Deadwood

Happy Dropout Day

Blow Me

156. The Truth About Meteorology

The weather is affected very negligibly by meteors.

Rain doesn't come from clouds; it shoots upward from puddles.

No-one has ever seen a kilopascal.

The principal learning from meteorology school is how to say 'precipitation' without drenching everyone.

They say that the reason we discuss the weather so much is that it's the one thing we all share in common, but you don't hear people discussing their anuses.

Every snowflake is unique, but so, technically, is every Meat Loaf song and yet, likewise, no-one can tell the difference.

There are only two types of cloud, ominous and fluffy.

Though hurricanes and tsunamis get the glory, it is, in fact, drizzle that is the worst type of weather.

The relative humidity is how stuffy your older relatives feel, and squawk about, as a handy small-talk substitute.

Humidity is named after Humus, the Greek god of sweaty scrota.

The 'feels-like' temperature sure sounds-like bullshit.

If someone can tell me the difference between showers and 'shower activity', I'll give him some handjob activity.

Hail is just frozen little clear drops of lava.

Nothing thrills a weatherman more than an impending storm. Gives him a warm front.

Ever seen a meteorologist predict the lottery numbers? No. They forecast squat.

Contrary to popular belief, snow doesn't drift. Snowflakes are highly social creatures that gather together for companionship and warmth.

The only irrefutable proof of an angry and malevolent deity is sleet.

All meteorologists, thanked sarcastically for the rain one more time, are apt to cut a swath of carnage through the greater tri-state area.

Wind is terrified of kites.

Staring directly into a solar eclipse is an ideal safeguard of optical health, but you must never even glance at the moon.

In some countries, you need a licence to buy an umbrella because it is such a potent symbol of masculine virility that the very sight of one is guaranteed to drive all women within two hundred yards into a wild sexual frenzy.

Hail is never the size of golf balls. It IS golf balls.

Fog is caused by cold and warm air masses meeting, but a bright sunny day is taken credit for by Trump.

The word 'inclement' applies only to weather and a visit from your in-laws.

After all is said and done, the most accurate means of tracking the weather is still the window.

157. Hurtful Things Hitmen Tell Each Other

You couldn't be more obvious if you were wearing a neon orange hunting vest accompanied by a marching band.

Giving someone sea bass and hoping they choke on a bone does not make you an assassin.

You reload slower than a geriatric gigolo.

Stilettos work for you only if they're heels.

Your 'victims' are just like new after a trip to the walk-in clinic.

When you say a guy's gotta go, you mean out with you.

My three-year-old niece garrottes cleaner than that.

If you want to send a message to your enemies, a singing telegram would be more chilling.

You make so much spatter we should call you Jackson Pollock.

You kill slower than Celiac Disease.

Stick to whacking off.

You know who's scarier? Casper the fucking Ghost.

Careerwise, try a whole new direction, like Life Coach.

Your targets don't sleep with the fishes. They sleep in, before a healthy breakfast.

158. Facts About Pizza

There are no bad toppings, merely those that are sickening to all right-minded humans.

You'd think it wouldn't take a great leap of creative thought to conceive of round boxes for round food, but they were designed by the government.

Cheese was actually the fourth thing they tried in crust. The first three were applesauce, gin and cicadas.

Pizza Hut and Papa John's have merged to form John Huts, purveyors of cheap pizza for those who love dysentery.

More inmates on Death Row choose pizza as their last meal than any other food, but as a final harsh punishment, they are given vegan.

'Pizza' is derived from an ancient Roman word meaning, 'It doesn't matter how little else we accomplish, this makes us awesome for all time.'

Wood-fired pizza is ideal for those with a taste for bark.

Anchovies were even less popular by their original name, colonic reek-centipedes.

The ancient Egyptians worshipped pizza as piously as they did cats, so their Siamese panzerotti was a big hit.

A slice is triangular because, and this is not widely known, so is your stomach.

In some countries that take pizza very seriously, it isn't just free if it's late, the driver hangs himself.

A dog can detect the aroma of pizza a block away, a university student on other planets.

Pineapple on pizza is a sacrilege akin to cinnamon on bacon, an offense for which, in some countries, you can be legally baked.

You can snort pizza, but it takes forever, and it burns, and before you're full, your date will be long gone.

Traditional Neapolitan pizza is topped with tomato, mozzarella and three flavours of ice cream.

Pizza was served at The Last Supper and Judas got upset because they forgot the green peppers. Everyone knows the rest of the story.

The NSA tracks all sales of pizza stones so that cruise missiles can be targeted at insufferable trend-whores.

The most popular pizza topping in Japan is whale, which requires a crust sixty feet wide and three barrels of tomato sauce.

Italian folklore tells of the mythical pizzzzza, a food capable of putting a man to sleep for a thousand years of the most wondrous dreams.

159. Christmas Traditions In Sudbury

Send threatening letters to Santa demanding more beer.

Smoke outside the corner store, think about the new year and work on your thousand-yard stare.

Strangle a hooker with garlands.

Visit the Stuff That Grew Museum.

Someone always gets pregnant at the big Polluters' Ball.

The mayor goes around peeing season's greetings in the snow.

Forget scenes of Mother Mary holding Baby Jesus and hold the mother of all bejesus hockey fights, baby.

Patronize a Nativititty bar.

Beat up the mall Santa's elves because tights.

Buy one of those winter globes that you shake and little gleaming flakes of sulphur gently snow down on the town.

Deal some smack and deal the missus a smack.

Each year, in remembrance of all those bravely gelded by the annual Yuletide Freezing Of The Hollyhocks, the townsfolk gather to weep icy tears of woe for their fa-la-losses.

Enter a fox hound in the great end-of-year Anyone Different Hunt.

Get loved ones the best gifts by looting early.

Go outside on the sidewalk with the kids and play hypodermic hopscotch in the soft, syringy snow.

Burgle the homeless shelter and steal the festive gruel.

160. Behind The Scenes At The Taxidermist

Stuffing a snake first involves snipping the ends off and blowing.

Bedwetting, setting fires and an interest in taxidermy are the three most reliable childhood signs of a future serial killer.

Industry rule of thumb - if it squawks, it isn't ready yet.

For the most interesting taxidermy result, your dog should die by electrocution.

During the last, declining years of his life, Elvis took a taxidermist with him on tour just in case.

Never buy the pies from the adjacent bakery.

Taxidermists always have a jar of bees' knees behind the counter, but you need to be a Freemason to buy them.

There are strict laws against stuffing loved ones after they pass, and especially before.

The least popular name for a taxidermy shop is The Gut Hut.

For travel convenience, you can have your pet stuffed with an air bladder for easy inflation wherever you go. The location of the nozzle, however, depends on whether the taxidermist likes you.

More than fifty people are murdered each year for telling taxidermists to get stuffed.

On the great plains of central Africa, dangerous wild beasts must be stuffed on the run, and this is a sign that you are the manliest of warriors or something.

The president has ordered that when he passes, he wants to be stuffed, and have a parade, but staff are accustomed to ignoring his loony edicts and besides, there's not that much stuffing in the world.

There is suspiciously little difference between industry-standard stuffing materials and Walmart socks.

It takes longer to train as a taxidermist than as a dentist, though most of the additional time is spent waiting for the nausea to wear off.

Premature ejaculation is a major problem amongst taxidermists, owing to the overwhelming thrill and rarity of boning something alive.

If you spend thousands to fly across the globe, trek through a hazardous wilderness, bring down a water buffalo with a high-caliber rifle, ship the carcass home and have it stuffed and hung on your rec-room wall, you should take up knitting.

Taxidermists' favourite word is 'chock'.

If you decide that the passage of time has dimmed your love for your pet, you can have him unstuffed for free.

Taxidermists scout talent at Build-A-Bear Workshop.

Animals are usually stuffed in a pose of majesty or ferocity, except for the wiener dogs.

161. Creepy Ways To Flirt

Buy her flowers, delivered to her bed as she sleeps.

Wave cheerily from the park bushes.

Read her the poem that you wrote about her, on your chest, in the blood of her cat.

Say 'Come here often' not at all as a question, and then show her the spreadsheet of exactly how frequently.

Say you've just come out of a serious relationship and you just want to get back out there and have some fun with someone who, with only minor surgery, could be made to look exactly like your ex.

Dress up in your finest lurkingwear.

Use a reassuring conversation starter like, 'Hi, I'm no threat.'

Brag about having Faces Of Death in all formats and tell her that, since some corpses are female, it's a chickflick.

Tell her it's fate that you met her on the Eve Of The Grand Becoming.

Show her your proudly-carved crotch notches.

Send her a nice You Harlot card.

Have cosmetic Pennywise surgery.

Opine that love is a desperate construct, a lie, a sham, a dark-web plot to keep us forever in bondage to those who seemed nice in the bar.

Arrange an introduction to your penis, Queen Victoria.

Smile warmly and say, 'Wanna be on the news?'

Remark how alluring she'd look in a freezer.

When she says you have nice eyes, pop one out with a spoon and say it's hers.

As she tucks into the expensive box of chocolates you brought, brag that you filled them all yourself.

162. More Unmotivational Sayings

If at first you don't succeed, kill yourself.

Even a broken clock is right if you don't care what time it is.

Keep your eyes on the stars and your feet on the ground and your manhood in Miley Cyrus.

A watched pot never boils, unless you're Superman.

An unexamined life is not worth living, nor an unexamined prostate worth having.

Do one thing every day that scares you, and one thing once that frightens you to death.

Good things come to those who wait alone in their dreary apartments their entire lives.

No-one can make you feel inferior without your consent, but you can be utterly unworthy without your knowledge.

You must expect great things of yourself before you can put them off.

Fortune sides with him who dares give up.

When the going gets tough, cry, really snotty and loud, with, like, actual wailing and running around.

Better the devil you know than Piers Morgan.

Better safe than hanging flayed upside down in an Estonian snuff dungeon.

People who are crazy enough to think they can change the world are the ones who do in fact get put away.

Do what you can with all you have, wherever you are, unless you're in labour, in which case you have an excuse to slack off.

Success is liking what you do, unless you like being a hobo.

Dance like no-one is watching, masturbate like no-one is listening in your parents' room.

163. The Dark Side Of
The Easter Bunny

His criminal record shows billions of counts of trespass.

It takes him ten seconds flat to sleepfuck everyone in your house.

He hides one of every ten eggs in a beartrap.

Like Santa, the Easter Bunny relies on legions of eager helpers, and his internship programme is considered the best training for future drug couriers.

Check your wife's panty drawer for nibble marks.

The vast majority of those 'eggs' are painted turds.

He is so profoundly deranged by rabies that you're well advised to get those 'treats' shots before ingesting them.

For reasons lost to the mists of time, mention his brother, Bugs, and the Easter Bunny will choke you with marshmallow chicks.

You know what big feet are said to indicate. So it is with large ears. The rest of the year, he's the famous bestial porn star Pubic Hare.

He often contracts out his rounds to Easter skunks.

He's still bitter about losing the Playboy gig.

He's so maddeningly infested he might as well be called the Easter Flea.

That's him in Monty Python And The Holy Grail.

How does he manage such exertions? A big old basket o' meth.

164. Fun Improvements To Guantanamo Bay

A selection of boarding waters, including mountain spring and sparkling, served by a dedicated CIA sommelier.

Snarling guard dogs no longer trained to kill but merely to drag your gonads to and fro.

Naked, shackled, stacked Pilates.

Formal dinners as the captain's table.

Classes on how to accessorise a predominantly orange wardrobe.

Light-hearted Scrabble rivalries between Those Who Say Barbed Wire and Those Who Say Barb.

Renaming of rendition to 'tourism' and extreme rendition to 'super-duper tourism'.

A choice of gluten-free, non-dairy and low-carb meals to be forcefed.

Arts classes to whittle elegant bamboo shards for your fingernails.

If you can't write, you may now scream your last will and testament.

Ghostly Johnny Cash shows.

GB Shakespeare Society productions of The Maiming Of The Shrew and Much Jihad About Nothing.

Frequent-fryer miles for those that often make it as far as the electric fence.

Relaxation in the fully-submerged Turkish bath.

165. Signs You Need Anger Management

You think all foods taste of bile.

You got fired by the Khmer Rouge for being too mean.

The local Hell's Angels bring you a basket of muffins each week with an apology note for the engine noise.

When you get between a mother grizzly and her cubs, her attitude is fine, take 'em.

You were never in a discussion that didn't end up needing crime-scene tape.

Your dates won't come out from under the table.

You replace crushed steering wheels on your car more frequently than tires.

The sight of spring lambs frolicking carefree in a sunny wild-flower meadow makes you punch a nun.

Your meditation mantra isn't Ommmm, it's Grrrr.

You frighten children because your fists won't unclench and the veins in your neck stand out like garter snakes.

Scorpions back away so fast they bump their curly bums on things and cry.

You scowl to the bone.

You tried knitting to relax but you always wound up eating the needles.

Your favourite word is 'conflagration'.

Everyone in your kung-fu class emigrated.

If the sky is too blue, the breeze too refreshing or the petunias too pretty, you are gripped by livid paroxysms of wrath.

In spite of your all-pork diet, you burn so many calories flying into furious rages about what's on television that you're chronically malnourished

There is no speck of your skin unadorned by Sam Kinison tattoos.

Your hobby is fuming.

166. Why The Least Cool Member Of A Band Is The Drummer

The first thing we're taught is that hitting isn't playing.

Generally, the most noteworthy thing they're known for is dying from inhaling their own vomit, or others'.

When working out new material with the band, the limit of their contribution is thud-thud-thud or thud-thud-thudud-thud.

Guitar blisters are cool. Ripped vocal cords are cool. But splinters?

Any instrument that can be played with equal panache by passing out onto it or dropping it from a van is never cool.

No other band member can so effectively frighten away sewer rats or encourage earthworms to come to the surface.

There's a reason the handsome singer is at the front and the drummer's at the back.

The ultimate oxymoron is 'percussion instrument'.

No other band member can be replaced with a nine-dollar device from eBay.

Every other instrument requires talent beyond the ability to count to four.

You never hear anyone say, "That Bach! What a wildman!"

No-one else considers trashing a hotel room rehearsal.

In prehistoric times, the first drummer played a hollow log, and he was Charlie Watts.

There are no sex cymbals.

167. Excuses For Photocopying Body Parts At Work

Misunderstood 'job openings'.

But the instructions say, 'Lay flat on glass' and 'Insert cartridge'.

So dedicated am I to this company that I don't take time off to see my doctor, just send him a picture of the affected area and he diagnoses me by post.

The Bible says be fruitful and multiply.

Ohhh, the copier needs more 'toner'. I misheard.

Trying to eliminate fear amongst female colleagues via the 'reduce' function.

My viewing habits are triplicate-x-rated.

Wanted proof that I am so a hard worker.

Was getting my Xerox off.

You sacked me first.

168. Horses' Favourite Movies

Sleepless In Saddle

Aclipclopalypse Now

Canter-bury Tales

Cat On A Hot Tin Hoof

Fifty Shades Of Hay

Filly Jack

Full Metal Feedbag

Jockey Balboa

Legends Of The Stall

Nags Of Our Fathers

One-Hour Photo Finish

Runaway Bridle

The Men Who Stare At Oats

Whinny The Pooh

169. Complaints Of Elton John's Husband

Endless rants about the failure of Save The Children to provide a chinchilla throw backstage in spite of the explicit instructions in the two-hundred-page benefit concert contract.

Loud, livid renditions of I'm Still Standing when you don't bring the sedan chair quickly enough.

Frequent extended Madonna visits while she tries to offload orphans because she bought too many.

Gets all in a tizzy when the wind ironically blows out his candelabra.

Makes eyes at his tiny backup dancers.

Becomes enraged when Bernie Taupin claims it's His Song.

Insists on wearing the duck suit to bed.

Storming from mall to mall in a furious, fruitless search for sufficiently vast sunglasses.

Ire on Liberace Sucks Night.

Never laughs when he comes home and you sing The Bitch Is Back.

Hair transplant failures blamed on lousy head.

Calls him Daniel in intimate moments.

It's just so unfair that being the rich one enables some people to let themselves go and become puffy while some others have to do sit-ups morning, noon and night.

Sheds even more furiously when you call him Moltin' John.

Stomach ulcers caused by silently repressing preference for Madagascar over The Lion King.

Sensitive to jokes about his little pianist.

Recurring nightmare that you're Keith Richards come to cut him.

Actually hisses during hissy fits.

Thinks his pasties make him look pasty.

170. Songs For The Accident Prone

Achy Breaky Part

Ouch, I Did It Again

I Guess That's Why They Call It The Bruise

Jumpin' Jack Splat

Paint It High-Visibility Fluorescent Yellow

I'm Still Standing (Wait, No)

You've Lost Feeling

The (Nine One) One I Love

I Wanna Hold Your Hand For Balance

Bohemophilian Rhapsody

Limp This Way

I Can't Help Falling

How Do You Mend A Broken Hip?

Tie A Yellow Ribbon As A Tourniquet

A Big Hunk O' Gauze

Let It Bleed Out

171. The Real Reasons Scotland Rejected Independence

A rogue nation is one thing, a brogue one something else.

Didn't want the only movie on TV to be Braveheart in perpetuity.

Inappropriate for the national anthem to be a soccer hooligan chant.

Neither Sean Connery nor Mel Gibson affordable as President.

Too cheap to buy votes.

Legislation ought not to be passed according to which party wins the brawl.

World leaders refuse to attend state dinner of battered, deep-fried intestines.

Tossing hats gleefully into the air won't kill anyone, but cabers would.

Years of day-long toasts to independence would paralyze productivity.

Hard to think straight when you're all fucked up on haggis.

172. Secrets Of Old West Gunfighters

Cattle rustling had nothing to do with stealing cows. It was much, much worse.

The movie image of gunfighters drinking straight whiskey is Hollywood nonsense, as they largely preferred kale and ginger smoothies.

Far more fearsome than the outlaws were the inlaws.

If you swaggered up to the bar in a saloon and ordered milk, you were asking for trouble, because, due to poor refrigeration, it was often sour.

After the bloodbath, the OK Corral was renamed This Corral Sucks.

Cowboys didn't want it known that cattle herd naturally. You need only follow them wherever they're going and pretend to point the way.

Handguns of the day were so imprecise and unreliable that most disagreements were settled by a beat poetry slamdown.

Old West nicknames were allocated by drawing them from a hat. Sissy Peterson, Cupcake McGubbin and Flounce Rickerson are names lost to obscurity.

Billy The Kid, contrary to myth, was not allowed guns by his parents.

Relations with native Indians were largely harmonious, so that you were apt to be butchered on sight and your pieces scattered widely over the plains only by the Cree, the Apache, the Iroquois, the Metis, the Comanche, the Sioux, the Cheyenne, the Blackfoot and the Shonee.

The Pinkertons ran a tough, fearless, incorruptible detective agency, but you could make them cry by mocking their gay name.

The most common baby name was Ol'.

Boot Hill was a real place, but a less popular tourist destination than Boob Beach.

John Wayne didn't really talk like that; his real name was Bee Gee.

It was considered honorable to shoot a man with his boots on, but only his boots.

173. Woes Of The English Minister Of Loneliness

There's no-one to appoint Vice Minister Of Loneliness.

The press have yet to attend a press conference.

Can't pardon the Unabomber.

Enjoys family-size TV dinners at his desk so he can have left-overs the following day.

The notches in his bedpost are just the chunks that he chewed out during nightmares about nobody turning up to his funeral.

During Prime Minister's Questions, asks only if the PM would like to catch a movie sometime.

The 'Ministry' is his parents' basement.

The Department Seal is a teardrop on an unopened condom.

Spells Valentine q-u-a-r-a-n-t-i-n-e.

Requested a windowless office so he wouldn't jump.

The sign on the Ministry door says Sigh.

Tries to introduce a bill to mandate that girls talk to him.

During election campaigns, is charged with staying behind to water the plants.

When he buys a pair of lovebirds, they enter into a suicide pact.

His greatest policy decision is whether to be ignored in a blue or brown tie.

Refuses a protective detail on the grounds that the guards themselves are higher-value targets.

Has photos of colleagues' kids on his desk.

174. How To Be Italian

Have wine for breakfast and bellow about the anchovies.

Be achingly gorgeous until your 25th birthday, at which point you should immediately quadruple your weight and develop a fascinating collection of facial abnormalities.

Tolerate any manner of depravity and corruption as long as it's done in an exquisitely tailored suit.

Emigrate to find a better life, but even after ten generations, refuse to lose the accent or cease longing for the old country.

Name all your kids Tony, even she who objects.

Marinate everything in olive oil, especially your hair.

Talk wildly with your hands and break four phones a day.

Change governments more often than your underwear.

Eat bread with a side of bread and a shortbread cookie.

With each passing year, believe that you get ever more irresistible to women, and that they yearn to see as much of your chest as possible without actually removing your shirt.

Court only women whose 'staches would shame Yosemite Sam.

Have fewer wallet photos of your children than of the Pope.

Go on strike to demand more strike time.

Favour fabrics that are shinier than good taste would typically require.

Train for years as a chef, work a hundred hours a week in the finest restaurants, collect Michelin stars like most people hoard Pokemon, but proclaim that your aging, anosmic mother is the greatest cook ever to walk the Earth.

Believe with every fibre of your being that each kind of pasta isn't exactly the same.

Use food as curse words. 'OH! Bafangool, uh? Gnocchi YOU, marone! Rigatoni al FORNO!'

Of all the colours of the rainbow, don't rule out any as unsuitable for pants.

Proclaim the immeasurable beauty of Venice while disregarding the eye-watering stench.

Forget your anniversary twenty-nine years running, but quote every word of The Godfather from memory.

Even on family vacation to Sicily, take a crack at conquering it.

Enjoy bottomless espresso so thick it is drunk with a knife and fork, and by noon have the metabolism of a hummingbird to explain your speech patterns.

Use phrases like 'goomba', 'reggiano' or 'extra virgin' as though they actually mean something.

Smack your kids while they're sleeping in case they do something when they wake up.

Never forget that yelling is the ideal substitute for being right.

175. More Ways To Spot
The Amish Cool Kids

Says he can get you any kind of sacramental wine you want.

Wagon wheelies.

Refers to perusing reference materials as texting.

Throws around foul language like, 'Fuck thee!'

Buggy rides six inches off the ground.

Has to be nagged to clean his loom.

Calls bitches hoes.

Suggestively pronounces his name Obi-DO-ya.

Refers to a barn raising as pulling an erection.

Calls his girlfriend Wench and protests that that's her actual job title.

When nobody's looking, reads the New Testament.

Wears his straw hat backwards.

176. Signs Your Mechanic Trained As An Interior Designer

Diagnoses faulty Feng Shui in your carburetor.

You routinely crash into trees as your brakes are made of velvet.

Sweeping floor-to-roof bay windshield.

Your fuel economy plummets on account of the Italian marble tiles.

Feels strongly that no vehicle can have too many windchimes.

Take a corner too fast and you get slapped by a curtain.

Oriental four-on-the-floor floormats.

You pull the lever to wash your windscreen and find yourself in a blizzard of potpourri.

Paints one door a different colour as the 'accent panel'.

Beanairbags.

While you enjoy having fresh espresso on tap during long journeys, the horrific burns are starting to impact your love life.

Fully-reclining driver's seat.

Stained-glass mudflaps.

Your roof-mounted storage box is replaced with a gazebo that makes your car sway terrifyingly in even the lightest breeze.

Replacing the gasoline with camomile extract smelled lovely until your engine exploded.

Vaulted cathedral glovebox.

To minimise environmental impact and ensure sustainability, your tires are made from cornhusks.

177. Troubling Side Effect Warnings

More oily anal discharge than optimal.

Might result in fingerprints that match those of serial killer at large.

Can result in dubious South African accent.

May cause continuous testicular implosion.

Some kidney stones the size of Shetland ponies and untreatable bowel tortion causing the worst imaginable lifelong searing torment and perpetually shrieking ululating Afghani prayers for the sweet release of death have been reported.

Blood might thin or thicken or curdle in your veins, but then again, it might just clot. Or not. You'll be ever so keen to find out.

May cause exponential growth of additional nipples, visions of Hugh Hefner's ghost in a bunny outfit, secretion of semen through eyeballs and body odor of mackerel.

Hearing impairment might result from the loud ceaseless drip, drip, drip of gonorrhea.

178. What To Expect When British Astronauts Encounter Aliens

An awkward initial meeting whereby the aliens are required to prove beyond doubt that they aren't French.

Despite instalinguistic translation capability, they are told they use English improperly and shunned.

Headmasters come running to welcome them with a sound thrashing.

It's weird that they're indistinguishable from crumpets.

Too polite to object to relentless anal probing.

The Splagnorxian ambassador is offended and armed conflict launched when his traditional greeting of drawing exposed sensor stalks toward his outstretched abdominal fissure is met with a curt nod.

First contact would not happen after 5:00 PM or at the weekend.

Immediate sharing of technology to help the aliens warm their beer.

New types of weather can be discussed at length during excruciating small talk so that critical topics such as trade and infinite sources of non-polluting energy might be avoided indefinitely.

In spite of their boundless knowledge, highly-evolved morality and pangalactic propulsion technology, the alien visitors are treated with grudging condescension and made to feel decidedly inferior.

Aliens immediately prostrate themselves in surrender to any life form so barbarous as to eat blood pudding.

The fools don't fly on the left side of the sky.

179. More Pointless Product Warning Labels

Some jigsaw puzzle assembly required.

Hamster not suitable for pulling carts.

Efficacy of snorkel diminished beyond Earth's atmosphere.

Use steam-powered penis enlarger with caution.

This end of drinking glass up.

Earphones' noise reduction feature may not entirely block Red Hot Chili Peppers.

Umbrella not to be inverted and used as portable plunge pool by Tom Cruise.

Floss teeth only, and gargle orally.

Hadron Collider not for reheating spaghetti.

Do not attempt to slow juggernaut with face.

Do not insert toy train into urethra.

Do not refer to microwave oven as 'space toaster'.

Moat not guaranteed to keep out Kevin Spacey.

Kite not for miners.

Jalapeno juice not for use as emergency eyewash.

Don't fling the caribou.

Do not share condoms.

Hitler wind-up doll might get too wound up.

180. Recurring Nightmares Of The Stars

Yoko: What if there aren't enough vocal coaches in the world?

Frank Stallone: The awful realization that he might pass the remaining days of his life as the only one who sees how much more talented than his brother he is.

Pierce Brosnan: Brought to trial for his crimes against the James Bond franchise.

Ronald McDonald: One child in the bunker manages to get a cell signal.

Elton John: Coke furies no longer excuse for being a colossal twat.

Reese Witherspoon: The afterglow of Legally Blonde wears away and she is now just too old to wear those skirts.

Kathleen Turner: Voice deepens to the point where it can only be measured by the Richter scale.

Mick Jagger: Learns to dance and sing, career over.

Ryan Gosling: People discover that he has the brains of an avocado.

Donald Trump: Melania learns enough English to understand all the conditions in the pre-nup.

Zach Quelsackacrapiam: Both fans die.

Jean Claude Van Damme: Catches a glimpse of one of his own movies in a TV-store window or while spying on his neighbours with binoculars.

Piers Morgan: Satan finally completes the extensive programme of renovations and upgrades required to prepare for his arrival.

Colonel Sanders: Word gets out about what else he considers finger-lickin' good.

Siegfried: The huge stack of dead Roys is stumbled upon by a hiker.

Christian Bale: A brain injury results in just chilling the fuck out.

Tom Cruise: The Thetans aren't less than two feet tall as L. Ron promised.

Will Ferrell: Told to be funny or shot, it's the latter.

Woody Allen: Soon-Yi gets old and he has to restart the spousal adoption process.

Samuel L. Jackson: He perishes from the shame of being in every movie ever made but not in every book, song and puppet show.

Paris Hilton: Her face freezes in only one expression. Wakes up and IT'S TRUE!

Russell Brand: The sound of the people of Earth telling him to piss off grows so loud that he genuinely cannot hear himself think.

181. More Headlines That Would Cause Panic

Containment Breach At Giant Boybands Farm

Teeth To Be Brushed Sixty-Six Times Per Day, Laugh Militant Dentists

Committee Of Tom Cruise, Victoria Beckham, Bob Geldof and Elon Musk To Decide All Baby Names

Studies Find That Those Who Swear By Vinyl Because The Sound Is 'Warmer' Are Extra Fertile

Outbreak Of Kardashians Now Worldwide Pandemic

Funding Approved For Release Of New Fast And Furious Movie Weekly

All Sports Banned Except Golf

Those Convicted Of Minor Offenses To Be Sentenced To Ice Capades In Lieu Of Fines

Twitter Becomes Trumpbook In Hostile Takeover

Legislation Prohibits Sale Of Shaving Cream To Douchebags, Man Buns Mandatory For All

Turns Out A Nutritious Breakfast Is Slow-Acting Deadly Poison

Loss Of Tonsils Causes Eventual Impotence

Computers Hacked Worldwide, All Browser Histories Now On CNN

Shoe Stores To Serve Only Women Accompanied By Spouses

Exhumed Carcass Of Margaret Thatcher To Appear In Playboy

Staff Meetings Now Truly Endless

Terminator Sent Back In Time To Kill Unborn JK Rowling

182. Original Full Rosters

Simon And Garfunkel And Yoko

Ernie & Bert Bacharach

The Jackson Twenty-Seven

Ross And Rachel And The Allman Brothers

The Kids Of Degrassi Street And Those Within About A Mile Or So

Al Qaida And The Pips

Alvin & The Chipmunks & 101 Dalmatians

David Cassidy And Goliath

James Cagney & Lacey

Crosby, Stills, Nash, Crosby Again And Young

Sonny And Sonny's Mate Luke And Cher

The Four Horsemen And Two Unicyclists Of The Apocalypse

The Great And Average Lakes

Tweety & Sylvester Stallone

183. What Bigfoot Tells His Kids

I take fine baby photos. You were born blurry.

As you grow in confidence, you'll know you aren't a hoax.

Yes, salmon again. Eat it or go to your lair.

Don't you dare growl spine-chillingly behind my back, young man!

It's all fun and games until someone ends up stuffed in a glass case at a low-end roadside museum.

Remember Uncle Patchy? That's why we don't allow gum in this family.

Be patient, little one, you'll be abominable soon enough.

I'm not a racist but no son of mine is gonna date a bear.

You don't need school - hunt, gather, tear asunder, repeat.

If you ever get lost, find a forest ranger and tell him you're a missing link.

Enough with the morning wood knocks.

No bath! How are you supposed to reek?

You'll learn to be a loner when everyone you meet becomes a laughingstock.

When the door is closed, don't come in. Your mother and I are fighting extinction.

184. Tips For Rookie Air Traffic Controllers

When tired, announce that you're going to bed. Don't say you're gonna crash.

It makes pilots nervous when you call them Sully.

Try not to think about the thousands of innocent lives in your inexperienced hands, and how just one tiny mistake will ruin countless families, causing untold misery for generations, condemning you to decades of ceaseless guilt, which you can be spared only by hara-kiri.

The sky is massive, so there's almost no way to screw up.

Remember that it's 'rapid descent', not 'plummet', and 'incandescent approach', not 'fireball'.

If you hear a pilot shout something that sounds like 'Heyday!' he's having a really good time.

It's Boeing, not Boing.

Nobody really knows what a vector is.

Sound professional by adding '-er' to every worder.

Pilots will like you better if you call them Maverick.

Sometimes birds appear on radar, so if a couple of blips bump into each other, it's probably fine. A water landing is as misleading a term as a mountain kiss.

Your popularity will not soar if you call it gaydar.

Pilots are resourceful, so at the end of a long shift, just shout "LAND!" and they'll work it out among themselves.

'Holding pattern' is ATC code for 'Gotta pee'.

When a 747 does cartwheels, it's a sign of a happy landing.

The airport firefighters almost never get to do what they've trained for; get them to like you by lying to pilots about their altitude.

185. You Know You're A Snowflake When...

Immediately upon meeting anyone, you apologize profusely for your skin colour, your gender and your face.

You wake up screaming over things that go Trump in the night.

In lieu of conversation on a date, you feel it's less risky just to colour the placemat.

You petition the UN weekly to have sarcasm declared a hate crime.

The only dirty talk you'll tolerate is a handwritten note asking you to consider the possibility of being asked politely, of your own free will, to mull the notion of potentially removing your overcoat.

Your appendix burst because you refused to have your condition labelled critical.

Your clothes are always dusty since, when you see a Facebook post with which you disagree, you don't come out from under the bed for days.

Your safe space is an actual safe.

You watch the news through those dark eclipse glasses.

You feel a debate has turned abusive when someone says 'Hmmm.'

The very existence of Pepsi is an affront to your deepest beliefs.

You have your auditory canals professionally spackled so you won't hear talk radio.

You can no longer walk, because, when you spot a bumper sticker or a lawn sign that concerns you, you weep on your shoes and get soggy socks and toe fungus.

You're petrified of rabid dogs, robbers and memes.

Your primal flight impulse is triggered by smiles, lest they be meant ironically.

You refuse to use any toothpaste that claims to 'fight plaque' as you're a pacifist who believes that oral hygiene is a matter of respectful negotiation.

186. Excuses For Returning Your Newborn To The Hospital

Gets the dingoes all riled up.

Won't sit still for tattoos.

Not a happy drunk.

Shows distressingly low aptitude for Karaoke.

Nowhere near as flame-retardant as anticipated.

Would apparently prefer that its rattle not be attached to a snake.

This one leaks.

Doesn't fit in the glove box.

Sucks at Scrabble.

Only marketable skill is shrieking.

I so don't do needy.

Requires more luggage than the Sultan of Brunei.

Worst getaway driver I ever had.

Great for picking up chicks at the park but refuses to make self scarce when we get home.

Functions as a really shitty kite.

Can barely grasp the premise of Goodfellas.

Dribbles when dribbled.

Was kinda hoping for Bam-Bam.

Unsoothed by my crib-death nursery rhymes.

Looks and acts too much like the president.

187. Neil Armstrong's Regrets

His name. Folks get him confused with Neil Diamond and demand he sing Sweet Caroline.

Golf was a lame sport to play in low gravity. Shoulda been rasslin'.

Wishes he hadn't acted amused over a Ralph Kramden 'To the moon, Alice!' gift photo. Now he can paper his house with them.

Shouldn't have signed that first mooning guy's butt.

Now nothing but g-forces can hit his g-spot.

Still calls Houston when he has a problem but everyone there has blocked his number.

Developed a taste for Depends way too soon.

Dinner guests don't come back when you serve it in a little tube.

The lunar module gave him claustrophilia.

During sex, burns up on re-entry.

Still gets death threats from the others on the mission when it's not his fault no-one ever heard of them.

Breathed at parades and contracted tickertape lung.

Moods entirely dictated by the tide.

No longer bludgeons those who come up to him and belt out That's Amore.

Could've just gone to Sudbury.

188. Things Not To Say To Avoid Offending God

Burning bushes certainly make a statement, but for clarity of message, try a fax.

Didst thou ever think of The Ten Asking Nicelies?

I get the whole 'mysterious ways' thing, but erectile dysfunction?

If I am without sin, Jesus died for nothing, so get off my back about the orphan porn.

It was great meeting thee, but there's a lot more going on with the Hindus.

You could've sent a plague of locusts but you were feeling extra wrathful so we got the Red Hot Chili Peppers?

Any particular reason why, in your majesty and omnipotence, you need chosen spokesmen at all, let alone the ordained kiddy diddlers?

I dunno, somehow the pearly gates just scream Look At Me.

I gotcher Palm Sunday.

If I say I'm an atheist, will ye disappear?

How do those who aren't even in Hell yet deserve rap?

Listen, pal, if I wanted to suffer for all eternity, I'd get married, all right?

I know they're traditional and all, but those annoying psalms make me want to crucify myself.

So bacon. Sin or not?

If there's no money in heaven, what do you flip when both boxers pray to win?

You had almost a week. Is this really the best you could do?

What's up with the plague of hipsters?

You know, you needn't do it. Thunderbolts pretty much hurl themselves.

189. Least Menacing
Boxer Nicknames

Raging Moth

The Clinching Clubfoot

The Quivering Quitter

The Staggering Stick Insect

No-Show Nancy

Kid Contusion

The Portland Potpourri

The Bleeding Bladder

The Brittle Bum

The Flailing Fleer

The Frail Fop

The Italian Scallion

The Jabbing Jezebel

The Mall Walker

The Pacifist

The Pleading Palooka

The Prone Groaner

The Quaker

The Stewardess

The Swollen Prostate

The Vapors

189. Least Menacing Boxer Nicknames

The Vegan

The Weeping Willow

The Flouncing Fairy

190. What The Contents Of Your Fridge Reveal About Your Personality

Keeping Camembert in the fridge in the hope that it will improve the odour suggests that you've failed to grasp the point of French cuisine.

It's perfectly normal to have a few beers chilling in the fridge, but being unable to close the door for the bottles while a tiny bag of lettuce rots on the counter might indicate that your diet lacks fibre, or solids of any kind.

Is there kale? If so, right now go fling it down the garbage chute in your trendy condo building and follow it.

From a store fridge, you are a cunning and strategic shopper who wisely takes items at the back, in the awareness that they put the lethally poisonous ones upfront.

Uneaten pizza indicates that you were arrested, killed or abducted by aliens before you could finish it.

Twenty kilos of five kinds of bacon means you're probably a human rights advocate or a superhero.

It may seem responsible to keep a polar bear in the fridge as opposed to somewhere warmer, but you must really ask yourself some serious questions about the need for a vast human-eating predator in your studio apartment at all.

The little round indents are for eggs, or, if you insist, your balls, but don't slam the door.

If there are leftovers in Tupperware from the Coolidge administration, which you fear to peer into because they are now essentially weapons of gastric mass destruction, either quit buying Tupperware or call it what it is, Eventual Garbage Mini-Bins.

Radiocarbondate that baking soda you believe can still absorb odours after all these epochs, and tell chicks you dig archeology. Science nerds are the new beefcake. If you have actual beefcake in there, it has evolved from something else and should be removed with tongs.

191. Romantic Comedy Horror Movies

Three Men And Rosemary's Baby

When Harry Met Carrie

The Thing About Mary

Runaway Bride Of Chuckie

My Big Fat Greek Chainsaw Massacre

Headless In Seattle

Saw Actually

Groundhog Day Of The Triffids

The Notting Hills Have Eyes

Breakfast At Pet Cemetery

Bridget Jones' Poltergeist

Cujo And Me

The Wedding Exorcist

Sweet Home Amityville

As Good As Friday The 13th Gets

Black Charlie Brown Christmas

Meet The Parents In The Woods

192. Signs Your Self-Esteem Is Dangerously Low

Your spirit animal is a lemming.

You don't even try to feed the pigeons because you know they'll say, 'Naw, man, we're good.'

You like when the restaurant hostess says, 'Party of one?' and you're invited, to follow her.

When a prospective employer asks where you see yourself in five years, in all candor you say down at the beach, pushing around a shopping cart of empties, wearing rubber boots and a towel cape and a tinfoil crown, mumbling about Socialism.

You only shop at stores called an 'averagemarket' as you don't deserve somewhere super.

You're sticking with Windows ME.

You avoid hookers because they'll just haggle you up.

You beg Jehovah's Witnesses to share the word of the Lord and they refuse.

You get fifty emails a day from Nigerian princes telling you to leave them alone.

You glue your mailbox shut on Valentine's Day just to be able to say you could've had one.

You're the president of the Piers Morgan Fan Club. And the membership.

You pretend to be on death row to find a girlfriend.

You think of your legacy mostly in terms of the stains.

Your Friday night fun is Netflix and pray for death.

You join eHermit.

Your ringtone is Milli Vanilli.

Your daily affirmation is 'I suck.'

193. Poorly Translated Warning Signs

Slow Death Zone

If Alarm Sound No Poop

Plank If Friendless

Emergency Be Gone

Ouch Tumble Into Gaping Chasm

Deer Crossing Holocaust

Asunder Area

Gate Of Aircraft Flying. Only Flying Persons Around Gate Or Leaving Required Not By Flying

Bridge Altitude Inadequate For Tallest Head Or Roof

Electrical Sky Wires Bring Sizzle Death

Safe For Next Only Of Kin

Bridge On

Plummet Here

Personnel Superior Into Furnace Only

No Shoplift Except Yoko Album

Tedious For Next Ten Years

Conflagration Of Leaves Unwelcome Around These Part

Feral Dog Boner Park

Friend Zone Forever Probably

Vehicular Stationing For Cripple And Such

Bleed Out Quiet

Picking Pocketing Rife Around Your Sack

Peril Ahead, No Queuing

Neighbourhood Watch Out You

Pee Never

194. The Meadow Frolic Rules

Only bees may pollinate the flowers.

No using the romance of buttercups to extend a doomed relationship.

No golfing in the meadow, but if golfing is your idea of frolic, you've probably already run afoul of the No Douchebags In The Meadow rule, so disregard.

No traipsing day and night through the meadow because your children will resent the abandonment and your wife will bone the neighbours in reprisal.

No frolicking devil-may-care, because if he might, he probably does, and then you're screwed.

Giant clown shoes disturb the tranquility of the meadow and increase the risk of injury from landmines.

If you're a cow, no grazing in the meadow, as the grass is sprayed with pesticides, and you'll need to be as healthy as possible for slaughter.

Anyone found skipping gaily about the meadow giggling childishly may be used for target practice by the indigenous meadow snipers.

If you see trash, pick it up, but if you spy puke, leave it.

No blasting butterflies with a flamethrower in the meadow without welding glasses.

No posting pics of yourself gamboling playfully in the meadow on social media because, given your personality, no-one will believe you're that happy.

No burrowing beneath the meadow like some grim spoilsport gopher of funlessness.

Do not lure naive young actors into the meadow with promises of work in commercials or meadow-based documentaries.

If you're a leper skipping through the meadow, pick up after yourself.

Do not feed the meadow trolls the good kids.

195. How To Tell Your Lover Is A Bomb Disposal Expert

Can only be aroused when you've been rendered inert.

Puts the clamps on your nipples with way too much care.

Won't apply lube until a beagle has sniffed it.

Instinctively flings dildos out the window and covers his ears.

Makes you sleep on the burned spot.

Sends in the robot to get a look at you first.

Unlike most sex partners, does everything he can to prevent you going off.

Doesn't like when you refer to it as banging.

His time with children consists mostly of shouting at them to stay back.

Nibbles your fuse so gently nothing happens.

Safe sex means head-to-toe Kevlar.

At the moment of climax, locks you in a concrete box for controlled detonation.

Sweeps your pubic hair for landmines.

No response when you call him dad, goes wild when you call him dud.

Your roleplay involves standing motionless for three hours while he removes your basque.

Foreplay is always The Hurt Locker puppet show.

He fills your Christmas stocking with nails and screws and other projectiles.

Refers to anal as 'planting a dirty bomb'.

Never says he's having fun, always a blast.

Sweats profusely when he probes you.

The only guy you've ever met who uses a sex accelerant.

His fantasies run largely to shrapnel.

Knows just which buttons to push and wires to snip in an argument.

Sets a timer before sex and keeps an eye on it nervously.

You learn very quickly not to bring up phosphorous in bed.

Doesn't realize how loud he pillowtalks.

Mistakes your IUD for an IED.

196. Lesser-Known Sayings of Jesus

Blessed are the douchebags, for they shall have fannypacks.

Check this out: Poof! WINE! How great art THAT?

I absolutely, 100% guarantee my Dad is tougher than yours.

I really hate Easter.

Blow me, ye winds.

I wish I could heal this manger mange.

For their sins? Me? Yeah, no.

It isn't a fishing trip, they're fishers of MEN, dear, and no, the hooker isn't coming.

It'll take a bloody miracle to feed this lot.

Lepers. I say unto them ew.

Mark! Will you, Matthew, Luke and John please stop writing down everything I say?

Turn these cheeks.

Seriously, your name is Pilot? Nice to meet you, Cap'n.

Wanna score some myrrh?

You're not my real Dad, you can't make me build shelves!

197. How To Celebrate A New Toilet

Copious cistern selfies.

Commemorative diarrhearama.

Hire a seat fluffer and paper sommelier for the day.

Mardi Gros.

Bar shitzvah.

Pass confetti.

Skip To Your Loo.

Diamond-encrusted tissue.

Use as novelty punch bowl.

Brass band to accompany inaugural flush.

Small parade of plumbers holding plungers erect.

Tickertapeworm parade.

Flushdance.

Play Commode To Joy on harp.

Peeñata.

Several days of dining on nothing but curry, chilli peppers and roadkill to show new toilet who's boss during maiden voyage.

198. Tools On The Ultimate Swiss Army Knife

A blade sharp enough to cut through an anvil or the plastic tag on a new pair of flip-flops.

Air horn to drown out the you-know-who Peppers.

Car stoplight nosepick gusto scoop.

Fold-out hipster douchebag torment rack.

Something to extract a lodged CD from a car stereo by causing maximum damage to the CD, stereo, dashboard and surrounding woodland.

Yoko talent-detection micrometer.

Tim Horton's lineup rescue flare.

Spousal work story earplugs.

Rap surrender flag (white).

Teenage loss of Internet access screaming tantrum defense shield.

Will Ferrell movie retinal acid drops.

Laser-guided, sub-atomic, pan-dimensional ultra-scalpel to locate the fabled soul of Piers Morgan.

Cotton candy machine Trump hair loom.

199. Bad Life Lessons
For Your Children

Be the best version of yourself you can with that gimpy eye and your pants on backward.

Ask yourself, 'What would Jesus do?' Then remember how it turned out for him and smarten up.

Follow your dreams, you follower.

Toilets aren't merely suggestions, as you apparently think.

Honesty is the best policy when your tell is stamping your foot and screeching like a microwaved gerbil.

These are the best days of your life, at this ice-cold orphanage, with no friends, and only celery to eat, in that iron lung.

Learn from each savage beating.

Be good to everyone you encounter on the way up. You can be a bastard later as you plummet.

Keep an open mind but not so wide that joining a Hondura death cult seems like a wise move.

Don't take things that don't belong to you, except, on Halloween, candy from strangers.

There are good people everywhere, but you're unlikely to meet them if they see you first.

From the very moment you were born and we looked into your eyes, we knew you were average at best.

Have dreams. Wishes. Goals. They crack me up.

Save a penny for a rainy day and see how far that gets you.

200. Musical Versions Of Action Movies

The Great Muppet Armageddon

Oklahoma Death Wish

Mummy Mia!

The Phantom Menace Of The Opera

Seven Brides For Seven Samurai

Chitty Chitty Kiss Kiss Bang Bang

Die Hard Jesus Christ Superstar

Jailhouse Twister Rock

Iron Man Of La Mancha

Aladdin Alcatraz

BrigaDoom

Beauty And The Beastmaster

Lethal Weapon Show Boat

Saw My Fair Lady

A Chorus Line Of Fire

The King And I, Robot

Rocky Horror Picture Show Balboa

201. World's Easiest Jobs

Air Guitar Tuner

Bacon Advocate

Bill Clinton Fluffer

Moon Counter

Paris Hilton Achievements Lister

Tito Jackson Fan Club President

Tapdancer Groupie Deterer

Curling Riot Policeman

Door-To-Door Piers Morgan Repellent Salesman

202. Dubious Weight Loss Tips

Instead of three big meals a day, have hundreds of small ones.

Just like dish detergent cuts grease, fat is repelled by shampoo. Have a big glass of Head & Shoulders before each meal.

Think cake is fattening? Think again - carrot cake!

Avoid gluten. Whatever the hell that is.

Walk five miles a day. Soon you'll be far from where your food is.

Don't eat pie, just brush your teeth with it.

In lieu of supper, knock on doors and beg the neighbours to let you suck the stains from their tablecloths.

After every bite, squaredance.

Drink a pot of coffee at bedtime. Tossing and turning is great exercise.

Skip breakfast for a week and you've banked five extra meals to enjoy any time you like.

Savour an all-you-can-eat buffet of steamed vapour.

Eat only egg whites, mixed greens and hash browns.

Do planks. Or, if that's too much exertion, play pranks.

Take out a gym membership. Or take out a guy named Jim.

203. Rejected Children's Toys and Games

Easy Smelt Blast Furnace

G.I. Tract Joe

Spiroagnewgraph

My Little Scorpion

Barrel Of Feces-Flinging Diseased Lab Monkeys

Sex Change Operation

Horny Horny Hippos

Cops & Grave Robbers

Tic Tac Toe Fungus

Midget Spinner

Connect 19,623

Swear Bears

Crap Gun

Nicotine Patch Kids

Pubik's Cube

Diddle Me Elmo

Batshit Crazy Eights

Blister Twister Third-Degree Edition

Duck-Duck Noose

I Spy For The Iranians

Kim Mah Jong Un

Monotony

Risk Of A Stroke

204. Disturbing Facts About Fruit

More soldiers are blown up by exploding pomegranates than IEDs.

Pears are so named because they mate for life. Separating them is what causes their bitter flavour.

The only significant difference between a cantaloupe and an antelope is that the former are sold with their hooves removed.

The word 'apricot' comes from the Gallic 'apres mort' or 'after death', as this is the only time they are palatable.

Apples are nothing more than sweet rancid onions.

Blueberries are sad.

That's not juice in the aptly-named kumquat.

Coconuts are neither coco nor your nuts.

Tomatoes are neither vegetables nor fruit, but a rare kind of red tuna.

Peaches and nectarines are the same fruit, except that peaches are feminists that reject the male oppression of shaving.

If you drop a single watermelon seed from the top of the Empire State Building, you have no life.

Strawberries have their seeds on the outside because when left alone in the fridge they masturbate ferociously and get covered in them.

There's a mere one-letter difference between a lime and slime.

It isn't mere coincidence that nothing rhymes with either 'orange' or 'xylophone'.

Partridge aren't fruit. What are you talking about?

You can tell if a watermelon is ripe by tapping on it - if it tells you to fuck off, it needs a few more days to mature.

In Japan, mangos are highly prized as sources of fibre and carnal rapture.

Bananas grow straight but are painfully bent by cruel multinational fruit conglomerates for easier transportation and for the hilarity of pretending they're telephones.

Plums' shape is why they were originally called bums.

205. More Wilderness Survival Tips

A dab of poison ivy will keep mosquitoes off your scrotum.

Enraged elk are less likely to gore you if you race around in circles shrieking and waving your arms above your head.

Try to appreciate the majesty of the forest or the stars in the sky or the wild boar gnawing on your face.

Many wild berries are packed with vitamins and nutrients and have such powerful laxative effects that dying won't seem so bad.

The native Iroquois could orient themselves by the clouds or something.

Forest fires are a lot more afraid of you than you are of them.

Bees can't climb trees.

It is typically best to wait until the second hour of a survival situation before turning to cannibalism.

Improvise a rudimentary shelter from an ordinary plastic sheet, fifty planks of wood, a ton of bricks and a truckload of cement.

Attract the attention of passing search planes using your satellite phone and homing beacon.

Make a fire by pounding two propane tanks together.

Unless you know exactly what you're doing, it's risky to suck out snake venom, especially directly from the snake.

Burrow to the core of the earth as a natural sunscreen.

Twigs and grit can be boiled into a foul-tasting gritty tea, which is precisely what you deserve for getting yourself lost.

206. Clues You're Too Old To Be A Rock Star

The guy you refer to as your drug dealer is just the delivery boy from the pharmacy.

You switch to a ukulele because it's lighter.

Sound check consists primarily of you yelling, 'WHAT?!'

You refuse a star on the Walk Of Fame because of the bending.

You used to wear disguises to avoid being recognized, but now that function is served nicely by your jowls.

Your backstage rider mandates a mug of hot cocoa and a crossword puzzle.

You trash hotel rooms by getting Deep Heat on the walls.

You find yourself wanting to turn that crap down.

The waist of your leather pants is migrating rapidly toward your chin.

Fans now hurl Depends.

Your addiction isn't to opioids anymore but to Oprah.

You insist your opening act be a barbershop quartet.

You once rocketed up the Hit Parade, now you ratchet up the heating pad.

Your guitar solos get longer to give you more time to remember the next verse.

You lose your temper at the Ferrari dealership because they won't sell you one in beige.

You now fret at customs that they might find your Rogaine.

Your compression socks are clearly visible through your skin-tight jeans.

Your Mom starts coming to your gigs.

Your lyrics mention your prostate more than they used to.

Your motto, 'Live fast, die young and leave a good-looking corpse' is now just, 'Live.'

207. Redneck Dating Tips

Don't whisper sweet nothings in her ear if they're just going to be drowned out by the roar of the NASCAR engines.

Polish up your tooth real good.

Show you're a man of means by upsizing her small Mountain Dew to medium.

Avoid comparing her appearance to Dale Earnhardt, except in the highly unlikely event that she's better-looking.

Coordinate your wifebeater and ballcap with the Burger King decor.

Try to remember not to call her Sis too loud.

Pose for romantic photos on the abandoned appliances in your yard.

Keep at least nine of the kids hidden until the second date.

When stealing flowers to give her, get them from the cemetery in the good part of town.

Be a gentleman and don't expect sex until you get to the KFC parking lot.

Compliment her on the near-symmetry of her breasts and how her eyes point in virtually the same direction.

208. Bad First Lines Of Novels

It was the best of times, and that was great.

A long time ago in a galaxy far, far away, Darth Vadar was breathing heavily around Luke Skywalker's sister, not knowing that both of them were actually his own children.

And so began Harry's fiftieth year at Hogwarts.

Wally The Asbestos Warthog laughed as the forest fire roared closer.

The day dawned black as night.

As the firing squad raised their rifles, Eduardo reflected on how it all had come to this. 'Aw, fuck, not another flashback,' he thought. 'Just shoot me.'

Dave now had the proof he needed that his wife was cheating on him, the briefest of glimpses through the high-rise apartment window as he plummeted by. Now what to do?

Ah, there's my sled, Rosebud.

Nobody believed there was a genuine threat from intergalactic pubic beetles until it was too late.

Once upon a time, they lived happily ever after until they died in a ghastly brothel fire.

'No!' he screamed. 'No, NO! In the name of God, NOOOO! Oh, all right.'

Santa wrung his hands with maniacal glee as he tossed the final vodka bottle aside.

209. Signs Your Teacher Used To Be In The Special Forces

He 'breaches' the supply cabinet.

Can hit you with a piece of chalk at four hundred yards and disembowel you with an apple.

Lays down suppressing fire when your team is batting.

He's good-natured until someone mentions Laos.

HIS drones put you to sleep permanently.

Instead of no talking says to go dark.

He teaches how to find Waldo in any book, not just Where's Waldo.

Letters home are stamped EYES ONLY.

PE lessons include much more bayonet practice than other classes.

Shouts, 'Cover me!' when exiting the staff room.

Storybooks are heavily redacted.

Report cards include grades for Gutting Insurgents and Withstanding Interrogation.

The class pet is a spitting cobra.

There's a board at the water fountain.

Uses a bamboo cage for detentions.

When he calls each name on the roll, students respond, "HOO-yeah!"

You take point in your row.

210. Tips For Founding A New Religion

Attract followers who face critical thinking challenges such that they believe with all their hearts that God wants them to have even less money so that you can have a plane.

Have a whole bunch more wives than everyone else because the sure sign of a prophet is that he's up to his nose in nagging.

As tempting as it is to include spacemen and monsters in your mythology, it limits your target market to lunatics and Hollywood midgets.

Everyone does sandals and a beard, so go for snowshoes and a sombrero.

Your holy book needs to be baffling and written in convoluted language, but, most importantly, heavy.

Choose a food that everybody likes and make it forbidden for a reason so random and arbitrary that it seems plausible.

It's best to decree that your followers must carry something very specific and sacred with them at all times - for gravitas, an anchor, anvil or shipping container.

Your biggest decision is one deity or many, though, if you plan to be a god yourself, then it's best not to build in much competition.

Knock out a few miracles early on to really cement your position.

Go for tax-exempt status. Or at least declare yourself payment-exempt.

Go out in a blaze of glory, or just with prostitutes.

Perform publicity-seeking stunts such as being struck by rattlesnakes to show you're the most enlightened of the critical-care faithful.

Have a big compound where you live off the grid and on the loose.

Become a noted theologian by writing a sci-fi novel.

Triple your annual income on a crying apology tour.

Forgive your enemies, but slander them in song.

Talk a lot about the purity your penis brings the virgins.

211. Upsides Of A Zombie Apocalypse

Drinking the blood of live rats aside, it's nice to get so much fresh air.

In light of all the putrefied flesh hanging from your face, nobody seems bothered by that mole on your chin anymore.

Government departments display no discernible reduction in efficiency.

A relief for those whose favoured mode of locomotion was always the slow lurch.

Lepers' dance cards full at last.

Popular new curse phrase, 'Kiss my resurrectum'.

Bieber by contrast slightly less revolting.

After years of working for a large corporation, roaming the Earth with a ravenous horde of the undead is vastly preferable.

Better to rot on the go than on hold with tech support.

More time to work on your poetry, though primarily with a flesh-eating theme.

Keanu Reeves now considered semi-lifelike.

Harvey Weinstein figures he now has a shot at all the chicks who said, 'Not in this lifetime, pal.'

Aged hippies, who followed the Dead before it was a thing, just carry on.

212. Behind The Scenes Of The Emergency Room

The most mangled get cookies.

It's fun to put up a No Walk-Ins sign.

STAT is a medical acronym for Sedate This Annoying Twat.

The only thing written on the chart is a score out of ten for how funny your injury is.

When a new shipment of rib spreaders arrives, you'd better hope whatever's wrong with you requires one.

Any pill they give you was taken from a rusty barrel labelled Placebos.

Complainers get the crustiest gurneys.

The diarrhea ward is cleaned with a leaf-blower.

The meanest game is to make you sing for painkillers.

The receptionist is the front line of order in a chaotic environment, which is why she always looks like her other job is catcher in a game of Czechoslovakian shotput baseball.

There is a mysterious correlation between cases of rudeness to medical staff and use of the testicular reflex mallet.

There's now a separate waiting room for the impaled.

When the staff run out of straws for their smoothies, they use catheters.

213. More Facts About The Japanese

Each year, thousands become billionaires when they are pressed into diamonds on packed subways.

Japanese workers begin the day with exercises just to give their unproductive Western counterparts a head start.

The most popular vacation activity is to spend only fourteen hours at your job.

Kabukake is a form of Japanese cum-drenched puppetry.

Sumo wrestlers are easily startled, and are best approached in heavy boots while ringing a bell.

Wasabi was originally created to murder Koreans.

In restaurants, rather than a basket of bread, you are served a bucket of snakes.

They too loathe Yoko.

Donald Duck is based on a character from Japanese literature called Happy No Pant Quack Bird Spouse.

The emperor is worshipped, but not as much as inflatable dolls.

In kindergarten, it is considered proper etiquette to work yourself to death.

Vending machines in Japan sell schoolgirls' panties but good luck finding a decent sausage roll.

The three most popular game shows are Eels In Your Pants, Plummet Pranks and What Can You Flay?

Saki is short for Nagasaki, and is peddled to westerners as revenge in that it's radioactive.

214. What Romeo And Juliet Would've Said To Each Other If They'd Lived

"This is getting too serious."

"I think we're gonna have to buy our parents a basket of muffins or something."

"A sleeping potion? That was your plan? Wake up in a CRYPT? What could go wrong, right? What are you, nuts? Do you KNOW how permanently creeped out I am? You're never planning anything EVER AGAIN!"

"I'll be back to make sure you're okay, beautiful. You just lay there in that shroud whilst I go have a few choice words with Friar Fuckhead."

"You know, school kids are going to study this forever. For the rest of time I'll be history's most famous emo loser."

"Why do all guys think they're way better at swords than they are?"

"Listen, you think I wanted to go? To a costume ball, are you kidding? I got dragged, all right? I had hoped to stay home and, like, you know, live and everything."

"Way to go, bitch. You invented the self-Cos."

"First of all, it might help if you could discern the difference between some chick and the sun."

"My mother was right about you."

215. You Might Be A Scrabble Addict If...

You named your dog QQUAZZY because 96 points.

You spellcheck faster than your computer.

You dumped your lingerie-model girlfriend and took out a restraining order when she drew hearts on all the blank tiles.

You insist violently that eieio is 'in the farming lexicon'.

You wish death by roaring flames upon long thinkers.

You always forget your anniversary, but etched indelibly in your memory is the time you knew a xanthippe is a Turkish dagger.

You rear-end folks twice weekly making words with the letters of their licence plates.

You stabbed a guy who put an S on the end of your jacuzzi.

You believe eight-letter words are the work of Satan.

Everyone knows your secrets because you keep them on a little wooden rack.

Your tax returns are rejected every year because you write out all the numbers in words.

You refuse to heed any warning sign where the words are written diagonally, resulting in you falling into seven mineshafts and one piranha-infested moat.

In your work as an air traffic controller, you make planes collide and their call signs form a twenty-point word.

You tore your family asunder rather than see things made into adverbs.

You would pick up the coronavirus more happily than a Q.

You pluralize everything you see.

You void your vowels in mixed company.

You are prouder of your high scores on the box lid than of raising fine children.

216. Unappealing Smoothies

Weasel Bits

Minty Compost

Next Of Pumpkin

Butt Or Scotch

PomeGranite

Snarling Bobcat

Raspberry Rasp

Mango Pineapple And Spleen

Quinoa, Buckwheat, Soy, Alfalfa And Essence Of Hipster

Placentavocado

Root Canal Beer

Gooseberry Sleuce

Botulemon

Blueberiberi

Laxative Swirl

Carrot, Celery And Self-Loathing

Grandmalon

Zesty Bog

Telltale Smear

Vanilla Vortex

Septic Summer Medley

Banana-Fana-Bo-Bana

217. How To Get Fired
As A Life Coach

Advocate keeping a daily journal, but mainly for counting bowel movements.

Teach the power of positive drinking.

Preach the motto, 'Bring 'em all down with you!'

Promote power naps as a way to reduce driving stress.

Measure self-confidence by how often you make folks cry.

Eschew a handshake in favour of humping clients' legs.

Three words. Always. Be. Yodeling.

Opine that it's parasitic children that ruin clients' work/life balance.

Pump them up to believe that, with confidence and a determination never to give up, they, too, can live in the subway.

Ask encouraging questions such as, 'Spare change?'

Instill an unshakeable belief that you can do absolutely anything you set your sights on in life but succeed.

Listen more than you talk, about your childhood in a Cambodian labour camp.

Tell them you make house calls. The poor house.

Dismiss mindfulness as hokum, but vehemently recommend Dr. Livingstone's Patented All-Ailments Restorative Elixir.

218. Even More Unmotivational Sayings

It is a simple mathematical fact that, on a planet of billions, there are always bigger losers.

Do not get confused between positive affirmation and public masturbation.

There's a curious sort of liberation in being bereft of hope.

Be proud and display on your desk the rocks your dreams ran aground on.

You can't know the secret burdens people carry, so pester them until they tell you, but don't listen.

No-one ever died regretting that he didn't spend more time at the office, except maybe JFK.

Seize the day, and for absolute clarity, the day does not live in your pants.

Man cannot live by bread alone, unless it's garlic bread with cheese.

The measure of a man is how he treats the least among us, and I'm afraid that's you, my friend.

Tomorrow's another day, usually.

Judge not, lest ye be judged and ye are appalling in every way.

A smile is infectious, though less so than that untreatable strain of herpes you've been concealing.

Always do your best. Well. Not YOUR best. Someone better's best.

You must love yourself before you can love another, and wash your hands first, too.

Happiness isn't what you seek, it's what you make, like that Princess-Leia-shaped bag of carnal mulch in the garage you think no-one knows about.

When you make others look good, you do too, except in your butt-ugly case.

A penny saved is a fucking penny. Aim higher.

219. How To Lose Your Job
As A Flight Attendant

Invite pests to stow their questions in the overhead compartment.

Instruct passengers to return their carcasses to their original upright position.

On the windows, paint startlingly lifelike scenes from your Engines On Fire line of artwork.

Announce that the captain has switched on the fasten seatbelts and shut the fuck up sign.

Describe how the seat cushions act as flotation devices except those that act as anvils.

Give whiners heavily-salted peanuts up the nose.

Tell diners the chicken is desiccated bludgeoned baby seal.

When people snap their fingers, snap their necks.

When lewd dudes make crude jokes about the Mile-High Club, tell them to stick it a mile high up their ass.

Sing a cheery song called Brace For Impact.

Say once you've had a black box, you never go back.

Make a panicked choking gesture when demonstrating the oxygen masks.

Be male and fend off, with increasing ire, inquiries about why you didn't simply become a figure skater or a dance choreographer.

During instructions about what to do in the event of a 'water landing', cough, 'Die'.

Insist that all babies be stashed silently under the seat in front.

Vigorously shake each tiny can of Coke to equalise the pressure.

If a mom asks if her child can see the cockpit, shrug and unzip your pants.

Refer to the economy-class passengers to their faces as a human debris field.

220. Reasons To Relocate Immediately To Tuvalu

It is not only legal but mandatory to slap someone who starts a sentence with, 'I'm no racist, but ...'

It only rains at night, the puddles smell of pancakes and the unique atmospheric ions ensure that smoking cleans your lungs with every drag.

Sales tax is -17.5%.

All signs telling you what to do end in Or Not.

Everyone's home has a spectacular view, even the gophers.

Dominos guarantees delivery in thirty seconds or it's free.

Even when you're over forty, doctors aren't fascinated by what's up your ass.

Tipping in restaurants causes great offense, except the fifteen percent you get from the waiter as a little thanks for the joy of serving you.

It's always sunny, even when it's cloudy, which it isn't, ever, owing to strict laws banning any form of condensation.

Crack federal snipers take out drivers with Baby On Board stickers.

Free HMO, HBO and Preparation H.

221. Bad Celebrity Perfumes

Tom Cruise's Space Dwarf

Some Assembly Required by Cher

Formaldehyde by Clint Eastwood

Weird All The Way To The Bank by Johnny Depp

Prune In Breast Cones by Madonna

Prince Harry's Illegitimate

Too Old For This by Reese Witherspoon

Fetid Bog by Kermit

Mel Gibson's Aryan

Incomprehensible by Guillermo Del Toro

Bad Life Choices by Lindsay Lohan

Self-Righteous by Meryl Streep

Ooze by Piers Morgan

222. Why We Need More Service Kangaroos

Full equality in society can be achieved only when aggressive service animals equip the disabled to join the ranks of muggers, bareknuckle boxers and street thugs.

Few pedestrians are injured bounding through traffic.

PTSD suddenly seems a very small problem indeed compared to having a kangaroo.

No need to teach them more than two words, boing and boing.

It's handy to be alerted to a phone call by a kick to the head.

You can lord your superior street cred over those that have a mere service wallaby.

They're the only known creature that scares away cows.

Always a nice surprise to see whose young they brought home in their pouch.

A welcome physical diversion from your emotional pain is a dislocated shoulder from leash pull.

Can be trained not to jump up on guests or the roof.

Take advantage of the little-known policy that kangaroos fly free on Quantas.

For a hobby, you can knit them cute pontoon socks.

They're quite protective of your remains.

In the event that an organ transplant is required, one can be obtained easily by booting it out of any passing donor.

They actually enjoy baths, the blood ones.

223. History's Lesser Icons

Alexander The Average

Billy The Little Kid

Chairman Meow

John The Pap Test

Lord Horatio Half-Nelson

Ludwig Von Beekeeper

Vlad The Inhaler

Abraham Linkedin

Adolf The Whittler

Alexander Graham Cracker

Prince Charles Manson

Christopher Robin Columbus

Contucius

Doc Lovely Holliday

Weevil Knievel

Fidel Castrato

Gangrenous Khan

Jack The Rapper

Johann Sebastian Barbara Bach

John L. Ed Sullivan

Joseph & Mary Stalin

Larry Of Arabia

Leo Toystory

Malcolm Y

Marie Curry

Marie Osmond Antoinette

Noses

Pontius Pilates

Vasco Da Gama Ray

Robert The Puce

Thomas The Jeffersons

William The Conjurer

Pablo Picasshole

224. Upsides Of A Long Car Ride With King Kong

Tolls don't apply to vehicles carried under the arm of an enormous primate.

One furry glare puts a swift end to 99 Bottles Of Beer.

Not a single word of complaint about your vile farts, though his routinely make your eyes bleed.

Motorists think you're friends with Tom Selleck.

Every gas station is self-serve and free.

The Satnav always suggests course changes very, very politely.

If a trucker cuts you off and flips you the bird, he's disembowelled through his windshield.

Your joke about Curious George peeing in the yellow hat always gets a laugh.

You make a fortune challenging local hicks to play Donkey Kong for cash.

No cop can get an accurate breath test from a gale-force roar.

Cool new car air fresheners. Goodbye Forest Pine, hello Musty Behemoth.

No need to stop at Scenic View sites only to have them obscured.

When you meet a couple of chicks at a diner, no more chance you'll end up with the hairy one.

He thinks the jack is adorable.

Brow ridge an effective bumper.

225. More Signs You're Being Cheated On

Leaves you with the kids on date night.

You seem to have a set of His His His & Hers towels.

You start a fantasy football league with the folks outside her door.

She slips you a daterape drug to get you out of her hair.

The sheer mental effort of remembering so many lies has caused a 2000% increase in her neural activity such that she can complete an 80x81 sudoku grid in her head whilst memorising all the profiles on Tinder.

You had no idea it was possible to melt a gusset.

She maxed three credit cards on date-site registrations.

Her answering machine says, 'Leave your name, number and which bar we met in.'

There are so many guys playing love songs on guitars outside that your lawn is voted the country's third-best music festival.

To save the time and trouble, the men's room stalls in town now come with her phone number pre-scratched.

The staple of your diet is chocolates from heart-shaped boxes.

She sucks so much commercial flight paths are routed away from your house to dodge the air pockets.

You spend more on Kleenex than rent.

When you call her and say 'It's me', she needs specifics.

226. Surprises In The Forthcoming Sharknado VI

Much to the dismay of zealous fans, episode VI is less a Sharknado and more a Tsharknami.

The Oscar buzz was just indigestion.

While V went straight to airplanes, VI is for rickshaws.

Not appearing by popular demand is Richard Dreyfuss.

The best defense against a nado of almost any marine creature is a sturdy umbrella.

Five minutes in and you're rooting for the sharks and not the awful surfers.

Samuel L. Jackson refused not to be in it.

A planned spinoff franchise, Dolphinwaterspout, was shelved, but homage is paid in some of the more lighthearted gore.

Actual sharks play themselves, like Harvey Weinstein.

The budget was cut dramatically when the product-placement deal was pulled, as ISIS feared it would sully their brand.

There's a brief appearance by bigshot fish Willy, but at a great distance and tremendous depth, so it's not like it's a highlight or anything.

One of the buddy sharks is Kevin Hart.

It's not the ideal date flick, as it appeals primarily to those for whom the very notion of a date has been a cruel joke for decades.

227. Uncommon Cheeses

Weasel's Crotch

Dickotta

Mozzarrhea

Sludgified Fowl Curds

Maggot's Pride

Festering Fresno

Up-To-Something Swiss

Smurfette Blue

Orange Potus

Stinking Doldrums

Quimembert

Pharmesan

Peckerino

228. Meryl Streep's Fears

She'll never be called upon to play, with utmost authenticity, a sumo wrestler, a young Palestinian boy or a birthing humpback whale.

Society will begin to value genuine sincerity and compassion over a flowy dress and a passing mention of some atrocity.

Jane Fonda might follow through on her threat to bring the pain.

Johnny Depp will someday portray her so convincingly she'll have no reason to live anymore, but there will be eternal debate as to whether she's just playing dead.

When she's morphed into every famous person alive in their biopics, eventually there'll be no-one left but Trump.

Her name will never be synonymous with artistic excellence and dedication and just continue to sound like a stain of some particularly noxious venereal disease.

Her body of work will be judged solely by Mamma Mia due to a freak electromagnetic storm that destroys all other recordings.

It's unseemly that she has more Oscars than friends.

Kevin Spacey won't get around to groping her till she's ninety.

Her status as Hollywood royalty will end when they find the naked pool boys locked in her love bunker.

The one thing she can't act is her age or she'd only play mummies.

Jennifer Lawrence starts to muscle in on the faux social awareness gig.

There's not enouugh room in the world for both Meryl Streep and Glenn Close But No Cigar.

The moaning in her hallways at night is the envious prehumous ghost of Al Pacino.

Her sex tape will get no views.

The weight of all those statuettes will tilt the foundation of the Yay Me wing of her house.

In the inevitable movie trilogy of her life, she'll be played by both Melissa McCarthy and an asthmatic llama.

It'll get harder to employ good people to unroll a red carpet in front of her wherever she goes.

She'll be nominated queen of the #NotMe movement.

229. More Unpopular Baby Names

Ostrichard

Phallex

Mary-Anus

Secretia

Scrotim

Pederastrid

Johndice

Bend

Tonylingus

Heimlichmaneuver

Adolfina

Charlottan

Randall Socksandal

Anathema

Glandrew

Accordionne

Malice

Nicolon

Ritard

Byle

Philatio

230. Seldom-Used Adjectives

Beige-hot

Chock-empty

Diarrhea-soluble

Fun-retardant

Llamentable

Pitch-white

Smurf-infested

Teste-scented

Bedpan-dipped

Beneviolent

Swandrawn

Cinnalicious

Demoosed

Blandtacular

Galifianacrimonious

Toejam-themed

Individually-stacked

ISIS-recommended

Knifelong

Lickproof

Maladmired

Nap-packed

Overjoyful

Semiboned

Phlegmish

Piersish

Pre-excreted

Scrotular

Semen-rich

Spittoon-fed

Ultratepid

Unprostitutional

Vajestic

Well-spawned

Yoko-inspired

231. Watered-Down Movies

The Bird

Imploring Private Ryan To Please Be Careful

Kinda Sad Max

The Slightly Tanned Knight Remains Seated

Could Perhaps Use A Shower But Still Quite Presentable Harry

The Empire Turns The Other Cheek

Taxi Cleaner

The Year Of Living Sensibly

There's Very Little About Mary

Casino Regulare

Some Like It Warm

The Ten Suggestions

One Half-Dead Mule For Sister Sara

To Wing A Mockingbird

It's A Life

Apocalypse Someday

Unsafe Weapon

Graze Bill

Restless Sleep On Elm Street

Debbie Can't Find Dallas

Ambivalent Bull

Flight Club

232. How To Tell You're Watching Too Much Porn

You can barely grip a pencil with your left hand, but you can crush a steel pipe with your right.

You're on a Samsung blacklist for burning out the motors of DVD players.

So much moaning comes from your apartment the neighbours assume it's haunted.

You have six oral professionals but no dentist.

You're so desensitized you only respond to hardcore Azerbaijani underground wombat tapeworm porn.

When you see a pretty lady, you imagine how foxy she'd look in thumbscrews and nipplepencilsharpeners.

You have to clear your browser history with bleach.

You think nuns on their knees in church look like slutty bitches.

You have so little sensation in your penis it took four hours to notice when you shot it with a nail gun.

It's impossible not to holler, 'You LIKE that?' when beating your carpets.

You think the guys who get the most sex deliver pizza.

Your favourite song goes BOW-chicka-chicka-BOW.

You are baffled when a flight attendant brings you merely a Coke.

Your computer cannot find enough free bandwidth to download critical security updates.

Your ejaculate is mostly dust.

Your chief exercise is writhing.

You're less worried about being caught masturbating than by the constant vibration weakening the supporting walls.

You are unaware that movies have endings.

To hold the remote and a drink, you need three hands.

You are not permitted in the root vegetable or baguette sections of the supermarket.

233. Why It's Tough To Be Married To An Assassin

Romantic strolls are mostly in the heating ducts.

His stupid cover story in fridge-magnet sales.

Your kids fail to learn valuable compromise/negotiation skills as all the local bullies are on crutches and tongueless.

Whenever you hug, you cannot escape the feeling that these could be your last moments on Earth.

Doing laundry involves the extra chore of removing tiny knives from the linings of jackets.

Forgets anniversaries but uses powerful drugs and hypnosis so that you do too.

The kids have to retrieve their allowance from a locker at the bus station.

There's only room in the trunk for one tiny bag on family trips to Disneyland because of the rocket launcher.

Passing bird pests take a double-tap to the head.

When a car backfires in the street, he barrel-rolls off the sofa.

While other kids are being taught life skills like swimming or baseball, yours can strip and reassemble a Kalashnikov in thirteen seconds.

234. In A World Without Coffee...

Short breaks in the workday would be called wank time.

The only cure for jetlag would be to just keep flying forever.

Every job seeker would find work as Tim Horton's tumbleweed sweepers.

The domestic morning homicide rate would soar and the streets would be clogged with medieval Bring Out Your Dead carts filled with the fast-decaying corpses of spouses who rashly said good morning.

Lawyers would desperately plead with unburned plaintiffs to claim respiratory distress from powdered sugar inhalation.

On every street corner, eerily, would be mere non-Starbucks establishments.

Receptionists would answer calls, "Yeah?"

Those that invested in complex expensive pod-brewing systems would simply continue not to use them.

The only thing instant that humans would still crave is gratification.

Seeing a sunrise would be unicorn rare.

Milk-frothing devices would now be deployed for gravy.

Long-distance truckdrivers would barely have the energy to rape hitchhikers.

At staff meetings, folks would just drink hemlock.

Double-filtering would just be what you do instead of telling dick jokes to your mother-in-law.

235. Why You Wish You
Were A Contortionist

If you go down a hot slide and burn your bum, you can blow on it.

Unblock your own drains just by wearing a pointy hat.

Save a fortune on clothes fully dressed in just pants.

Nothing says self-love like whispering sweet nothings in your own ear.

You find your IKEA easy chair more comfy unassembled.

After an argument, you can storm off in all directions.

Masturbation orgies.

Unbeatable at Hide & Seek.

You literally sit around the house.

Sleep on quadruplet beds.

Wow women by making love to them in many positions at once.

You regard Cirque Du Soleil as essentially loitering.

236. Signs You Need A New Lawyer

Accepts fees in arms.

Begins addresses, Ladies and gentlemen of the jewry...

His entire summation is always a rueful shrug.

Chases ambulances on his daughter's bike.

Consents to throwing away the key.

Crossdresses for cross-examinations.

Calls pleadings grovelings.

Giggles when anyone says briefs.

Has contempt convictions for calling the judge Your Otter.

His law library is just a load of John Grisham books.

His motto is, 'You can't lose if you flee.'

More urinals than most offices.

Insists on referring to you as the perp.

Makes air quotes and winks when pleading you not guilty.

Refers to something called attorney-client-blog privilege.

Can't read agreements without his contract lenses.

Takes it as a compliment that he's propping up the bar.

Undue reliance on the whoops defense.

You see him at the roadside with a sign Will Sue For Food.

237. More Classic Male Logic

Dogs do not play poker naturally, ergo a painting of them doing so is art.

Underwear which is mostly holes and a few sparse remaining fibre molecules is a precious nostalgia treasure worth fighting to retain in perpetuity.

On the eve of the most magical day of your life, when you betroth yourself to spend forever with the woman of your dreams, it is only fitting, in reverence of tradition, that your friends pay naked sluts to grind on you.

Shopping isn't an activity. If you don't know why you're going to the vending establishment, you're meandering aimlessly through life. Park car. Enter mall. Make intended purchase. Return to car. That's Nature's way.

I have only two feet, and thus need only two shoes.

Candles have three uses and three uses only: birthday cakes, church and power outages.

If it cannot be fried or barbecued, then it probably isn't food.

If the door of the dishwasher closes, it's loaded correctly.

You can barely drive. The fast-forward function of the remote is beyond you. How can you think you're qualified to operate the thermostat?

I might have made the wet spot, but you made me make it, so you should sleep on it.

Maybe we aren't geniuses, but we know a trap when we hear one, and those pants make your ass look microscopic.

If the ref on TV could see, would he have made that call? No, but he can hear, so I yell.

We ask women where things are because they, like, know?

238. More Classic Female Logic

We ask if these pants make our butt look big because we fret about your reputation as that poor man who can only get a fat-ass.

We buy an eye-catching array of shoes to draw men's gaze away from our tits like pitiful loser horndog lasers of lust.

If something is on sale, you're spending less on it, thus saving money, so buy two.

There is nothing more beautiful than cushions, and it is not possible to be surrounded by too much beauty.

Remembering the birthdays and anniversaries of a handful of close friends and family members is as rudimentary an intellectual challenge as distinguishing between twelve profoundly different shades of off-white.

You don't expect the salesperson to keep schmoozing you after you've signed the finance agreement, and likewise the marriage register.

How is it that you have developed a sniper's aim at things floating in the toilet but can't hit the hamper with clothes?

Fishing takes all the excitement of golf and removes it.

The line between makeup that makes one look sophisticated and that which screams whore is both thin and variable, depending on which bitch has wronged us in this life.

The most intimate way to bond with your man is to show interest in his activities, so he'll love when you ask questions during sporting events.

The penis is a dangly abomination with two functions, neither of which it can perform with any degree of accuracy.

The quality of a movie is directly proportional to the volume of self-discovery that takes place and indirectly proportional to the number of aliens that are horrifically slaughtered.

An extra-large option on the menu is not a gauntlet of challenge to your manhood.

239. Hitler's Cravings

A hint of what the holy hell else a guy's gotta do to impress a chick.

An astrologer who can go one lousy week without being executed.

Not being being bitched at for 'parading around' in his under-wear, when he literally is.

A delicious saurbagel.

A nice, long, luxurious, hot shower, for Goering, in the name of God.

The candor to acknowledge that the first and second Reichs were actually also pretty good.

Just once, a pair of those hilarious Groucho nose glasses to don mid-fuhrer-furor.

The slow death of everyone who ever even met Charlie Chaplin.

A Leni Riefenstahl movie without quite so many nude dudes in it.

240. Subway Etiquette

When killing yourself, leap down, not up, as windshield wipers weren't made for spatter.

Smoking is prohibited unless you're cool.

Stow your gnu.

If you have questions or feedback, pull the red lever to summon the driver.

Spitting in the subway is a fifty-dollar fine. No charge for explosive diarrhea.

You have great taste in music, so crank it up and share the wisdom.

Avoid 'manspreading', particularly your cheeks.

No luggage is too large to take on the subway. Other passengers don't mind, and their shins will heal in no time.

Strike up an engaging conversation, but not with others.

When it's crowded, it's perfectly acceptable to sit on someone's lap or face.

The rhythmic motion of the train puts people in a relaxed, contemplative frame of mind, ideal for hearing your take on what Jesus wants.

Announce you're the train marshall and frisk everyone thoroughly.

241. Things That Are Appealing But Lethal

Rattlecakes

Wounded Grizzly Care Bears

Lacerate-Me Elmo

Tae Kwon Donuts

Feather Boa Constrictors

Apple Cyanide

Flesh-Baked Bread

Cottonmouth Candy

Easy Electric Chair

Coiled Spring Flowers

242. Signs You've Had Too Much To Drink

Disgusted with your behaviour, you get yourself in a headlock and toss your ass outta the joint.

For ease of intake processing at Booking, you carry a set of mugshots wherever you go.

You become convinced that the tiny man who controls the light in your fridge is secretly pissing in your yoghurt.

You confuse a jar of jalapenos with your eyedrops.

You perform a symbolic sea shanty illustrating the history of liver damage throughout the ages.

It takes a battalion of sexual professionals with a complex system of ropes and pulleys to coax your manhood into a droopy little mockery of an erection.

Chicks won't pick you up, nor taxis, buses, cruisers or ambulances.

Visiting Eastern Europeans advise you to slow down.

You fight the hydrant that won't go home with you.

You feel you lurch in a way that wows the babes.

You lose your battle to hold the floor down.

You shout 'Drinks on me!' and wait for the grateful applause to die down before pouring one over your head.

You try to build a fort out of peanuts.

You lure a young lady back to your place but suffer a mental block about which of you wears the condom.

Tom Cruise starts to make sense.

You vomit on the rug and think it's art, you're Jackson Pollock, and so it is.

You've taken so many shots they call you Clyde Barrow.

243. More Things Said By No-One Ever

It's best to be upfront with potential girlfriends about my necrotizing rectal run-off.

Nice new full-torso tattoo, Mr. Bieber. Now you're SO much less a tool!

CRANK that Yoko!

Why must airlines provide so much legroom?

Do you have any American beer?

Shawshank Redemption would have been better if Zach Truckloadafuckwit were in it.

It's a blind date so I'm wearing this golf outfit.

What a lovely mustache, Widow Gotti. Do you wax it?

I tried to force myself on Harvey Weinstein but he wasn't interested.

I haven't worked very hard this year, so you'd best reduce my salary.

My idea of heaven is eternal Ice Capades.

Please don't call ahead when you visit, Mom, I'm keen to be surprised.

This movie popcorn is scandalously cheap, and mmm, this sure is butter!

For our honeymoon, I've booked two weeks in Sudbury.

Who's president again? I just never hear anything about him.

Game Of Thrones would be terrific if not for all the violence and nudity.

Please let the in-flight movie be Hangover 3.

244. Advantages Of A Career In Septic Tank Maintenance

The boss never complains when you soil yourself on the job.

When you get promoted to supervisor, you no longer have to blow obstructions out of the hose.

Be the cool dude who makes caked-on hip again.

Win any bet on which turds will float.

Develop a self-image as an eye-watering James Bond.

Chat with the veterans pining for the old days before gloves.

Get famous posting vids on EwTube.

Feel the pride of being the one folks come to with their putrid problems.

All the used condoms you could ever want.

Know a slew of sexy seepage secrets.

No worries, she'll quit school before Bring Your Daughter To Work Day.

It's a fun conversation-starter that your degree is on 3-ply paper.

You are rife with so many infections your saliva's nearly all penicillin.

If there's one ironclad rule of the female libido, it's slags dig sludge.

Make a name for yourself in the crusty-crafts community.

The shimmering allure of the haze wafting up from a tank on a hot Spring afternoon.

These days, it looks vastly more impressive on a resume than working for the president.

Wild tank-themed parties.

Tinder photos that make 'em say, 'What IS that?'

Get good enough to shudder in the Olympics.

Dames buy you clothes and a week at the spa.

Become a fester parent.

Your business cards are scratch 'n' sniff simply by virtue of being on your person.

You make a few extra bucks stress-testing new deodorants.

You always get the whole lunch counter to yourself.

Nobody ever steals your truck or anything within five hundred metres of your truck.

Your raging halitosis doesn't even make the top ten unpleasant things about you.

Your loungewear is hip-waders.

When you tell folks you work with tanks, they say thanks for your service.

245. How Inmates Have A Mid-Sentence Crisis

They stop complaining they got fucked by their lawyer to gripe that they didn't.

Finally concede that, all things considered, the warden's not such a bad chap.

Start finding checkers more exciting than a riot.

Begin to really take care of themselves by exercising fourteen hours a day instead of just ten.

Ask that the raping racket be kept down after nine o'clock.

Start weeding the yard and saying grace over the gruel.

Their dreams turn from their celly to their celly in a red sports car.

Start to prefer self-conjugal visits.

Trained chorus line of bedbugs.

Quit dragging the metal mug across the bars in case the dentures fall out.

Write perfumed love poems to Mr. Right Guard.

Rather than tough, start looking fetchingly contrite.

Skip visiting hour to spend more time thinking about what you did.

Advise gangs settle their differences with contract bridge instead of shivs.

246. Things You Don't Want To Hear In An Elevator

Allah, bless this humble servant's glorious sacrifice! Five, four, three...

Hi, I'm Richard Simmons.

I smell toast, or my name isn't Grand Mal Sal.

I wish I didn't always go berserk in confined spaces, but my tank was shelled in Iraq, you know? So I try not to worry about it.

Is the explosive dysentery clinic on this floor?

Nobody move, I dropped my murder hornets.

Hey, wanna see something really turgid?

Since it's just you and me, how about we bond?

This elevator almost always gets stuck. But don't worry, I'll entertain us. I can yodel!

Well, looks like we're trapped. I vote we eat you first.

Does this look infected to you?

Yeah, I gotta go, Mom, my phone is dying. No, not me, my phone. Stop worrying, it's just a little bit of smallpox. If it were a big deal, they'd call it largepox, right? Ha ha!

If I hear one more dinging sound, I'm gonna stab someone.

247. Dubious Statistics

One in three marriages ends in divorce, one in death, and in the third, both parties simply waste away yearning for either of the first two options.

Before entering your home, the need to urinate increases five billion times each second it takes to recover your dropped keys.

Only 90% of hipsters are douchebags, but the rest are in there trying, so...

Just 17% of people eat enough fibre, and 17% care about fibre.

If a crumb crumbled makes ten new crumbs, how many people is Tom Cruise dismembered?

One hundred percent of penis enlargers don't work, I've...heard.

The tightness of underwear elastic is always 10% greater than your available strength when trying to reach a particularly fierce scrotal itch.

Sadly, merely ten percent of catapults are used for cats.

Eleven percent of Cher is Cher, dropping to eight or nine at her next appointment.

The resultant longterm damage to a man's self-esteem is 1500 times more profound than a woman's palpable disappointment at seeing his junk for the first time.

Only one in seven horses is hot.

If the average volume of canine urine is ten fluid ounces, spanning the sixty thousand acres of land excitedly anointed in the course of just a single walk, that low liquid density over such a wide area means that, in effect, mathematically, dogs don't pee.

248. You Might Be A Perv If...

During sex you call out Lassie's name.

Despite using the Internet sixteen hours a day, you've never heard of Twitter or Amazon.

There are no virgin fire hydrants in your neighbourhood.

On all your walls, there are only framed photos of your anus.

You climax when you hear the term 'flogging a dead horse'.

You know the tensile strength of your own windpipe.

You ask strangers on the bus to bugger your nostrils with sea urchins.

You list your address as the waterpark.

You identify as omnisexual.

You routinely forget your keys but never leave the house unlubed.

While most people react to a baby panda by saying, 'Awwww', you say, 'Phwoarrrr!'

Your houseplants wear pasties.

Your hobby is lurking.

249. How To Be American

Declare relentlessly and with absolute certitude that your country is the best in the world despite having never been anywhere else.

In the unlikely event that you do travel, display the social graces of water bison and know that, in order to make yourself understood by those who do not speak 'American', you need only increase your volume to ever more ear-splitting levels.

Accept that you're going to ruin at least one gun dropping it in the toilet.

Consume more porn than any other nation but erupt with outrage when a mother breastfeeds in public.

Believe with every fibre of your being that the only way to reduce violence is to ensure everyone's armed to the teeth.

Gape in wide-eyed wonder at anything more than seventy years old.

Employ, as your primary mode of opinion sharing, the bumper of your truck.

Shop for booze and fireworks and guns in the same store, because what could go wrong?

Know what God wants, and don't ask why it's always money.

Choose a school where the most students have textbooks and the fewest are slaughtered.

Have as your spirit animal a bull in a china shop.

When in doubt, bomb.

Adopt as your favourite verb 'to supersize'.

Barge out of bed in the morning.

Insert every other food in pizza crust.

Know of no natural wonder that can't be fracked.

Consider yourself bilingual if you trashtalk.

When you want to do a little reading, buy a stamp.

Be convinced that in anatomy texts you'll find 'bazoongas'.

Salute the flag and demonstrate zealous patriotism at every opportunity, but decry as fanatical extremists any others that do the same.

Think of Europe as a quaint little place with castles that can be explored thoroughly in five days.

250. Benefits Of Global Warming

An end to seasonal todger shrinkage.

Camels finally get to show off their high-diving skills.

Christmas cookouts.

Every home that has a tub will have a hot-tub.

Learn key mechanical skills affixing wheels to toboggans.

Hawaiian Tropic overtakes Google as most powerful corporation.

Man's new best friend? The squid.

Everyone loves the seaside.

Massive home-building boom, though mostly houseboats.

Picassoesque melting skyscrapers.

Rock battles are more manly than snowball fights.

Scuba sherpas.

Skimpier outfits for nuns.

Slithering whales.

Mosquitoes get a shot at wiping us out in Winter too.

Sperm elk.

Those succulent Saharan lobsters.

Those lovely withering willows.

Sudbury temperatures will soar to minus thirty.

Surely the end of the Ugg Boot.

That'll teach those iceberg fuckers to mess with the Titanic.

Yeti less intimidating on the beach.

You needn't mow barren, scorched dirt.

251. Why Dinosaurs Make Great Pets

Always glad to chase a stick or a Scout troop.

Grooming consists merely of hosing off the gore.

It's a great upper-body workout scratching an armour-plated belly with a rake.

They're adorable when they respond to correction by roaring at jet-engine volume and stomping the town into a pancake.

Coughed-up hairballs can be knitted into dozens of beautiful blankets and rugs.

Nuzzle unwelcome guests to death.

Risk of burglary reduced to nil no matter how many iPads and Faberge eggs you display in open windows.

When they run in their giant exercise wheels, they generate as much power as the Hoover Dam.

No food costs; they live happily on a diet of Jehovah's Witnesses and paperboys.

Just as cats bring you little presents of dead mice, raptors lovingly gift the bowels of hipsters.

Nothing lifts your spirits after a stressful day at work like a block-long wagging tail and a drooling mouth that could swallow a Subaru.

Backhoes make handy pooper-scoopers.

However fierce they may look, they'll always cower if you make a sound like a meteor.

If a seeing-eye triceratops inadvertently leads a blind man into traffic, it really doesn't matter.

No-one makes big bucks off a dog park.

Scales are dandy toboggans.

Fertilise a billion roses with a single crap.

252. How To Be German

Schedule brief sausage breaks throughout the day, between the main lunch and dinner sausage buffets.

Attend to your work without smiling or idle chit-chat until the designated minute for smiling and idle chit-chat.

Oppress those kids on the lawn.

Learn to play another nine instruments that go oom-pah.

Study great works of romantic poetry such as Das Grossenshlammenpfeinegoranklakkenkrugerschmeizendammensteiffen.

Learn to get absolutely bone dry following a shower so that leather undergarments slide on with ease.

Adopt the attitude that you might as well hork down sauerkraut and beer in a country where statistically you are much more likely to die by Doberman.

Become a social scientist and toil to make the breakthrough that explains lederhosen.

A fury a day about immigrants clears the lungs.

Play your little fraulein a suggestive tuba tune.

March right out and enjoy that sunshine, SCHNELL!

Go to an authentic local eatery and order the favourite, Supper In A Stein.

Toast marshmallows and sing ribald campfire songs over burning books.

Paint a brightly-coloured poster about the bondage of the workers by the Zionist bankers.

Call everything a 'fest', even a funeralfest.

Develop sexy love-making technique via no-nonsense foreplay and orgasmic precision.

Practice charming smalltalk by putting all the witty adjectives at the end.

Be a hit at well-organised parties by memorising volumes one through seven of The Giant Book of Fart Jokes.

Teach your children important life skills such as lining up their toys in order of fun.

Learn to enjoy all foods doused in strong mustard and fermented yard waste.

Lie shamelessly about your carbon emissions.

Live life with carefree whimsy with one shoelace slightly longer than the other.

Embrace equality and respect in all things, with the obvious exception of buxom serving wenches.

If you cannot afford to buy something for your children, develop the reflex of blaming Greece.

Adopt an expression of utter bafflement when anyone makes even the most fleeting reference to the war.

253. Lesser-Known Reindeer

Bleeder

Fireball

Ghastly

Hater

Isis

Lurker

Amok

Arthritis

Dirtydancer

Dine-And-Dasher

Flasher

Gassy

Gory

Groper

Nag

Re-Entry

Sketchy

Venison

Vertigo

Vomet

254. Grounds For Dismissal From Ikea

Believing it's immoral to sell lamps that are incompatible with every bulb ever conceived except the Flinkenshvarblingen, available only in a pack of sixteen hundred.

Failing to say the name of the limited-edition range of spoons without choking on your own tongue or dowsing a customer in phlegm.

Holding out false hope that patrons might someday make their way home to their families, while sweeping up the skeletons of those whose dreams of the exit proved fatal.

Putting two dots randomly above the wrong vowels in a string of seven in a row.

Telling a customer about the secret shortcuts that bypass the seventy thousand square feet of picture frames.

Applying barcodes to boxes in such a way that they can be found and scanned easily without your repeatedly flipping and rotating heavy boxes to the soundtrack of the cashier's drumming fingers.

Developing the Stockholm Syndrome that afflicts all employees.

Directing shoppers too specifically to where their purchases can be found in identical boxes on sky-high shelves in a warehouse the breadth of the Northwest Territories.

Ordering an insufficiently vast quantity of giant artwork featuring rope bridges over chasms.

Failing to recommend the thin oddly-shaped crackers from no known place in the solar system.

Hinting that any colours exist in nature beyond black, white and beech.

Letting slip that ninety tealights for three dollars is still no bargain.

Making the new guy unpack the wee cacti.

Claiming that Ikea is Swedish for slow death.

Making vacation plans for an epic exploration voyage to the farthest nether regions of the parking lot.

Mentioning the word 'union' when informed that you will henceforth be paid in Billy bookcases.

Referring to shoppers as buggy bitches.

Wistfully remarking that you remember the outside world.

Using a Duracell battery to avoid replacing the company-branded ones every eleven seconds.

Employing a tiny pencil as a shiv to lobotomise yourself.

Warning parents that the ball pit is actually bottomless.

255. Signs Your Partner Is A Ghost

Moans even when you aren't having sex.

Cries during Ghostbusters.

Every time you turn on a light, goes toward it.

Gives you presents for Christmas future.

It's always chilly under the blankets.

Leaves voicemail in TV static.

Locking the bathroom door doesn't seem to deter her from strolling right in.

Only German word she knows is poltergeist.

If you leave the toilet seat up, she reaches into the darkest recesses of your soul and rips your deepest fears out so that you might confront head-on, just for a moment, the gaping void of nothingness that is your significance to the infinity of the universe.

The dog pees when she enters the room.

When you get stiff, she says it's a start.

About the twist at the end of Sixth Sense, she says, 'What twist?'

Whenever she's sure of something, says she's dead certain.

Your kids are named Heebie and Jeebie.

256. Tips For Dating Tom Cruise

When mentioning friends or siblings, call them Tom-friendly names like Splat, Slurry or Frond.

Reassure him that the baby gates are for his own safety.

When he reminds you yet again that he does his own dangerous moves in movies, don't ask him to perform the stunt of shutting up.

Don't tell him you think it's best that he hasn't won an Oscar, since it would tower over him in photographs.

Don't tell him the award you think he should get is Scariest Smile On A Fanatical Twerpy Zealot With The Gleaming Crazed Eyes Of A Coked-Up Crowd Sniper.

If the evening turns amorous, you will first be whisked away with stiff whisks by Tom's retinue for cleansing with industrial disinfectants.

Do not ask to see Tom's spaceship, because he will show you, and you won't like it.

Sudden shafts of light from the heavens should not be remarked upon as these are merely Tom's texts.

Do not mention Nicole or words that sound like Nicole, such as Nickelodeon, Nicaragua, nicotine, nick or coal.

Any mention of Snow White should also include reference to her seven perfectly normal-sized companions.

Don't engage him in debate as to how a fully-cleared Level 8 Operating Thetan is distinct from a Cloud Nine Loon-Sized Batshit Wackjob.

Pretend he hasn't mentioned in all previous conversations that his nickname among peers is Laserhead, for his legendary ability to focus, and perhaps don't bring up the monikers he doesn't know about, like The Diva Dick, The Oddest Duckling and The Littlest Homo.

Avoid cracking wise in bed by asking him to go up on you.

Do not refer to flights of stairs as mission impossible.

You must have a bag of kittens on you at all times in case Tom needs to wipe his bum.

You'd be weird too if you were bullied in school, stuffed into a backpack and worn to class by the teacher.

Most film sets are boring, but it's fun betting when he'll snap and gore a gaffer.

If you read his kids bedtime stories, avoid Tom Thumb.

If Leah Remini comes within range, you will be required to hold Tom's jacket while he punches her furiously in the ankle.

257. Travel On A Nazi Airline

Their motto is Vengeance From The Skies.

The flight attendant is the luftwaffenbevereichcartenschtuar-tessenfraulein for short.

Turbulence is known as Jew breath.

If you need a pillow, ask and one will immediately be brought to stifle the noise as you are shot.

Flight crew includes one pilot and eleven gunners.

Crying babies are weak and stored in the cargo hold.

Flight attendants in leather thigh boots sounds sexy but isn't.

After landing, you are expected to establish a beachhead.

Passengers will be scourged until they can repeat from memory every word of the emergency instructions.

In the event of a water landing, you will maintain morale by cheering as the pilots and crew are swiftly rescued, and then you and your spirits can sink.

The pilot flies into frenzied roaring furies over obstacles in his path, proclaims they are not there and hangs those responsible for telling him.

Seatbelt and No Smoking signs replaced with one that says 'SCHNELL! SCHNELL!'

The man who puts gas in the aircraft is Herr Goplanefueller.

The frequent flyer programme is Mile Kampf.

The in-flight movie is always Triumph Of The Will.

Air speed increases once the leaflets have been dropped.

For ease of recall, you will find your seat number tattooed on your wrist.

258. Unsuccessful Breakfast Cereals

Al Frankenberry

All-Brain

Asbestios

Cap'n Crotch

Cocoa Puff Adders

Chocobarbs

Dreaded Wheat

Oat Grain Clusterfucks

Drearios

Fetid Funless Festerflecks

Fruit Slurry With Bits

Gangrene, Anthrax, Botulism, Hemlock & Raisins

Honey Bunches O' Radioactive Iron Filings

Ricin Krispies

Special KKK

Tinkle Sprinkles

Trump Chunks

Turned Trix

259. More Musical Versions Of Action Movies

Dirty Harry Hair

Calamity GI Jane

Dr. Jekyll And Mr. Hamilton

Enter The Band Wagon Dragon

Singing In The Reign Of Fire

The Bourne Silk Stockings

Taken On The Town

Big Trouble In Little Detroit

Annie Get Your Top Gun

Indiana Jones And The Last Cabaret

Gentlemen Prefer Superman

Goodfellas And Dolls

South Pacific Heights

Mad Max Mikado

Sniper On The Roof

The Lion King Kong

Bye Bye Birdman Of Alcatraz

Rapid Grease Fire

Kiss Me Thor

Les Expendables

260. Modern Commandments

Thou shalt not kill time on public transit bellowing into thy magic pocket trumpet.

Judge not lest ye be judged a douche by snowflakes.

Driveth not thy vehicle like a cunt, nor judge thy time more precious.

Thou shalt not break bread without sharing it, online.

Thou shalt LOL or ROFLMAO at the faintest amusement.

Thou shalt not steal, though music, movies, apps and memes are fine.

Honour thy mothers or thy fathers.

Grope not, excepteth ye be Kevin Spacey.

Render unto Trump that which is Trump's insatiable need to take credit for everything.

Thou shalt not covet thy neighbour's ass though she post it for all to see.

Thou shalt not bother, for effort is beneath thee.

Yap thou not during sportscasts on the Sabbath, woman.

Thou shalt not take the Lord's name in vain, unlesseth the Leafs be cast out from the playoffs by some bogus little bullshit penalty call and a powerplay goal in overtime.

Allude vaguely unto thy posse regarding thine illness or injury or sadness and unto ye all shall provide hug emojis.

Rock not a fannypack in the name of God almighty.

261. Clues Your Blind Date Is An Arsonist

Accelerants come up more frequently than you might expect.

Writhes and moans at the sound of sirens.

Orders flambe for every course, and salad, and drink.

Asks for his steak a degree of well-done so severe that the chef personally comes out twice to verify the order.

Holds forth knowledgeably on the melting point of the decor.

Mysteriously able to find a fireworks display on a wet Tuesday in April.

His taste in movies runs primarily to Backdraft and Towering Inferno.

He orders you both a Molotov cocktail.

Doesn't smoke, though he sure smells of it.

Lets slip that he's never found a woman hot enough.

Names the candle on your table Ignito.

Asks to sit in the flashpoint section.

Touches himself when you say the colour of your dress is burnt sienna.

Throws an epic tantrum when you mention your job as a sprinkler salesman until you explain that they're for lawns.

Takes you to Burning Man months before it starts.

262. Movies For Drug Addicts

Dependence Day

Dude, Where's My Vein?

Castaway Spoons

Lawrence Of Arrhythmia

A Drain Cleaner Runs Through It

Armgeddon

Harry Potter And The Stoned Philosopher

Total Relapse

A Man For All Seizures

Braveheart, Beat!

How Green Was I?

All That Autopsy Jazz

The Bourne Marks

263. Tourism Pitches For Planet Earth

Free parking in November for intergalactic annihilation frigates.

More water in a single rainshower than you've been fighting a brutal war over for the last seven centuries.

Snack on the many free-range hipsters!

Sucker hordes pay a ludicrous price for the most basic gamma-photoproton galvinator.

Marvel at the majestic landscapes, dine like royalty on the many exotic plants, laugh at the sad uni-penised males.

The invasion will go unopposed as they record it and post it.

Their culture teaches them E.T is adorable. They don't know that's how we spell EAT.

Humans explode satisfyingly when subjected to even the lowest-power molecular discontiguiser rays.

Meet Supreme Leader Cruise and get him to do anything you want.

Gasp with wonder at scenes of breathtaking natural pre-globofracking splendour.

264. What A Lousy Guardian Angel Does

Plays on his phone while you fight quicksand.

Hits on the paramedics who scrape you off snowploughs.

Boasts of peerless cockblocking prowess.

When he says he's 'got your back' he means he's WAY behind you, well clear of any trouble.

His sage advice is always sucks to be you.

Says things like, 'Ohhh, I thought the running of the bulls was toMORrow! How'd it go? Really? Ouch, geez. Sorry, man.'

Blames simple inattention for your sleep violation by dwarves.

Advises you to hide in the house on Saturdays and Sundays since he doesn't work weekends.

Requests frequent updates on your being lost in Detroit so late.

Gives an actual rat's ass.

Keeps you virtually carjack-free.

Doesn't like hovering, and flies only south, always south.

In spite of your peanut allergy, every day you catch him trying to slip a Snickers into your lunchbox.

Encourages you to wear ill-fitting shoes so you're the slowest to flee angry mobsters.

Tries to appeal to your ego by saying, 'Think of me as your very own Judas.'

Boasts that he's banged your last five girlfriends and your dad.

You get shoved into oncoming traffic more than seems like coincidence.

265. Why You Should Not Use Paparazzi As Wedding Photographers

Zoom lenses so long ushers sustain eye injuries.

They try to bribe the flower girls to spill the beans on the bridesmaids.

You hear the word 'jackals' somewhat more than at most weddings.

Fights break out when the bartender enforces the No Scum rule.

Honeymoon consummation marred by whirring shutter motors and clicking.

When the priest asks if anyone knows cause that the couple shouldn't marry, ten hands go up.

No-one can hear the vows with those jackets over their heads.

Lacking a grasp of the point of wedding photos, they try to get you at your frumpiest or most enraged.

They insist shots of the bride be from above to get more cleavage.

A pack of them bays instructions to kiss the bride.

They hide in the cake.

266. The Point Of Earlobes

Additional air-braking for decelerating athletes.

Just an interim step in the evolution of human wind chimes.

After five days, the Lord looked upon that which He had wrought and said unto Himself, 'Needs more dangly bits.'

They're basically just exterior side-mounted tonsils.

Without them, we'd have to wear earrings on our eyelids, making blinking too strenuous, so that our retinas would dry out, and we'd be a nation of blind folks who can't even cry about it.

If you lose one or two, Cher has extras.

Earbums would be ridiculous.

Ancient humans lacked notepaper for staff meetings and hunting-gathering seminars.

Only one other thing to laugh at in the Garden Of Eden.

A very certain sort of early slutty sapiens knew they drove elephants wild.

They're the delicious little sweet spot in earmuffs.

Tough target practice for fetishist snipers.

They prevent those self-impressed, fancypants frontal lobes thinking they're all that.

They're the go-to place if you feel something must be impaled.

The principal focus of erotic thoughts in the Victorian era.

Scientists now believe they may have evolved in humans quickly under pressure as some sort of early-warning auditory Red Hot Chili Peppers defense system.

There is no better way to check the temperature of a bath or a vat of magma.

Fun swing for dwarf rhesus monkeys.

267. Deleted Bible Stories

Adam Sandler And Eve

Could God Make A Kidney Stone So Big Even He Couldn't Pass It?

Jonah And The Good-Sized Trout

Moses' Burning Bush

Noah Wyle's Ark

Shaking Down The Money Lenders

Moses Demanding The Children Of Israel Quit Following Him Everywhere

The Friendly-Fire Smiting Of The Righteous

The Blind Man And The Cliff

The Incorrigible Samaritan

The Epic Three-Day Crucifixion After-Party

The Drunken Rant On The Mount

The Prodigal Orphan

Three Wise Guys

When Mary And Joseph Were On A Break

268. How Apples Are Hazardous To Your Health

Granny Smith is so protective of her apples that if she catches you eating one, she'll cut you into neat little segments.

Cider is concentrated liquid suffering.

Infants fed excessive applesauce become serial killers, or worse, bankers.

An apple placed in a sock and swung at the head can generate impact such that the grandchildren of a mugger will be born too dizzy to walk till they're twenty-seven.

According to the laws of nature, there is technically no significant difference between apples and murder hornets.

It is only recently that apples came by the bushel. They used to be sold by the invading horde.

Eat a seed, become a tree. Fact.

Never forget that all of your stress about fashion stems from some chick eating an apple.

As tempting as it sounds, do not attempt to consume the Big Apple, unless you're Godzilla.

A mere ten minutes in an oven superheats an apple to a higher temperature than summer on Venus.

Fuji apples will zoom down at you from the sun and crack your skull.

The word 'orchard' was chosen because it has a more pleasant ring than Mafia burial ground.

Put two varieties of apple together in a pie and they will fight to the death.

The native Shawnee considered apple pie such lethal poison that you weren't considered a man until you could eat a slice.

The apple inspired the less-popular party craze Bobbing For Piranha.

269. Signs You Play Too Many Video Games

All the people you know have names like DungeonDude, LightSabre3691 or CaptainThrust.

If you approached your career with the same zealous fervor with which you hunt for Easter eggs in Assassin's Creed, you wouldn't still be cleaning out the grease trap.

If you see someone about to get hit by a car, you yell, 'Up, up, left, X, JUMP!'

One of the best decisions you ever made, in your view, is the Zelda tattoo.

You dump your girlfriend on her birthday because you need the money for a bigger memory card.

You feel the best way to demolish a house is to fling birds at it.

You hope to find a woman like the hookers in Grand Theft Auto.

You call any setback in life a glitch.

You are gender-confused ever since Ms Pac-Man.

You refer to the offspring as your next-gen platforms.

You tell the optometrist your vision has gone all pixely.

Your CV is just a list of high scores.

Your fridge is broken but your console has more advanced cooling than your local blood bank.

Your over-developed right arm was caused by your Wii controller, not what everyone thinks.

Your thumbs are so gigantic people can see you hitchhiking for miles.

You've achieved so many extra lives you genuinely believe you are immortal.

270. Reasons To Skip Plan B And Go Straight To C

Plan C is like a bronze medal - ideal for plucky underdogs who got where they are because somebody much better made a blunder of some kind.

They never say 'First time's the charm' or 'Second time lucky'.

C is for the middle people, average, mediocre, just about good enough, not entirely useless, largely non-threatening, no real risk of changing anything, dull, bland, sound like heaven?

Plan B is usually along the lines of, 'Okay, let's split up. I'll go that way, with this dead flashlight, walking backward...' Plan C is always something much more sensible, like, 'Yeah, no.'

Plan B is never conceived in safety but in fact grave peril, whereas Plan C was always ALL about the bunker.

Plan B is usually similar to Plan A, and thus equally unrealistic, whereas in Plan C you actually start as a transient so that there aren't such unpleasant surprises and you can think clearly.

Plans A or B seldom involve the cool stuff, like cock-fighting or black-market kidney smuggling.

If Plan B were so good, you'd have done that in the first place and wouldn't be in the sort of disastrous shitfest that warrants alternative plan-making.

Plan C is a lot more fun, since its key strategy is always a binge of some kind.

It's no coincidence that 'Plan C' is almost an anagram of 'panic'.

If you have no Plan B, people will be too busy arguing that you can't skip straight to Plan C to naysay it.

The Iroquois had a saying, 'Plan B is we let you run first.'

Two words - Caitlyn Jenner.

271. Unsuccessful Fast Foods & Snacks

Pizza Latrine

Bugger King

Cinnabong

Whites Castle

Turkish Prison Delight

Penis Brittle

KKKFC

Mr. Subhuman

Manchu Trough

Contraceptive Sponge Toffee

Bloodtrail Mix

Bubblegumdisease

S'morgues

Scummy Bears

272. Protocol For Trump/ Un Summits

Don't call it a receiving line. Trump hears 'receding', and the world sees how he is about his hair.

There is no way to fake knowing the words of Hymn To The Glorious Benevolent Supreme Leader's Gracious Wondrousness.

Ignore Trump's insistence that it's merely good etiquette to let him try executing someone too.

When discussing television, it's best to avoid M*A*S*H, as Trump didn't understand it.

Open with the story of how you won the election, and close with it, and tell it in the middle.

To break the ice, share jokes about the freedom of the press to beg for mercy.

Do not permit spouses to compare notes on whose husband is fatter and more despotic.

It's insensitive to use starving waiters for swizzlesticks.

Build trust by agreeing that it's perfectly normal to have raging trouser tents for siblings and/or offspring.

Don't hand out Rogue Nation bathrobes.

At the bargaining table, avoid tweeting 'SAD!'

Focus on the upsides of starvation, such as no Trump Grill.

Ensure that the teams of aides chasing their magnificent leaders around with small desks and lamps don't crash into each other.

The harder hair gets the higher chair.

Try not to initiate a global thermonuclear extinction event over whose suit fits worse.

No matter how much she begs, do not permit Melania to defect.

In toasts, minimize use of the phrase 'sea of fire'.

Do not refuse food on the grounds that you've already eaten this month.

Don't accept offers of pug snacks.

When the epiphany strikes, don't blurt that you both look like pufferfish with hair.

Okay, fine, perhaps just some stray hors d'oeuvres.

Be polite. Allow time for others to brag about you too.

If you can't finish your meal, it's perfectly acceptable to ask, unironically, for a doggy bag.

Suggest, don't insist, that the floor cleaners be shot if your tie gets dirty.

273. Facts About Moose

A moose can carry hundreds of times its weight in air.

Aboriginal peoples used moose for hatracks and wives.

Owing to an all-lichen diet, moosemeat is technically a vegetable.

Cows have four stomachs, but moose have countless spleens.

In ancient times, hunters would use a hollowed-out moose as a primitive submarine for hunting aquatic creatures such as other hunters in hollowed-out moose.

Technically, a goose is a downy moose.

Moose can't tapdance. Don't be ridiculous.

Moose communicate using Morse Code by bashing their antlers together but, since it's in Finnish, nobody has the slightest idea what they're saying.

Moose semen is nature's most potent breath freshener.

Nineteenth president Rutherford B. Hayes kept a pet moose at the White House. It is for this reason that he is oft referred to as that crazy bastard with the moose.

The word moose comes from the ancient sanskrit muuse meaning vastly flatulent.

The young of the moose are known as chinchillas.

Their diet consists chiefly of veal.

There is less difference than you think between a moose and a yoyo.

274. Rookie Submariner Mistakes

Referring to the gunner crew as torpedophiles.

Forgetting to take the lens cap off the periscope.

Expecting to get a laugh saying, 'This place is a dive! Dive!'

Reversing into an iceberg.

Wearing tapshoes during radio silence.

Cracking the window in your cabin for fresh air.

Complaining the food is sub-par.

Breaking the tension of stalking the enemy with an epic drum solo.

Announcing that you have to take a leak.

Steering all conversation onto the weather.

Seldom surfacing from your beer.

In silent running, scurrying about on tiptoe loudly hissing at everyone to shush.

Complaining incessantly about the poor cellphone signal.

Walking around only in swim shorts and flip-flops with a towel on your shoulders.

Using someone else's bunk to stow your fishing gear.

Confusing the captain's quarters and the head.

Making lewd jokes about gangplanks.

275. Snowman Dating Tips

If she gives you the cold shoulder, it's a good sign.

Don't make her boobs bigger while she sleeps.

Lie when she asks if those big white balls make her ass look fat.

Don't get the colour of her eyes wrong. It's easy to remember. They're coal colour.

Don't make a big deal about her frigidity.

Compliment her on the crispness of her nose.

A stroll on the beach is romantic but lethal.

If you offer her a cold one, make sure she's very clear about what you mean.

Wanna drive her wild? Little frostbites on her (no) neck.

Don't pack extra snow around your crotch to impress her, it never works.

Taxis are expensive. Take Ubrr.

If some thug with a hairdryer jumps you, let him roll you.

A gentleman never takes advantage when a lady gets slushy.

No girl fails to be impressed by industrial-strength a/c.

Be interested, ask questions, but don't grill her.

Avoid self-repair with yellow snow.

Tell her she's pretty, not hot.

Three little words: Netflix and windchill.

276. Yet More Unpopular Baby Names

Luftwaffe

Mortis

Arachned

Stevenndiagram

Pustule

Thrombosis

Blasphemy

Nostrilla

Tedius

Botulynn

Syria

Gonadam

Hip-Hope

Academia

Hades

Dominatrixi

Slimon

Haggis

Phlegmbert

Dementia

Hemophilia

Yoko

277. How To Stay Cheerful
On Death Row

Start a rousing round of Four Hundred Billion Bottles Of Beer.

Journal about your future plans.

Tutor newly-arrived inmates on their convulsing technique.

Plan a hilarious 'Sorry, wrong number' prank in case the governor calls.

Enjoy the compliment of being referred to as appealing.

Whistle while you wither.

Make lovely commemorative programs as keepsakes of the big day.

Renew your subscription to Outdoor Life.

Write Green Mile fan-fiction with an alternate ending where magic unicorns whisk the poor, misjudged inmates away and the guards have to fry each other.

Masturbate furiously on laundry day.

Write a fan letter to Trump and he'll pardon you.

Name your cool hand Luke.

Develop multiple personalities and insist they have a legal right to be killed separately.

Dig a tunnel of love.

278. Movies About Sudbury

Singin' In The Acid Rain

Back To The Past

On Molten Pond

Loathe Actually

It's A Wonderful Life Anywhere Else

One Shade Of Grey

The Beer Hunter

Some Like It Sulphurous

You Got Jail

Here For Eternity

A Beautiful Mine

High At Noon

The Incest Bride

As Bad As It Gets

Pretty Ugly Woman

279. Clues Your New Roommate Is A Cannibal

Hangs around crash scenes with a fully-loaded spicerack.

Installs a six-foot microwave.

Keeps filling the tub with chopped veggies and stock before you get in.

A few too many framed photos of Jeffrey Dahmer in his room.

Compliments you daily on how succulent you look.

Has a What Would Hannibal Do? bumper sticker but looks at you blankly when you mention anything about elephants, Alps or the A-Team.

His skull beer mugs look disconcertingly authentic.

Is visibly disappointed when his Hawaiian Pizza is just ham and pineapple.

Orders barbecue sauce in oil drums.

When shopping for a new freezer, makes you get in to see how roomy it is.

Switches your shampoo for a blend of soya sauce and balsamic vinegar.

When you stub your toe, passionately argues for amputation.

When you're looking at the tank to select the lobster you want, he's looking at the other diners.

Has no stereo but twenty types of tenderizer.

You slowly notice the absence of those noisy kids that used to play in the hall.

You quit barbecuing since he kept trying to push you onto the grill.

280. If Dogs Ran The World

Mailmen added to the terrorist watch list.

Cancer research curtailed as funds diverted to fight the scourge of mange.

Every meal thoughtfully served in a garbagecan, drinks in a toilet bowl.

Frasier renamed The Eddie Show.

Koreans, in cages, marinating.

Hydrants, hydrants everywhere, as far as the nose can sniff.

Makers of sex dolls go bankrupt, artificial leg sales soar.

Shade unknown as trees razed to deny squirrels safe harbour.

Constitutional amendment enshrines absolute right of dogs to be up on the couch.

Leash laws repealed, collars grim exhibits in a slavery museum.

#FetchThis movement goes viral.

Public holidays each week for rolling around in something stinky.

281. Facts About Comets

The ancient Egyptians believed that, if you see more than one comet in a single night, you're a liar.

A comet hitting the Earth would be an extinction event, unless it struck the White House, in which case the planet would be saved.

Some comets are so small they could fit in your pocket, which would hurt like fuck.

If you look directly at a comet, it will damage your eyes, but only if you simultaneously sandblast your face.

Copernicus theorized that comets were merely atmospheric refractions of sunspots, but then he also postulated that it was best to be drunk all the time, so...

Nobody is impressed by a sun-dried tomato anymore, but serve comet-dried and you'll thrill your hipster friends.

Meteors and comets are identical except that comets have their tails in front.

Comet detergent sells much better than when it was called Space Grime.

They say Halley's comet crosses Earth's path only once every sevety-five years, but actually it just hides behind the moon most of that time.

Bill Hailey claimed until his death that he was the one who wrote Great Balls Of Fire.

Comet watchers were understandably viewed as nerds in school by the girl watchers.

The only thing that streaks by faster than a comet is the weekend.

Santa actually has many reindeer called Comet because as soon as they're off the sleigh, they bugger off across the galaxy and don't come back for seventy-five years.

282. Failed Sports Illustrated Special Editions Other Than Swimsuit

Railroad Transients' Hostage Edition

Acute Gastric Distress Edition

Ewes & You Carnal Barnyard Secrets Edition

Kim Jong Un Potatofaced Maniac Edition

Deep Inside Christopher Walken Edition

Premature Betty White Memorial Edition

Skin Grafts That Didn't Take Edition

Fungal Lymphatic System Vietnamese Polecat Porn Edition

Rip Your Head Off For Breathing Eggshell-Walking Menopause Edition

Indecent Exposure Central Park Edition

Crones Of Salem Exhumation Edition

Piers Morgan Lycra Bicycle Shorts Pray For Death Edition

Worrisome Bulbous Protrusion Edition

Your Mother Nattering All The Way There Edition

Deep Space Where No-One Can Hear You Scream Safe Haven From The Red Hot Chili Peppers Edition

283. What Annoys Stalkers

When Facebook recommends you as someone your victims may know.

Restraining orders that mandate maintaining a distance of two hundred yards when you were schooled in the metric system.

The objects of your affections are usually insufficiently grateful for a surprise breakfast in bed.

You cannot claim disability benefits for hearing loss caused by rape whistles.

You get no credit for being the first to post a Like on their media posts or shower curtain.

Somehow there's less joy in painstakingly locating a single pubic hair when you can buy a sack online for a buck.

A newspaper with eyeholes is WAY more conspicuous in real life than in old spy movies.

They think you're gay when you come out of the closet.

They invent new pepper sprays faster than a fella can built up a tolerance.

The lyrics to Every Breath You Take are lovely sentiments and in no way creepy as fuck.

No matter how skilled you are at hacking, you can still be defeated by a tiny piece of tape over a webcam.

When trees go bare in autumn, you are easily spotted in your camo pants.

There is no longer the merest shock value in sending someone a pic of your junk.

Not vacuuming behind the couch is inconsiderate of those who have dust allergies.

It's sad that sweet nothings are so hard to hear one stall over.

No matter how peculiar what you do to yourself in the name of godly devotion, some jerk has already started a craze of it online just for fun.

You can legitimately claim to be seeing someone if you pull the fire alarm and there she is.

284. More Things We Tell Our Kids About How We Had It Rougher

Our allowance was a nickel a year and we had to put five cents on the mortgage.

Our parents didn't coddle us like wusses and darlings, they loved us through fear and revenge.

School trips were to the local prison lasting six to ten.

Our entertainment was studying with a funny hat on.

The only toys we had were those we'd carved from the bones of the siblings that died in threshing mishaps.

We knew the value of a dollar and the precise definition of elbow grease.

Our playground slides were blazing hotplates of third-degree burns, and we loved it, and our favourite toy was a stick to poke our eyes out with.

There was no masturbation, because our adolescent hands were cramped from twenty-hour days jackhammering granite for no readily apparent reason.

My father told me there are no free rides as he charged me ten bucks for a lift to gramma's funeral.

The house was slightly warmer if we learned to run in our sleep.

There were only two TV channels, and both of them were just a guy yelling at us to read more.

Before we could sit up unassisted we could hay the fields.

If we misbehaved we were beaten. If we then behaved well, we were walloped again for inconsistency.

You went to church every Sunday no matter what, as that wafer was your weekly meal.

Your word was your bond, and if anyone ever broke a promise, his house was torched and his pets skinned alive.

There was no gumball at the bottom of our ice cream, or ice cream, or fancy digestive systems.

If another kid punched you, you punched him back, you didn't go running to your mommy like a crybaby, 'cause mom really hated those, and she'd hurt you with a wooden spoon in ways that would give the Spanish Inquisition restless nights.

285. Pet Peeves Of Great White Sharks

That stupid movie should've given people a mortal terror of Richard Dreyfuss.

Pitiful seals who think the best defense is flapping.

Even though more people are killed each year by vegetables, there's no movie called Potatonado.

The Discovery Channel has one shark week and the rest of the year it's Hitlerama.

Sharkfin soup is infuriatingly delicious.

Take the kids to Sea World once and they keep them there forever.

Bigshot whales who think they're all that because they can sing and we're too cool to.

The acrid taste of surfboard.

The injustice of the fact that everything gets to evolve but us.

No matter how slowly and non-threateningly we approach people, we never get hugs.

Signs that say you can't feed the ducks when, after all, they ARE the food.

Peer pressure to immediately eat anyone who falls off a ship, even if you've only just finished a hearty meal of plane-crash victims.

The same old jokes about dorsal sex.

Other sharks that insist on putting 'great' in front of their names like great big copycats.

Those who think it's mean to call swimmers chum.

That slick clickety-click Flipper chick gets a flick and I get dickety-dick.

286. Excuses For Getting An Erection At A Funeral

It's what he would have wanted.

You haven't heard of mourning wood?

Misinterpreted laid to rest.

This is my creamation.

It's the lesser-known sixth stage of grief.

Back off, padre, you handle grief your way and I'll handle mine.

How was I to know which bones are offensive?

I'm trying to raise your spirits.

Vicariously stiff.

Vulnerable chicks dressed in black really do it for me.

You say dirge, I say turgid.

They go low, I go high.

You can't miss this.

287. Signs Your Kid Is Mentally Ill

As a baby, she changed her name to Lady Googoo.

Can't explain the blood in his water pistol.

Chases and bites the mailman, skins him and wears his hide to school.

Cries when you suggest visiting Legoland but is ecstatic at the prospect of dredging a swamp.

Takes his imaginary friend to the imaginary woods and kills him with an imaginary pipe, planting his imaginary head on an imaginary spike as a real warning to others.

Uses Lego bricks to construct a gallows to hang traitorous teddybears.

Hears voices in his head and in his bum.

His bath toys run largely to leeches.

All bedtime tales must be of Vlad The Impaler.

Rocks without a rocking chair.

Instead of horsey on daddy's knee, plays rabid boar.

His iPod holds only the entire oeuvre of Charles Manson tunes.

Says he doesn't understand why the teachers at his school are always sobbing.

So that his Christmas gifts will remain surprises, refuses to open them.

Spells out names in his alphabet soup and calls them his disciples.

The other children not only won't play with him, they dig moats around their houses with their bare hands.

Nuclear crimson furies over the fact that Froot Loops are neither loops nor, if you want to get technical about it, froot.

Uses Playdoh to make models of tapeworms and other parasites.

Will colour only outside the lines, beyond the book and past the city limits.

288. Pet Peeves Of Door-To-Door Salesmen

Having to flee those who frantically flushed their crack when you knocked.

Chatty old ladies who are keen to tell you everything else they won't buy.

The bitterl- dawning realization that all those adult movies about the famed Roadside Home For Wayward Nubile Nymphos might've been bullshit.

Those who are offended to be called Mister Man Or Missus of the house.

When they shout through the door that they don't want to talk about Jehovah.

When you irk the boss and get the anvil beat.

When the door is answered by Louis CK.

Unfounded rumours of Peruvian doorbell scorpions.

Repeated head injuries from plummeting Amazon drones.

Amish folks who want to trade your wares for some burlap and a lamb.

Trump fans who'll be sold nothing but a bill of goods.

Whiskey-craved cougars who do want to see what you have, but only in your pants.

289. Signs Your Personal Hygiene Needs Attention

More than one pandemic has been traced to your socks.

Mouthwash jumps back out of your mouth.

Folks put plastic bags on their phones when you call.

Tramps offer you change.

Wags at the car wash say too bad it isn't a convertible.

You're a role model to skunks.

You love how your job as a septic tank swabber makes you smell better.

Moths hurl after eating your clothes.

You don't wear boxers or briefs but barnacles.

You feel responsible for the threat of global wilting.

You fail to perceive the difference between quarantine and your life all along.

You find camel spit freshens your breath before a job interview.

Your shower curtain is mostly moss.

290. Why You Should Have A Support Combine Harvester

Scientists have determined that the calming effect of sedatives is negligible compared to a vigorous threshing of the sheaves.

It senses when you're down and will gently harvest your face.

It's a secure, cozy feeling when it settles on your feet at night.

Making the giant fluorescent Please Don't Touch, I'm Working vest will keep local tailors gainfully employed for months.

It's entitled to free admission to Disneyland, and you can make millions in compensation when they refuse to let it ride with you on Splash Mountain.

It may lead you out into traffic, but that's more of a problem for the traffic.

You get more public empathy if you breastfeed it.

Just to name it Harvey.

You get quite a few extra seats on airplanes.

Even in a crowded shopping mall, the paramedics will have no trouble locating the patient having a seizure near the food court being protected by a snarling combine harvester.

You welcome company to shreds.

For small apartment life, get a little lap combine harvester.

No fleas, and you get used to the weevils.

291. More Recurring Nightmares Of The Stars

Steven Segal: Sudden, remorseful self-awareness causes him to just stop it.

Dr. Phil: Oprah takes him up on his offer to wax her car to a high sheen daily with his bald pate in abject gratitude.

Barry Gibb: The testicle clamps come loose and fall out of his trouser leg during a live performance.

Kiefer Sutherland: Acting skills indistinguishable from an asthma attack.

Cher: Global warming kicks in, leading to extensive melting.

Leonardo di Caprio: Remembered only for Critters 3.

Meghan Markle: Boyfriend not a prince, just a ginger Nazi.

Tom Cruise: What if the Thetans aren't two feet tall as L. Ron promised?

Paulie Shore: Cat escapes the bag, fan mail all in his own handwriting.

Bill Cosby: No woman will ever again want to sleep with him. Or near him.

Oprah: Head grows freakishly, impossibly, even more massive, so that she topples over whenever she walks, cracks face.

Richard Simmons: Annoyed population of the earth rises up as one and slays him.

Jesus: Joseph real dad.

Godzilla: Outbreak of realisation that metaphors can't hurt you.

Simon Cowell: Shirts whose top four buttons are held closed by tungsten carbide bolts and military-spec Kevlar shackles.

Elon Musk: Sometimes things don't happen just because you have a weird name and say they're going to.

Keanu Reeves: A role that requires emotional range beyond that of a rice cake.

Has-Beens Everywhere Who Unexpectedly Had Resurgent Acting Careers: There never was a Quentin Tarantino.

292. Traditional Divorce Anniversary Gifts

Heavily-used pair of yapping-inlaws earplugs.

I Still Miss Your Sister t-shirt.

Leftover powerful fight-or-flight-suppressing pharmaceuticals that got me down the aisle.

Dick-Withering Shrew On Board wacky bumper sticker.

Your-Taste-In-Music-brand suppositories.

Viper stole.

Framed etchings of fantasies of the friends of yours I thought about during sex with you.

Bullet I dodged novelty broach.

Vial of the thick gray dust of my hopes and dreams.

Commemorative gilded ball-and-chain bolt cutters.

Fixed-in-down-position toiletseat bolts.

Hot bitter popcorn.

293. Moments In Life More Horrifying Than When Your Parachute Fails To Open

Turning up for your first day of work at the Democratic National Committee wearing a Make America Great Again cap with your Crooked Hillary tattoo visible because you forgot your pants.

The awkward silence in the bar as you realise that dwarf tossing actually means throwing them.

Your turn to be groped by Kevin Spacey comes around and your appointment falls right when the clocks go back in October.

When your explosive diarrhea strikes nasally on the first date.

The computer is already at the repair shop when it occurs to you that you didn't clear the browser history of the Rwandan necrokindergibbon blowtorch porn.

Accidentally leaving the lid of your scorpion tank open while taunting them for being trapped in a tank.

You're spray-painting obscenities on a car and you realise it's your own, and you're a cop.

The tests come back negative for tapeworms but positive for eels.

You're violently shrieking well-deserved abuse at Piers Morgan on TV when you notice it's not the TV but a mirror.

You're kissing your grandma goodnight and she won't let go.

You realise that the sexy cougar you've been making real progress with for the past hour is your Uncle Malcolm in drag.

You're a rock star, and you don't party, so you don't pass out and drown in your own vomit, but you have near-death experiences in others'.

Your recurring nightmare about being wed during sleep paralysis to a gang of Trumps in orange tighty-whities proves prophetic.

The exploratory surgery turns up a new route to the Indies.

Ants ruin your Treblinka picnic.

The prehumous ghost of Yoko sings in your shower.

294. How Scorpions Show Their Sensitive Side

Astonishingly eloquent poetry using little-known rhymes for 'neurotoxin'.

They purr, if by purr you mean lie in wait.

They sing like angels, at your funeral.

Scorpions are exceptional parents and hardly ever kill their own young, though they will gleefully slaughter loads of yours.

Ask a scorpion for help and he'll assist you without hesitation, particularly if what you need help with is being stung by a scorpion.

After fatally stinging you, they send a basket of muffins to your grieving family, with more scorpions hidden inside.

Scorpion mates hold tails during romantic strolls through your hair.

They refer to lobsters as their wet brothers from other mothers, and to curious housepets as corpses.

Some are deeply unpopular among their fellows, such as Pierce Morgan and famed scorpion music snot Sting.

Most of Shakespeare's sonnets are now believed to have been written about scorpions.

They wag their tails exactly like a dog doesn't.

Scorpions do more charity work than any other venomous, charity-worker-hating arachnid species.

The sting is really just a cry for help; your cry for help is totally legit.

They share 99% of the DNA of Yoko.

295. Seldom-Sent Greeting Cards

I'm Sorry Your Shortcomings Make Me Sad

My Bad For Forgetting To Feed Your Dog Or Kid

Congratulations On Your Flabbergasting, Odds-Defying Engagement

Happy Housewarming, But Before You Warm It, You Might Want To Have It Fumigated

Way To Be Old As Fuck

My Bad For Amputating The Wrong Leg

Congrats On Being Less Of An Ass This Week

On The Occasion Of Your First Prison Assault

Props For Your Promotion To My Worst Mistake

Stop Yapping In The Name Of Human Mercy

Well Done Finally Getting That Gimpy Eye Seen To

Who Knew You Could Eat So Much Cheese?

You Made Manager! And Here We All Thought The Odds Were Against Your Even Making Bail

With Deepest Sympathy For The Ugliness Of Your New Arrival

Sorry For Dowsing You In Excrement

Best Wishes For A Speedy Recovery After I Dumped Your Ass On National Long Overdue Day

Get Unwell Soon, You Vile Sack O' Crap

It's April Fool's Day And I Miss You

Yay! No More Fleas!

Way To Make It Through Your End-Of-Rehab Party

Sad To Hear About Your Coma, Read This Later

Deepest Apologies For The Horrors To Come

296. Clues You're Obsessed With Your Phone

Any book longer than 140 characters is wordy.

Hookers are your second-favourite service provider.

If someone doesn't text you for 24 hours, you start the grieving process.

When you wake up, you reach for your phone before yourself.

You are in a Sirious relationship.

You can't remember where you live, but you know your IP address.

You evaluate music on how it would sound as a ringtone.

You once drove two hundred miles to retrieve your phone from the diner where you left it, figuring your pregnant wife whose water broke could fend for herself till the next bus.

You disconnected your brother's iron lung to plug in your charger.

You respect all cultures and faiths, but you'd stab an Android user in the throat as soon as look at him.

You try to clear your trouser history.

You attempt to enlarge photos in books by spreading them with your fingers.

You work tirelessly to ensure that your baby's first word is lol.

You'd rather have a larger screen than a bigger anything else.

You'd sooner refresh a page than the air you breathe.

Your blood pressure is inversely proportional to the number of bars.

Your children freeze in winter, but your phone has a shock-resistant, temperature-regulating, aviation-grade protective cover.

Your hand slips into your pants when a story about 5G comes on TV.

Your idea of dirty talk is, 'Whooooo's your data?'

297. What Hotdogs Are

Chaff content of sumo wrestlers' mawashis.

Congealed grunge-band runoff.

Calcified misery of a million ugly teenagers.

Past-prime gas bladders.

Dessicated skank.

Factory-reject value-brand discount Spam.

Fermented Larry King gum curds.

Leper windfalls.

Oprah hugehead dandruff porridge.

Ox nostrils and wienerdog-wiener roadrash.

Porn movie set jacuzzi surface crust.

Post-coital licorice panties.

Dental spit-sucking machine swirl.

Fat-farm aerobics-class spandex wringage.

Pureed love doll.

Milk curdled by exposure to ghost of Joan Rivers.

The pig parts even the French won't eat.

Unburnable residue from strippers' thong incinerators.

Week-old, fast-food-restaurant greasetrap McPutridity.

298. Dream Interpretations

If you dream of unscrewing your kneecaps and having them glazed and hollowed out and used for ashtrays, you should consider simply staying awake.

When chased in dreams, you always run in slow motion, which still enables you to escape in recurring nightmares of pursuit by elms and post offices.

Dogs dream of slurping away at their rectums, but if you have that dream, it's a sign you are perhaps too fond of dogs.

Dreams about dreaming are a surefire sign that you are best avoided at parties.

Dreams of being naked in public generally arise from indecent exposure convictions.

Flying dreams chiefly afflict those who were raised by starlings.

Dreams about sex are perfectly normal; dreams of fellating an infinite queue of baboons, applauded by nuns and your Great Aunt Imogen perhaps not so much.

Dreams that you were molested by Cosby usually turn out not to be.

If you dream Yoko can sing, you're Yoko.

It's important to discuss your dreams, just not with me.

You will stop dreaming of sex with your boss if his snoring wakes you.

Daydreams are exclusively about bacon.

Everyone dreams of Danny DeVito as the goat overlord of the underworld. Right? That's common?

Don't worry about dreams in which you murder loved ones. The government's dream-monitoring satellites are effective only about 80% of the time.

If you appear in your own dream as an animal, then that animal is your spirit guide and will be your constant companion for all time, but if you appear in an animal's dream, then you are its spirit human and can look forward to picking up its dream poop for eternity.

In dreams, we frequently solve problems that elude us in a waking state, which is why six-hour naps are such a boon to workplace productivity.

Dreams about water indicate either latent hostility to your mother stemming from the moment you achieved self-awareness in the womb and were overcome with terror at being forced into a cruel world and an uncertain future or you have to pee.

Lucid dreaming is the same as regular dreaming but way the Christ more scary.

Dances With Wolves was Kevin Costner's favourite wet dream.

299. More Dubious Statistics

The human body is more than 60% water. The rest is Pringles, and bugs that fly in while we sleep.

Seventy percent of adults know that the capital of the USA is Washington D.C., though that falls to five percent if the sample is limited to Americans.

Something helpful does get accomplished at two percent of one seventy-fourth of staff meetings.

The process for converting an image to JPEG format makes people at least four times more attractive, except in the case of passport photos, in which complex government facial mutation software makes everyone look like a sleep-deprived swamp troll.

Modern mathematical models can now show in quantum terms that your wife's work stories, viewed algorithmically, do indeed 'bend back' on themselves outside the space-time continuum as we know it, expanding at once virtually to infinity yet still somehow always 'ending' where they started.

The quality of a movie is inversely proportional to the number of helicopters in it unless it's Apocalypse Now.

Since ten percent of humans are gay, odds are, to a guy in line behind you at the bank, you're the one who got away.

The concept of Absolute Zero is a notional construct of the theoretical likelihood of that waitress at Olive Garden that you believe thinks you're mysterious going out with you.

If your road rage takes the form of remarks that the offending driver 'got his license in a box of Crackerjacks', you are older than ninety-nine percent of the population.

Having the latest iPhone makes you 0.00001% more attractive to 0.000000003% of women, though you'll think it basically makes you Thor.

The volume of pizza available is always 40% less than the volume of pizza that you want, though the reverse is true ten times for salad.

When you order a grande, iced, sugar-free vanilla latte with caramel drizzle and soy milk at Starbucks, there is a one hundred percent chance you're a douchebag and nil chance you know it.

300. Clues The President Is Amish

Frequent stops to let the motorcade graze.

Replaces button with nuclear hook-and-eye.

Believes that the deficit can be reduced by boosting candle production.

Campaigns on a platform of pine.

First Lady's only duty is making soup for Congress.

Flea market watched more closely than the stock market.

Has no time for Big Oil, but supports Big Molasses.

Potluck summits.

Only permissible party fundraising is selling corn by the roadside.

Peacekeeping runs more to beekeeping.

Presidential bunker stores apples and oats for winter.

Refuses to meet Muslim women on account of how they flaunt themselves.

Secret Service fiercely protective hens.

The hardest part of choosing his cabinet is deciding what varnish to use.

Travels on Ground Force One.

Presidential seal too showy, replaced with executive shawl.

Visiting dignitaries hosted at Barn David.

White House staffers' duties mostly quilting.

War Room has actual hawks.

301. More Bad Life Lessons For Your Kids

Share, especially needles.

Add 'sponging off society' to the Skills section of your resume and double the eyelid piercings.

If you continue to masturbate with the zeal and fervor you now exhibit, you will perish long before graduation. Put all that passion into algebra.

Women will break your heart, but not all. Some will also crush your soul. For sport. They're witches.

Don't blow folks in alleys for inferior crack.

Take time to spend time with others. Not us.

Hitch your wagon to a star, but let's face it, you're not gonna be a world-beater in a wagon.

Stay in school for an ungodly long time to get a job you can toil at miserably forever until your soul shrivels and dies, and eat well.

In troubled times, keep a stiff upper lip. People will pity you for having Bell's Palsy and be nice.

Keep an open mind, but not so wide that joining a Honduran death cult seems shrewd.

Remember, you're the less fortunate child that other parents use to make their kids appreciate what they have.

No matter how little is in the tank when you borrow it, bring the car back full, and same with my stash.

You've got good genes, just not sure whose.

302. What Makes Santa's Elves Snap

Another year of being paid in Christmas spirit instead of money.

All meals in the North Pole canteen are candy-cane-flavoured.

Pitiful digitless shift bosses who are gonna tell YOU how to run a Barbie lathe.

Referring to the eggnog cooler as the elfcum dispenser.

Touching documentaries about child sweatshop labour that should be titled Oh, But Fuck Elves, Is That It?

Those creepy lying Pinocchio puppets who claim you gave 'em the Spacey.

The epic drunken annual rip-roaring Caligulan debauch that erupts the instant Santa leaves never has non-narwhal hookers.

Boozy demands from Mrs. Claus to help with the mistletoe.

When Santa pushes for increased productivity so he can diversify into the Eid, Hanukkah and Diwali markets.

Snowflake snowmen always turning the heat down.

We work our asses green all year. The man gets a hundred kilotonnes of cookies on his rounds, but can he be fat-arsed to bring some home for the staff? Nooo-ho-ho.

303. Best Ways To Crash A Party

Have the Queen drop you off.

Ask if your puppet can use the bathroom.

Offer to show everyone the shrunken head of Justin Bieber if they let you in. Any dried fruit will suffice.

Unicycle pyramid.

Burst in with an armful of pitchforks and declare that Kevin Spacey was seen in the neighbourhood.

Materialize through a gaping fissure in the space-time continuum and head for the hors d'oeuvres.

Hide in the cake and burst out with the stripper.

Ride in on a bear, carrying pizza.

Dress as a cowboy and claim to be part of a wandering troupe of Village People tribute performers.

Streak the party, but hang around for a drink.

Dress as Wally and congratulate everyone for finding you.

Weep uncontrollably and beg for asylum from the lame bash next door.

304. Most Memorable Things About Hitler's Wedding

Not one person chooses to speak now as everyone opts whole-heartedly to hold their peace.

No-one knew Goering could jump until the bouquet was tossed.

Oscar Schindler was in charge of the guest list and managed to invite ten thousand people.

You don't often see a black leather tuxedo.

The groom's frothily sentimental speech about the rape of the working class by the Zionist vermin was deeply touching.

The comical way that violinist was fed to the guard dogs.

Hardly any ranting during the vows.

How everyone laughed when Himmler got bunker confetti up his nose.

Mengele personally fused the tiny bride and groom on the cake and transplanted some extra legs.

Tinking glasses replaced by ominous murmuring.

The massive bow that was put on Poland.

It was so hilarious when the priest briefly pretended to be a rabbi before vanishing forever.

The wedding video by Leni Riefenstahl was epic, beautiful and featured more naked dudes than anyone remembered being there.

The bombs made the marching tunes skip.

The photog who snapped a smiling Furhrer shot was shot.

Little chocolates and cyanide capsules on the honeymoon pillows.

The ballroom was decorated for the reception with barrage balloons.

305. Navy Seals' Christmas Presents

A Hellfire missile painted like a candy cane

Joke bombs inscribed God Rest Ye Not So Merry, Motherfuckers

Matching Kevlar scarf and mittens

Popcorn strung gaily on the garroting wire

Swiss Army nutscracker

Wall calendar of scenic Guantanamo Bay

Artillery-cancelling earmuffs

Bodybag stocking

Chocolate bayonets

Confetti flashbangs

Dental records scarf

Eggnog-flavoured sodium thiopental

Human remains ugly sweater

Night-vision tree lights

306. Why Snow White Is A Bitch

Once free of her evil stepmother, to celebrate she started hitting the bong pretty hard and embraced a promiscuous lifestyle, earning her the nickname the High Ho.

Insisted the song be changed to Whistle While I Twerk.

It's only because Snow White had smashed every other mirror in the palace that the remaining one was frightened into proclaiming her the fairest, when in fact she had one eye so gimpy it gave her courtiers whiplash cringing.

She was more fond of huntsmen whose 'h' was another consonant.

Many hard-working squirrels and bluebirds found themselves unemployed when she realised she could save a fortune outsourcing housekeeping duties to less adorable forest creatures such as weasels, rats and cobras.

Given her awful, erection-shrivelling voice, Snow White is the real woodcutter of the tale.

Sensitively eschews the less politically-correct term dwarves in favour of little people, but always puts air quotes around 'people'.

Set Sleepy up with Cosby.

The dwarves had cool names like Axemaster, Thundercrotch and Lil Satyr before she came along.

Tells Grumpy he'd be Happy if he got better meds from Doc.

The Huntsman fails to kill Snow White, not out of mercy but because he loses the will to live due to her endless whining about the smell of the forest.

There were originally nineteen dwarves, but a dozen died from exhaustion trying to supply Snow White's appetite for truffles.

Being proclaimed The Fairest In The Land went straight to her head and she became an insufferable diva, ruling the forest with a despot's iron fist, inflicting floggings on the dwarves for such offenses as misspelling 'obsequious'.

Snow White consumed so many fairies, sprites, imps and trolls that most magical woodland folk relocated to the relative safety of gang-controlled Caracas.

Maintained a posse of underground circus backup dwarves Sleazy, Sketchy, Isis, Dealer, Mossy, Daddy and Vlad.

The Queen disguised herself when visiting Snow White on account of the machinegun nests.

First happening upon the bear's cottage, Snow White found barbecued Goldilocks just right before moving on to the dwarves.

307. Lesser-Known Sports Injuries

Tennis Spleen

Jockburst

Athlete's Face

Waterpolio

Curdling

Steeplechafes

Luge Rash

Shotpox

Pingpalm

Slipped Discus

Basketballs

Clubfootball

Synchronized Drowning

Badmintongue

Ebowling

Golf Bladder

Motorcrosseyes

Flu Jitsu

Sickboxing

308. Signs Your Blind Date Is An Alien

Exclaims she's so happy she feels like she's walking on sulphur.

Recoils violently when she sees you have only one scrotum.

Shows you a picture of her parents that has eleven people and a sort of mule in it.

When you ask what her lovely perfume is, she says Eau d'Olfactozoid Gammawaft.

When you stare at her iridescent sensor stalks, she shouts, "Down HERE, buddy!"

Whispers sweet frequencies in your ear.

Chokes with laughter when you say your Honda Civic is confined to sub-light speeds.

Compliments you by saying that your face reminds her of a quantum spatial anomaly.

Demolecularizes the waiter when he fails to put the dressing on the side.

Tips the valet with a five that has a picture of Tom Cruise on it.

Eats her chicken wings by dropping them into a pouch on her shoulder.

Her dirty talk is along the lines of, 'I suck like a black hole.'

Contentedly hums Yoko tunes.

Asks that you clarify which of the nine genders you are.

Likes to go walking hand-in-hand-in-hand-in-hand-in-hand.

Makes a scene at Pizza Hut when they refuse to do half pepperoni, half epiglottis.

Reassures you that her ex-boyfriend probably won't take you to a radioactive asteroid and nebularize you repeatedly in the balls.

Says her favourite music is vectorfield pulsar pop.

Claims you take her breath away, but makes air quotes at 'breath'.

Tries to pay the bill in Thralaxian Numericredits.

When you get her phone number, it's 75 digits long and some of them are symbols you don't recognize.

Wants you to meet her mother. Ship.

309. The Truth About Amazon

The only difference between Amazon and THE Amazon is that the former has more scorpions.

Amazon deliveries kill seven polar bears a day, not because of carbon emissions, but since Amazon drivers get paid in bear-bludgeoning hammers.

Your Prime membership entitles you to unlimited thoughts about how great Amazon is; all other thoughts are 99 cents each.

In truth, there's not much that needs to arrive within a day. A firetruck, perhaps.

Analysts predict that Amazon gift vouchers will be the de facto Earth currency within five years.

If an unusually large Prime box arrives at your home with what appears to be airholes cut into it, do not open it, as it's Kevin Spacey, gropery from whom is now included in your (ahem) membership.

The only organisation that the Mossad fears is Amazon Customer Services.

You can now order literally everything, including a gangland hit.

Sign up to new Amazon Lifespan and not only will you benefit from 10% off all orders, but your family won't have to worry about funeral expenses, as Amazon will retrieve your body, harvest your organs and send a tasteful gift card to your next of kin.

310. Things That Alarm Her Majesty

Corgi farts.

Running out of gin by teatime.

Fergie's sun-eclipsing camel toe.

God Save The Queen has always sounded so ominous. From what? It's never been clear. That song is so creepy.

Having to meet tacky dignitaries when you're exhausted from a Breaking Bad binge.

Pretending that monarchs of silly little made-up countries are just as good as genuine royalty.

Her picture on that gay Canadian money.

No advice convinces Harry that it is perhaps not the best PR to go to parties dressed as a Nazi.

Political correctness that prohibits the thrashing of servants even when they richly deserve it.

Prince Philip's relentless leering.

That the palace chef no longer makes Serf Surprise.

The appalling amateurism of ISIS beheadings.

Scars from sitting on the crown.

The capacity of the Scots to be uppity.

The torture of the tedious 'I was on a break' plotline.

The dearth of qualified wipers.

The extreme unfunniness of Zach Crackabagulengro.

The flimsiness of modern gussets.

The intense fury inspired by the mere sight of Helen Mirren.

The enduring popularity of Di The Slut.

The overwhelming urge to carve a bloody swath of carnage with the sword during knighthood ceremonies.

The startling similarity of Charles' ears to satellite dishes.

That weird-ass tan you get from wearing long white gloves all the time.

311. What Ducks Are Quacking About

Meghan Markle. Why should ducks be different?

How you can only get away with claiming your ugliest child is really a swan for a couple of months.

How bad ducks go to Hell, or Peking.

That stupid platypus and why they have to be associated with it when it frankly looks more like a Botoxed beaver than a duck.

Daisy, hell, yes, they would!

That's their way of lowing.

The embarrassment of getting it on with a hot chick only to find out she's a decoy.

The mirthlessness of the endless down-on-a-duck jokes.

Birds of prey don't get uncool games named after them. No-one plays Hawk-Hawk Goose.

If there are ducklings, why aren't there whippoorwillings?

The anti-fowl Hollywood conspiracy that prevented the finest movie of the Eighties from hatching a dozen sequels and left poor Howard T. Duck turning tricks on Wilshire Boulevard to pay the coop rent.

Sure they'll kill you, but those lead weights are freakin' delicious.

312. Childhood Traumas That Led To A Career In Banking

All toys were secured with little chains.

Since your friend returned your Mr. Potato Head just one day later than he said he would, you broke his nose with a pair of plastic feet.

You were discouraged from your ambition to be an insurance actuary on the ground that the family had no truck with daredevils.

You made your stuffed animals queue for cuddles and when they got to the front of the line, you poked them in the eye.

When you played house with your cousin, she always foreclosed on the mortgage and made you play Cardboard Box Under A Bridge for the rest of the day.

You were named your PIN number and thrashed daily with a balance sheet.

Withdrawal.

Bedtime stories off the books.

Your parents took half your allowance for letting you forage in the recycling bin.

You were taught that the most lofty dream to which the human spirit can aspire is assistant branch manager.

You were kept in a vault.

You would give even more candy to the kids with the most candy but take it from those who hardly had any.

Your father made you calculate the depreciation on the Lego bricks that you foolishly took out of the box and played with.

When you asked Santa for a less dreadful personality, all you got for Christmas was a briefcase and a not-too-bright tie.

Your mother quoted Gordon Gekko to you in the womb.

You were taught that the grandest badge of virility a man can display is a receding hairline and no chin, so that your lower lip IS your neck.

Your bedtime story was Guess How Much I Loan You.

The kids who were willing to play with you were given a boring calendar.

The only GI Joes you were allowed were mercenaries.

You were criticized by teachers for your low interest rate.

313. Banned Olympic Sports

400m Breast-And-Ass Stroke

Decatheterlon

Four-Man-And-Leopard Bobsled

Freestyle Queue

Grand Mal Discus Throwing

Guilt Tripping

Javelingus

Tax Evasion

Long Hump

No-Pantathlon

Parallel Gay Bars

Drunk Old Broad Jump

Purse Snatch

Smack Shooting

Spluge

Stolen Goods Fencing

Sumo Sprint

Synchronized Period Swimming

Tae Kwon Dozing

Undressage

Water Polio

314. Other Unpopular Margarine Brands Besides 'I Can't Believe It's Not Butter'

Butter As If

Not-Quite-Rancid Gullibility Mucus

Not At All Butter But Not A Solid Or A Gas So Okay, Why Not?

The Resemblance Of This To Butter Is So Passing That It Might As Well Be Called 'I Can Totally Buy That This Is Creosote'

This Is So Unbutterlike I've Developed Serious Trust Issues

The Butteresque Spread For People Who Loathe Themselves Even More Than Margarine

If This Is Butter Something Has Gone Horribly, Horribly Wrong

So Greasy It Won't Even Stick To The Bread

Petrochemical Pride

My Perception Of Butteriness Is So Skewed That This Has The Potential To Be Butter, I Suppose, Though I Don't Specifically Recall, In My Experience With Butter, The Sensation Of My Tongue Dissolving

Easily Weaponisable Toast Lubricant

Non-Dairy, Flavour-Neutral, Semi-Permeable Lipido-Joy

Emulsify This!

The Fact Is That This Could Very Well Be Butter. Anything Is Possible These Days. But The Magic Can't Happen Unless You Believe. So Just Believe, Okay? Look, I Have A Family To Feed. Not With This, Obviously, But Help A Brother Out, Will Ya?

Don't Proclaim Your Beliefs On A Condiment

Butter My Ass

315. Romantic Lines From Passive-Aggressive Love Letters

The day I met you is seared in my memory.

I yearn to see your body.

The moment I see you each morning, I get a jolt of adrenaline.

You are the eagle of love to the salmon of my destiny.

I love you to little woodchipper bits.

All of my previous disastrous relationships served only to prepare me for you.

Do you know how much I love you? Is the cat out of the bag?

I'll lay the world at your feet, and yes, yes, then I'll pick it up.

My love for you is stronger than any flight impulse.

No matter what you might have valid reason to think, you're beautiful.

Our meeting was titanic fate.

To compare you to a rose would be an insult.

You make me want to be a better whatever the hell you want me to be.

You make the birds sing. And migrate.

You play the strings of my heart like Whack-A-Mole.

You were made for me, they said.

316. Little-Known Laws Of Physics

A body at rest should be buried before it reeks.

The wave theory of light is the best hypothesis modern science has devised to explain the enigmatic phenomenon of Trump's hair, just as the notion of Absolute Zero is the measure of the literacy of his tweets.

Two atoms of equal size and density collide with a sound that is of no interest to anyone.

The hertz measures sound frequency. The Red Hot Chili Peppers' sound frequently hurts.

The only constant is change, so that could change.

Acceleration is how fast you eat celery.

Theoretically, if you could stare directly into a black hole, you would be looking through a space-time portal into the vast, lightless expanse of your ex-wife's heart.

Any fast-moving object, no matter how large, can be rendered harmless by smashing it into thousands of tiny pieces that will fall on you like angel kisses.

The shortest distance between two points is a job at the White House.

Topper's Third Law Of Nadular Impact Conservation states that the kinetic energy of any projectile making contact with the testes is instantaneously transformed into expletive sonic energy.

The nucleus of an atom is composed of empty space and tiny shards of AOL disks from the 1990s.

317. Things Overhead At A Red Hot Chili Peppers Concert

I wonder how they play in such similar keys.

Surely this is a hate crime.

They're just as good live.

You know how time flies when you're having fun? What's it called when it moves backward five or six eons?

Bugger. Ten seconds in and I've already flung all the rancid tomatoes I brought.

Spontaneous human combustion isn't a myth, right? It does happen. RIGHT?

Leo Fender really should have listened to his mother and become a pigpen polisher.

Flea misspelled it.

Excuse me while, for a more enjoyable experience, I mosh on my face.

If you waterboard me, I'll waterboard you.

After I beat cancer, I saw each moment of life as precious, but I was younger then, and foolish.

I would've preferred actual scalpers.

I wish they'd califinish.

I wonder what the music lovers are doing tonight.

I knew it was a bad sign when Yoko opened.

318. Changes Now That The Boy Scouts Admit Girls

Dwindling popularity of spitting and farting contests during wilderness retreats.

Outhouses pristine and smell of lavender.

Males now spending less time in tents playing with own wieners and more time fetching items for female Scouts.

Camping trips confined exclusively to areas free of bugs, snakes, bears, dirt and trees.

Life-saving skills practiced only up to point where rescuers' hair might get wet.

Less emphasis on navigation skills and more on asking for directions.

The hopscotch badge is new, and only one gender will get beaten up for having it.

Kayaking now mostly yakking, skipping stones just skipping, roughing it now fluffing it.

Campfire songs feature much more Katy Perry.

Piles of Ugg boots at Scouts events visible from space.

Scavenger hunts now just to gather ingredients for potpourri.

Statue of Baden-Powell to be replaced by a randomly-selected Kardashian.

Troop camaraderie now restricted to individual bitterly feuding cabins.

Now both main varieties of child molester are drawn to leadership roles in the organisation.

319. Facts About The Japanese

After national disasters, thousands queue up politely waiting their turn to loot in an orderly fashion.

In the wake of Fukushima, the bedside lamp industry has failed, as most now read by the cheery glow of their testicles.

The Earth's oceans have yet to spawn a creature that the Japanese won't gleefully consume with just a splash of vinegar and soya sauce.

There is no smoking in public, but masturbating furiously on the subway to loli hentai is mandatory.

In kindergarten, it is considered courteous to work yourself to death.

In restaurants, rather than a basket of bread, you are served a bucket of snakes.

Sushi is for tourists - the classic Japanese diet is mostly potatoes and deep-fried cheese.

Kamikaze is the Japanese word for, 'Those fools didn't add enough fuel!'

The Yakuza started as a jazz dance ensemble that became homicidally enraged while waiting for their big break.

Japanese KFC outlets serve their chicken live and are wildly popular.

Tokyo Disney slaughters more Komodo dragons than any other family theme park.

Japanese people are actually quite tall, but they don't look it because they are very far away.

Only Japanese men can pleasure Japanese women on account of their seventy-six additional erogenous zones.

Burping after a meal signals to your host that the food was good. Hurling means you never had better.

The Japanese feel that the River Kwai looked nicer without a bridge.

320. Yet More Unmotivational Sayings

You can't always get what you want, unless what you want is ceaseless disappointment.

I find that the harder I work, the more luck I seem to have finding victims.

If you don't have anything nice to say, you've probably met me before.

Knowing is not enough; we must apply. Wishing is not enough; we must be delusional.

The grass is always greener on the side where the dogs pee most.

All good things must make you fat or poor.

It's no use crying over spilled milk, it's dropped cocaine that's truly heartbreaking.

Hope for the best and pretend to be surprised when the worst inevitably happens anyway.

Don't bite the hand that feeds you, go for the legs. More meat, and it stops them escaping.

If you can't beat them, join them, earn their trust and slaughter them as they sleep.

Take the road less travelled and you'll find out why.

You miss 100% of the shots you don't take at Zack Gofloganoctopus.

If you do what you always did, you will get what you always got, syphilis.

People who live in glass houses should not do naked squat thrusts during daylight hours.

Keep your friends close and your enemy's loved ones as human shields.

Every dark cloud has a silver lining, except for those supercell storm clouds that spawn tornadoes that wipe out trailer parks, inflicting untold misery on thousands of helpless innocents.

No-one can make you feel inferior without your consent, unless you're a git.

The starting point of all achievement is desire, especially if you desire to achieve a wank.

321. The Dark Side Of Aromatherapy

Most aromas are at least one part crotch sweat.

Big Aroma continues to keep secret the wonder smell that causes immediate and permanent penile gigantism.

There are more than two thousand varieties of hibiscus essential oil but only one kind of hibiscus palsy.

Those in the sewage industry marinate free.

Unscrupulous aromatherapists will just chew a car air freshener and breathe it on you.

The Wet Dog Method is no longer considered good science, nor the Frying Eel Technique.

When two competing aromatherapists meet, they squirt each other with lavender until one of them dies.

Citrus scents promote calm, well-being and vivid hallucinations of chasing your grandparents with a whisk.

You will find yourself most emphatically unwelcome if you request the happy ending aroma treatment.

Healthcare cuts mean aromatherapy is now the approved treatment for a skull fracture.

When they say, 'Okay, all done', they're saying 'dung', and to them that will never get old.

You have to pay extra if you have an unusually large nose.

322. Sexy Things CIA Agents Say To Flirt

Wanna be my handler?

Welcome to Homegland Security.

I'd double-tap that.

I'm here to be debriefed.

I'll give you rug burn notice.

I always maintain situational awareness of your cleavage.

I wanna infiltrate your dark site.

Those are some sweet assets.

I do wet work.

Let's go undercover.

Get a load of this extraordinary rendition.

I'd like to introduce you to a very special agent.

Have you seen The Bourne Turgidity?

I'm not in Virginia anymore.

Everyone will want oversight of this congress.

323. Clues Your House Is Infested By Cows

Inexplicable mooing when the postman knocks.

Never any hay left in the cupboard.

A search of the internet reveals no hooved termites.

No matter how hard you try, you cannot get the bed sheets to lie flat.

Odd proliferation of shower towels marked Clarabelle.

You keep finding your leather jacket in the trash.

The heaps of crap on the rug are larger than the dog can manage.

Fridge overflowing with milk, though you haven't bought any in weeks.

IKEA troughs mysteriously assembled overnight.

You can't squeeze even one more thing into the closet.

Marginal increase in how much your spouse complains about your smell.

Pamphlets extolling the benefits of vegetarianism mysteriously slide beneath your bedroom door.

Medication appears in your bathroom cabinet for 'stomachsaches'.

Endless stream of cowboys and rustlers peering through your window.

You can never find your favourite castratin' shears.

You have to start ordering cud in bulk.

Your browser history runs to stampedophilia.

Pile of the carpet chewed down to less than a millimetre.

You catch mad cow disease from your own pillow.

Can't hear the doorbell for the bells.

In the morning, the couch sags.

Suddenly there's a separate curd fridge.

You wake sweaty from nightmares of electric fences.

Dozens of extra flip-flops in the hallway, always in sets of four.

324. How The French See The World

There are two kinds of people, those with a lick of sense and those who dislike runny cheese.

Inexplicably, the name Frenchmen and women all say they most call out during sex is Gerard Depardieu.

Sophistication is defined by one's ability to smoke nonchalantly while sneering.

The only inedible part of livestock is the barn.

They see the world through the eyes of the brilliant French thinkers and philosophers throughout their history, encapsulated in their motto, 'C'est la vie' or, 'That's life', which tested better than 'What can you do?' and, 'Aw, screw it.'

Wine, wine everywhere, and nary a drop not to drink at breakfast.

The world is a complex geo-political network of shifting power structures and military/industrial forces best surrendered to at once.

If it's on your property, it's food.

No greater, sexier, more spectacular human has ever existed than Charles de Gaulle.

They regard the smell rumour as a bigoted stereotype spread by ugly foreigners.

Humanity is a sea of diners and patrons heaped upon whom no amount of contempt could ever be enough.

They are rightly proud of the richness and grandeur of French culture that has enriched the world, despite their bizarre worship of Jerry Lewis as the One True God.

No human can possibly have a breakfast-time hunger so great that it cannot be satisfied by a flaky pastry and a thimble of hot chocolate.

There is nothing a beret does not go with, including a massive head wound.

If you have a stressful, high-pressure job, it might be acceptable to shorten your lunch to three hours.

A rain shower will suffice.

The French language is beautiful in every way and the volume of phlegm required to pronounce it only heightens its allure.

If you think you've added too much butter and cream to a recipe, you haven't.

Ugly fat chicks make the best subjects for paintings.

325. Items In Bill Gates' Yard Sale

Old mansions that got dusty.

Sweat-stained DOS Makes Me Horny t-shirt.

Stack of thousand-dollar bills that his time was too valuable to stoop and pick up.

Faberge eggs the kids failed to find at Easter.

The stuffed carcass of Steve Jobs in an unspeakable position.

A sprawling fifty-ring circus featuring, in tutus on unicycles, all the chicks who wouldn't date him in high school.

Pile of old Apple products with the best ideas removed.

Wyoming.

The plane that flies him to the bathroom.

The grieving next-of-kin of executed barbers.

Diamond-encrusted diamonds.

Worn-out iPad-smashing mallet.

The shrieking, squawking, couch-sized hulk of the first modum.

A solid gold copy of Who's A Dummy Now?

The original horizon of his livingroom.

The floppy discs that gave him ED.

326. Terrible Band Mergers

Barenaked Men At Work

Crash Test Cannibals

Cranberries Jam

Pink Sabbath

R.E.M. Speedwagon

Rage Against The Police

The Jackson Dave Clark Five

AeroSmiths

Manic Street Pixies

The Queen Kinks

Yes U2

Cheap Beach Boys

Depeche Floyd

The Red Hot Mamas And The Papas

The Allman Brothers Clash

Def Soundgarden

Dead Byrds

Martha And The Van Halens

Megadeth Vanilli

327. Tips To Manage Stage Fright

Repeat positive affirmations in your mind, such as, 'Kill me, Jesus.'

Have a small sip of wine to calm your nerves. And twelve of tequila.

Remember that the audience wants to like you, or to watch as your soul is crushed in an epic toe-curling crash-and-burn of catastrophic proportions.

It's natural to be nervous, but squelching onto stage in trousers saturated with urine is just a tad too natural for most audiences.

Even pros get nervous. And they are way better than you.

Realize that only very rarely does a crowd rise up as one and slay a presenter, ripping him limb from limb in a grisly frenzy of gore.

Think, what's the worst that could happen? Living in a box under a bridge, covered in your own filth, being slowly devoured by mice?

Start with a joke. Your qualifications, for instance.

Relax by mentally counting backward from twenty, or picturing a peaceful place, or mainlining opioids.

Think of the great, heaping stacks of money to be made by those far more charismatic than you.

Use puppets. Not in your performances, but use them.

Tell yourself that you're actually helping people, but don't fall for it.

It's helpful to recharge one's batteries by taking a much-needed break once your presentation starts.

Lead them in a prayer that you'll be fine. When their eyes are closed, make a break for it.

328. More Reasons To Move To Tuvalu

Pandas shag morning, noon and night, so there are baby ones everywhere.

You tend not to sweat the small stuff much, given the daily free leprechaun concerts in the parks and the cropdusters spraying cotton candy.

They always, ALWAYS bring you enough ketchup.

The only Pepsi available is Crystal, and likewise meth.

Spiders have no legs. Or bodies. Or heads.

The KFC branches also sell fish and chips.

You may play the Red Hot Chili Peppers only in flooded mines, in other countries.

Free repairmen are on call 24/7 to fix the wine plumbing.

Fresh flowers sprout from your nostrils while shaving.

If you're nice to everyone, you're blown by enchanted faeries.

Pumpkins grow with eyes and mouths already handily cut into them and a lit candle inside.

The national motto is Tra-La-La.

Though banned themselves, hipsters are required to stand at the border like reverse Walmart greeters and shoo away the similarly insufferable.

Mobile signal is a consistent twelve bars, except in caves and bunkers, where it drops to eleven.

329. Seldom-Used Units
Of Measurement

X-rating: the amount of time in quarter-billionths of a nanosecond between sending an SMS to your boss and realising you put kisses on it.

Spaceytime Continuum: the nearly imperceptible interval between the loss of your personal inviolability and meeting Kevin.

Stressibel: the discomfort level of Yoko sound above audible.

Waltribrunal: the size in dozens of lawyers of the legal team assigned to litigate against a kindergarten that hands out Winnie The Pooh colouring sheets to orphans without the express written permission of Disney.

Dinstant: the fleeting picomoment of hope at the start of a new Red Hot Chili Peppers release that this time it might be good.

Babenami: the number of pretty girls that flirt with you relentlessly within seconds of changing your Facebook status to 'in a relationship'; the Inverse Babenami is the number that don't when you switch back to single.

Underslice: the difference between the amount of pizza you have and the amount you require.

Tentdrain: the volume of blood diverted from your brain to your cheeks when you get a boner during a root canal.

Dentbaffle: the volume of inexplicable plaque on your teeth despite how often you claim to floss.

Infernometer: the ever-diminishing distance between Hell and managerial types who pepper their corporospeak with terms like 'moving forward' and 'bottomline'.

Eterniticktock: a measure of staff-meeting time.

Loveloss: the spiralling rate of decay of how attractive you find romantic partners through increased exposure to their intolerable personality.

Microfraction: the snack-to-air ratio in an alleged bag of potato chips.

Tim-lapse: the photographic shutter speed needed to view movement of the line at a Horton's.

Peeco-acre-ounce: the area over which your dog can spread a small volume of urine.

Epochalypse: the length of time it takes your wife to tell you about some social calamity.

Extorhalation: the volume of air inhaled by a back-street mechanic as he calculates a price that is seven or eight hundred percent of the actual cost of fixing your alternator.

Calorfactor: the number of times more delicious an item of food becomes as the calorie content is doubled.

330. Signs The Mayor Has A God Complex

Pledges to deliver us from deficit.

All 'fact-finding missions' are to a compound in the woods.

Ruins the weekly farmers' market by flipping over the tables and banishing the vendors.

Proclaims that the city shall have no other mayor but him.

Insists that all construction projects be completed in six days with a seventh to rest.

Press releases are on stone tablets.

Changes city ordinances to commandments.

In winter, attempts to part the snow.

When asked directions, says He is the way.

Most of the agenda of working lunches consists of saying grace.

Kills hundreds of jobs in the graven-image industry.

Annoys the press by referring to them as locusts.

Describes rain showers as a warning shot.

Takes on staffs' sins at the City Hall Christmas Party.

His ceremonial mace is in the shape of a lightning bolt.

Is forever pointing out successes he has 'wrought'.

331. How To Know You're Boring

Your wildest sexual fantasy is two women. One to keep the other awake.

Sloths develop cheetah-like turns of speed when you approach.

Folks block your number, fling their phone in the lake and, as an added precaution, follow it.

Belgians make jokes about you.

The police employ you as a hostage negotiator to teach a course called Surrender Through Monotony. The longest protracted stand-off you've seen is six minutes.

Those who talk to you and then watch golf die of the comparative excitement.

Your accountant and insurance broker alibi each other to avoid lunch with you.

The guy at the hardware store suggests you'd probably prefer something less 'in your face' when you try to buy beige paint.

Dogs hump the air rather than your leg.

Your nickname is The Ghastly Death Of The Party.

The publisher edits your autobiography to read simply 'Zzzzzzz'.

Highly-paid anaesthesiologists put a hit out on you.

The speaking clock killed itself during your call.

Your online profile includes as Interests droning, repeating yourself and sapping everyone's will to live.

Pillow talk is exclusively with your pillow.

You learn sign language to communicate with the deaf, who beg you not to bother.

The only Latin word you know is tedium.

When you count sheep to fall asleep, they leap off a cliff.

The lethal combination of you talking and the music of John Tesh is banned by the Geneva Convention.

332. If Days Were 36 Hours Long

Extended Directors' Cuts would be the default versions of movies - DVD extras would be raw footage of the crew building the set.

More time available to appreciate the richness and magic of life on hold with tech support.

Fewer days marred by accidental momentary exposure to rap on the car radio before shattering index finger changing stations.

More of the weekend to devote to dreading Monday.

Greater opportunity for old people to explain in detail what a young person's 'problem is'.

Extra minutes to loathe Piers Morgan with the finely-honed intensity that comes only with practice.

The Standing In Line At Starbucks slice of the daily activity piechart would be slightly less depressingly wide.

Online compilations of the best of Lithuanian sprained-ankle public-park cat-o-nine-tails auto-asphyxia porn gratifyingly expanded.

Kevin Spacey could grope less frenziedly to achieve his daily quota.

More Trump tweets per news cycle means the apocalypse is hastened, and nowadays that fact breeds the contentment we used to enjoy.

More narrative depth to your wife's tales of the harpy in Sales & Marketing who thinks she's all that and is thus toxifying the work environment.

Free Bird by The Allman Brothers now playable in its entirety in a mere day and a half.

More daily prayer time that Will Ferrell will get funny.

Competing social media platforms race to be the first to offer 36/7 live footage of actual paint drying.

Awkward one-night stands so excruciatingly long hookups replaced with monopoly tournaments.

333. How To Dump An Astronaut

"I need more space."

"You've got the wrong stuff."

"All systems are go."

"Dear John Glenn ..."

"I know you try in bed, but please, less Milky Way and more Emission Control."

"We just no longer move in the same orbits."

"Not even Hubble can see this working out."

"After the first stage comes ejection, you know that."

"You just don't understand a woman's g-forces."

"It's one small step for man onto a shuttle to anywhere the hell away from me."

"You're a pain in my asteroid."

"This docking port is no longer available for your vessel."

"You used to make me feel weightless, but now my life's a black hole."

"The only thing visible from space is your ass."

"It can never work. You're Apollo and I'm more Soyuz."

"When I said I loved you to the moon and back, I didn't mean literally."

"Your booster is simply inadequate for the payload."

334. Bad Wine Reviews

Had I crawled on my face across the searing sands of the Sahara and a single sip of this affront to the human palate was all that stood between me and dying of thirst, I hope I'd be mourned.

Round, full-bodied and oozing with regret.

If loathing were distilled into liquid form, this surprising Cabernet Sauvignon would have the potency of a thousand ex-wives.

Not only would this ode to bad taste never again pass my lips, I wouldn't breathe the air into which a thimble of it had evaporated.

I tried to force it on a wino at gunpoint, but he threw rocks to drive me away.

Never before has a simple fluid been more deserving of its own section in the Criminal Code.

As a wine connoisseur of more than five decades' experience, I was prompted by this sparkling abomination to pursue a career in exotic mime.

Ideal with fish, this robust medium dry white has an undernote of rotten haddock.

A roundhouse kick to the palette with all the subtlety of a dumpster fire into which the corpses of many fetid skunks have been thrown.

A sassy little upstart bouquet, busy but never precocious, marginally less robust than cistern seepage.

This noxious concoction has all the appeal of congealed toxic sea urchin with the aftertaste of a Croatian weightlifter's jockstrap.

With warm notes of elderberry and juniper, this wine still manages to flay the flesh from my throat more thoroughly than a pint of rusty razor blades.

After the first alarming swirl on my tongue, I couldn't reach for the glass again fast enough, to dash it against the wall.

My mouth leaped away from this vile slop in instinctive self-defense, so that I fell backward from my chair, striking my head a mighty blow on the floor, occasioning brain-stem trauma such that the only speech of which I am now capable is the reflexive epithet YUCK!

Serve at room temperature, if it's Room 101.

This wine would benefit from being allowed to mature for a millennia or two or, at the very least, until an hour after my time on Earth has ended.

335. Celebrities' Sexual Peccadilloes

Keanu Reeves' repertoire of sexy talk has expanded to an impressive six words, only two of which are 'matrix'.

Kevin Spacey has yet to encounter literally anything, living or inanimate, that cannot be groped with frenzied gusto, from cheese graters to culverts to blast furnaces.

Paris Hilton actually has an entirely different facial expression during sex, if by different one means the same.

Hillary can only get close.

So aroused was Danny De Vito by the notion of a pregnant Arnold Schwarzenegger that he was filmed for Junior exclusively from the neck up.

Yoko cannot perform if there is music.

A certain Commander In Chief can function only if told that his hands are gargantuan.

Cate Blanchett's sexual technique is so aggressive that she drains the very life essence from her partners, an act which arouses her still further.

Hef is now into auto-necrophilia.

Meryl Streep's roleplay in bed involves so many characters it's basically an orgy.

Judge Judy gets off on denying your every motion.

It requires two hours of lurking in bushes before Dustin Hoffman is ready to commence foreplay, which typically involves a further two hours of lurking in bushes.

Osama Bin Laden was in a state of near-perpetual arousal thanks to the satin Stars And Stripes assless boxer shorts he wore secretly beneath his robes.

The Pope needs to hear you confess. Slowly.

336. Unimpressive Native American Names

Drinks Like A Bulgarian

Knows When To Use Apostrophes

Likes Big Butts And Cannot Lie

Scowly Fucker

Seated In The Back Of The Plain

Too Much Petting Coyotes

Actually Celebrates Columbus Day

Bleeds Out Easily

Breathes Like Darth Vader

Cheats At Archery

Dances With Dances With Wolves

Makes Wonky Teepees

No Taste In Moccasins

Understood Donnie Darko

Won't Shut Up About Brando

Creepy Near Bison

337. Little-Known Laws

In most major cities, it is forbidden to cause a disturbance by continuously blowing your horn or goat.

In Dublin it is illegal to gesture disparagingly with a potato.

If you try to hijack a plane, an air marshall can take your peanuts.

Authorities can't force you to remain safely in your homes forever, but they can issue alerts that Kevin Spacey's whereabouts cannot be accounted for, so that panic at this time is advised.

You face a fine of five bucks for being ugly in North Carolina.

It is not illegal to perform Puppetry Of The Penis in public for a valid artistic purpose, to pay a bet or debt, on a drunken dare from your buddies or in a spirit of majesty and wonderment and braggadocio.

It's unlawful to hang around the monkey cages day after day at the zoo, praying they'll fling poop.

Residents of the Dakota in Manhattan have again been granted the annual Christmas restraining order that prohibits Yoko carolling in the building.

Courts have rejected the argument of a driver accused of fleeing police that he wasn't 'leading' anyone on a high-speed chase, the damn cops just kept following him at high speed. The judge sentenced the defendant to a term of seven years' dry buggery in penitentiary night and day, citing the tried-and-true Nice Try Pal Doctrine.

338. Sudbury Tourist Attractions

Chlamydia Boulevard

The Moderately-Sized, Slightly-Ass-Shaped Rock

The Standard-Sized Dime

Sure Would Forest

The Rubble Telescope

The Colossal Potholes Of Roads

Beer Hound's Leap

The Taj Mall

The Offal Tower

Viagra Falls

Museum Of Bitumen

The Hanging Gardens Of Gravel Lawn

Land Fill O' Lakes

The Grand Mal Canyon

The Great Pyramid Schemes

Machu Peepshow

Yellowsnow National Parking Lot

Big Bend

339. Most Mortifying Ways To Die

Choke on the umbrella in a virgin cocktail.

Ambushed by a unicycle gang.

Fracture skull despite being the only one in the Barbra Streisand moshpit.

Bleed out from penile Slinky lacerations.

Accidentally switch pacemaker to samba.

Insist your parachute be made of anvils.

Trampled to death by Smurfs.

Paper aeroplane crash.

Expire from a broken heart at the outcome of America's Next Top Model.

Hack out own heart to impress Meghan Markle.

Boner snapped off in Barbie Dreamhouse.

Overdose of diarrhea pills.

Go lion-tipping.

Contract the vapors.

Grisly scrapbooking mishap.

Murdered for attending Star Wars convention dressed as Sulu.

Good Friday caroling.

Total brain atrophy caused by three Adam Sandler movies back to back.

Overdose on hemorrhoid opioids.

340. Worst Excuses For Standing Up A Date

Hooker stole my pants.

Unexpectedly ran out of fucks.

Concluded that life is a gaping abyss of despair and torment and hopelessness and flung myself down a well.

Huge Depends malfunction.

Flowers were more expensive than anticipated, couldn't afford bus fare.

Got in brawl with the other personalities, rassled self to ground, broke clavicle.

Couldn't find a shirt to match my electronic ankle bracelet.

Was sure Angelina would call and didn't want to miss it. She didn't, but she will.

Was re-alphabetizing my Beanie Babies and lost track of time.

I was there but I'm invisible so you ignored me.

Couldn't wait, invented time machine, accidentally went back to before date was made.

Jumped for joy in gleeful anticipation, hit head on ceiling, bled out, had near-death experience, blinded by bright light at end of tunnel, stupid guide dog got me lost.

Mom threw jealous hissy fit, won't let me go.

My conjoined twin thinks you're a bitch.

Penis enlarger didn't come.

Realised subscription to SlutFest.com is cheaper.

Restless Leg Syndrome walked me out of the country.

Reviewed your online profile and decided to give homosexuality very serious consideration.

Too chafed by masturbating to the sight of your number in the phone book.

Was growing my hair.

Worried about date going wrong, debilitated by attack of Pre-TSD.

You seem like a Monica and I'm a Ross and that's just gross.

341. Things That Make
You A Monster

Standing in line for an epoch at a fastfood place and only when you get to the counter perusing the menu thoughtfully and thoroughly until global warming has time to pass the tipping point.

Singing along at a concert in the apparent belief that your performance is vastly more talented and popular than the entertainer folks paid big bucks to hear, absorbing hate rays that will eventually kill you as surely as a delayed-fatal kung-fu vibrating palm strike.

Fully reclining your seat on a plane and then requesting additional pillows to prop yourself upright.

Proclaiming that you 'work hard and play hard'.

When a woman bends down to pick something up, saying, 'While you're down there...'

Writing a cheque, at the variety store, for Twinkies, after a lengthy search for a pen.

Standing in a clueless clot of people at the bottom of an escalator despite not being Chinese.

Crocs.

Donating canned goods to the local food bank but peeling the labels off first.

Eating a box of caramels immediately before visiting the dentist.

Under any conversational circumstances whatsoever, believing that it is called for to deploy the phrase 'at the end of the day'.

Installing a 5000-watt stereo system to play Barry Manilow.

Offering to craft a balloon animal for a child and making a snake.

Supporting Trump on the ground that he's 'shaking things up'.

Saying you're some band or politician 'nation'.

Standing behind the rope line at live golf and imploring the ball to comply with your exhortations.

Ordering a triple cheeseburger with extra bacon, fries, onion rings, a sundae and a diet Coke.

342. Unedited Famous Quotes

Ask not what your country can do for you, ask what you can do for your country now that your first idea of helping was to vote for that asshole Trump.

We choose to go to the moon in this decade and do the other things not because they are easy, but because they are supercool and chicks dig astronauts.

A horse, a horse, my kingdom for someone to tell me what the chess pieces are really called.

The great strength of the totalitarian state is that it forces those who fear it to adopt the same haircut.

Fourscore and seven years ago, you started one of your work stories.

The only true wisdom is in knowing you know nothing about my secret stash of Venezuelan pole-vault ebola porn.

I came, I saw, I conquered, I had a wank, a nap and then another wank.

I shall return this screwed-up bookcase to IKEA.

Life is what happens to you while you're busy trying to remember your online banking password.

Don't cry because it's over, cry because it's your fault.

Dance like nobody's watching because that's some embarrassing shit.

We have nothing to fear but fear itself, and spiders.

Blessed are the meek, for they're easy to roll.

I took the path less traveled by, and now I'm lost and starving and stalked by coyotes.

We shall fight on the beaches, we shall fight on the landing grounds, we shall fight in back alleys behind pubs, we shall fight in underground bareknuckle brawls, we shall bitchslap each other with reckless abandon, we shall never sober up.

Alas, poor Yorick, or Yanni or Laurel.

Those who believe in telekinetics, raise my hand. And don't stop there.

We are what we repeatedly do; excellence, then, is not an act but a habit, especially excellent meth.

343. Things Dogs Wish We Knew

The fact that you crap in the house sickens us.

Before dining, proper etiquette requires that you first hork it up.

If you'd just once try it, instead of being so weird, you'd be dragging your ass across the carpet all the time, too, we assure you.

You don't know true tranquility of spirit till you've rolled in a disemboweled hare.

We happen to know that chocolate isn't the least bit poisonous to us, you greedy, selfish bastards.

We may have to come when you call us, but you don't see us walking around with neatly-tied little bags of your poop, now, do ya, pal?

On the food chain, squirrels are essentially chattering hors d'oeuvres.

Give us no credit, laugh all you want, but if we didn't bark our heads off, you'd have been slaughtered long ago by noises.

You're humble to deny it, but your leg is sexier than you think.

There's no dignity in eating from a bowl on the floor, only in loudly slurping one's sphincter when the vicar comes to tea.

If we could learn to speak only four words, they would be, 'You fetch it, dude.'

Don't talk down to us when you're so dumb you can't even see ghosts.

We're don't get why you throw out your very best stuff, like sticks.

344. Proof Trump Is A 'Stable Genius'

The Oval Office is referred to as The Egg Room.

He can't remember the name of his Florida estate, but thankfully, when mumbled, everything sounds like Mar-A-Lago.

The Situation Room has been renamed the We Got It, Don't Worry About It Room.

Keeps asking Pence if his term's up.

Seethes with bitterness that Obama gets credit for being the first black president when he's the first orange one.

Can't find his way to the Map Room.

There's a sign hanging from the door of Marine One that reads Jump Up.

The briefing notes for his meetings with Angele Merkel have the words 'Do not grab by pussy' at the beginning and end of each paragraph and a diagram on the front cover.

He calls the device with which teams of artisans do his hair a 'towel' without the 'r'.

He's more comfortable reading briefing materials if, tweet-like, random words are capitalized.

When Melania approaches, aides whisper, 'Wife.' If it's Ivanka, they hiss, 'No!'

He'll only answer the phone that has wheels and a face.

Keeps calling the cops to say he's being followed by men with wires in their ears.

The challenging nuclear codes have been replaced with a sequence of Looney Tunes characters.

The main reason for the high turnover of staff is that he forgets who works there and has security toss them out.

Refers to Putin as Val (demort).

His tighty-whities been labelled 'Mr. President' as a gentle reminder each morning.

Writes 'Republican' on the back of his hand each morning.

The Beast was nicknamed The Donnymobile so he wasn't too frightened to get in.

345. Budgeting Tips

Gas prices are high. Simply push your car everywhere and tell folks it broke down.

You need toilet paper or underwear, but both is hedonism.

Strategically start relationship-ruining fights just ahead of gift-giving occasions.

When blasting off your ears for fear of unwitting exposure to the Red Hot Chili Peppers and the crippling cost of the resultant lifelong anti-anxiety medications, use the acetylene welding torch to fasten your glasses to your face while you're at it, as they'll slip down the sides now.

Avoid a costly funeral by dying in a sinkhole.

Call the moss on your shower curtain Spanish and folks'll think you're stylish.

Lay your own eggs. It's cheaper, and you'll get paid an appearance fee on TV.

Consolidate multiple loan and credit-card payments into a single monthly thrashing.

No need for window washers if you move to a monsoon country.

Set up a trap line. Bait it with kale for hipsters. Steal their fannypacks and sell them at douche lawn sales.

It costs a fortune to raise children, what with college, clothes and three meals a week, so have a wank instead.

Seagulls know where to go for snacks. Befriend them.

Avoid donating your hard-earned money to charity by being oblivious to the suffering of others.

Dental treatment is expensive, but dentures are cheap. Do the math, let 'em rot.

346. Alternative Theories To Evolution

When they heard that Darwin was coming, all the most fucked-up-looking finches moved to the Galapagos.

Humans ceased walking on all fours when they tired of being taken roughly from behind by lemurs.

While Africa is the cradle of human civilisation, it was the colder northern climes that were the cradle of pants.

It took eons to grow a second one, but the thinking was that we were going to need another leg to live up to our reputation as bipeds.

Human nostrils were once much larger, enabling our ancestors to breathe more freely when fleeing prey and to act every bit as well as Kiefer Sutherland.

We first crawled from the sea onto land seeking not locomotion but a Starbucks.

Humans developed opposable thumbs out of sheer frustration owing to their inability to hitchhike.

Our brains grew in size as a result of the pressure to be better than chimps at sudoku.

Genetics explains everything except why so few parents slay their awful children.

The species, for the most part, also lost, along with a tail, a unibrow of muskrat bushiness, except for Brooke Shields, who has not evolved.

It never really caught on, but you still gotta love the prehensile dick.

Our first survival strategy was playing dead, which was dumb when we could've just strolled away from killer sloths.

We lost our shells in primitive rigged shell games.

Human males took to hunting and gathering when the females discovered the power of bitching and nagging.

Two minutes after the first human walked erect, a second one pushed him into a well. It was another forty thousand years till someone else gave it a go.

Verbal communication developed so that humans wouldn't die from their inability to express the agony of stubbing their hairy toes on the first failed square wheels.

Between the Stone Age and the Bronze Age, there was a brief, but ultimately unsuccessful, flirtation with Taffeta.

347. Signs You're Not Cut Out To Be A Hell's Angel

Your idea of a good time is less drunken brawl, more Dirty Dancing and yoghurt-covered raisins.

You insist it's troupe, not gang.

You consider your fighting style jazz-tap.

You spent your share of the last heist on mistletoe.

You throw around the silent treatment when no-one wants to play Frisbee.

You wake screaming from dreams of ladybugs.

You much prefer lilacs to leather.

You feel the need to apologise whenever you slit someone's throat.

The only tattoo you're willing to get is Hello Kitty.

You spent two days scouring eBay for training wheels to fit a Softail Deluxe.

You throw hissyfits when someone skips the daily road-safety briefings.

At night you sneak around changing Hell to Heck on the jackets.

You sulk when they don't put a little umbrella in your boilermaker.

You skip an actual stomp for the musical.

You steer all clubhouse conversation off marauding and back onto lawn bowling.

What makes you mean is when Beyoncé doesn't answer your fan mail.

You are late to home invasions when your tarot readings go long.

While the others were casing a bank, you were staking out a red-crested wren.

Your favourite part of a crime spree is the community service sentence.

348. Complaints Of Inflatable Sex Doll Sellers

Frantic phone calls from customers who get stuck in the inflation nozzle.

Those who toss them out once they get full.

Those slut-shaming crash-test dummies.

Even at a hundred percent discount, it's impossible to move the Angela Lansburys, but the Angela Merkels fly off the shelves.

Having to explain that no, lower cost notwithstanding, a dead hooker would not at all be the same thing.

Japanese businessmen trying to return theirs because they got too old.

Trying to laugh convincingly every time a customer makes the joke about unwanted inflatable pregnancies.

Gripes of kinky porcupines.

Germans wanting discounts for bulk-shipment orgies.

Special orders from Santa to elfin specifications.

Poorly-translated instructions that read, 'Welcome friend! Enjoy many giddy joy love make with option of all pleasure crevice!'

Endless stream of customers asking for advice on treating friction burns and genital mildew.

Dunces who put the studded bras on backwards.

349. The Dark Side Of Butterflies

Most people who claim to be attacked by sharks were actually gored by butterflies but are too embarrassed to admit it.

Muhammad Ali's less elegant first draft of his iconic saying was, 'Bleed from the bladder, sting like a bee.'

Crumbled and sprinkled on ice cream, butterflies taste like crap.

Caterpillars don't turn into butterflies, scorpions do and the chrysalis stage really pisses them off.

They look pretty, sure. But don't get between a grizzly butterfly and her cubs.

Butterflies can smell fear in more than seventy languages.

Make any joke with 'butt' in it and see what happens to you.

A staggering eighty-four percent of extinct species fell prey to butterflies.

I Can't Believe It's Not Butter was originally called I Can't Believe I'm Eating Butterfly Cum.

Butterflies mate by sodomizing you in your sleep.

The only purpose of a dreamcatcher is the slim chance that a butterfly might get caught in it, giving you a few precious seconds to escape.

Butterfly nets don't work. You need a butterfly Hellfire Apache helicopter.

If you counted every butterfly on the planet and calculated their combined weight, you'd clearly have too much time on your hands.

On the dark net, the most popular depravity is wingless butterfly suppository porn.

The best way to stop a butterfly attack is just to die.

When a butterfly flits through your window, it's either casing your apartment or checking out your girlfriend.

They soar higher than any eagle, to give the prairie dogs a chance.

The surest way to perish is by fly-by butterfly shooting.

350. Why The Grim Reaper Was Only Ever Invited To One School Dance

Dance partners couldn't escape his cold embrace, and he told the others, 'You're next.'

Urgent need for Tic-Tacs.

His idea of humour was, 'Pull my long, bony finger.'

The goth kids kept crowding around for autographs.

When they played Stairway To Heaven, he said, 'Not necessarily!' and laughed for an eerily long time.

Wore a scowl all night, and a cowl.

Couldn't be seen in any selfies.

Kept getting paged and rushing to the nursing home across the street.

When asked the time, would say only, 'It's later than you think.'

Browbeat the DJ into playing only dirges.

The lonely kids lining the walls were even more lifeless than usual, and still there the next day.

Encouraged everyone to smoke while muttering something about job security.

Says he likes when the school throes a party.

Argued with the security guard at the metal detector about his razorsharp 'crutch'.

Worn out by dancing, suggested they rest in peace.

Filled the ashtrays with dust.

351. How The Wild West Was Tamer Than We Thought

The mythic showdown at high noon was more of a bedtime puppet show.

Steers are self-herding, thus their name, so the cowboys used to mostly just let them graze, while the cowpokes excitedly watched.

Far more were felled by fierce pollen allergies than gun battles.

A house of ill repute was one that didn't comply with building regulations.

When snake-oil salesmen came to town, they also brought olive oil, balsamic vinegar and a wide variety of other fine salad dressings.

It was a hard life in the Old West, made slightly less difficult by the availability of inexpensive chamomile tea and scented candles.

The Gold Rush was known then as The Gold Take Your Time And Wait Your Turn.

The OK Corral was right next to the much more notorious Fine Ferns And Penelope's Pretty Good Pies.

If you tried to order whiskey in a saloon, they gave you milk and teased you good-naturedly about your little white moustache.

You mostly got up a Parcheesi posse.

Outlaws cried so loud about their saddle sores you couldn't hear the whorehouse band.

They tamed the wilderness mainly by plucking the daisies.

Frontier homesteads were kept tidy by woodland creatures singing future Disney tunes.

Every town had a peach cobbler.

'Pardner' was short for 'Pardon, may I pet your wiener dog?'

Gambling was betting your rivals would surely do well.

Spittoons were to collect glass, metal and other recyclables.

If a fella took your horse, you challenged him to a quick drawing-up of contracts for legally-binding arbitration.

The staple diet on a cattle drive was beans, black coffee and brie.

The ten-gallon hat got its name from its built-in hydration system for maintaining electrolytes on long rides.

Cowboys and Indians actually got along really well, as both were pestered non-stop by Hare Krishnas.

352. The Most Fun You Can Have In Antarctica

Go clubbing with seals.

Make a realistic snowman by attaching a carrot nose, coal eyes and your own frozen penis that snapped off in the night when you rolled over in bed.

Pray for the springtime balm of a polar vortex.

Frolic nude in dreams of narwhals.

Enjoy an ice-cold beer, soup, burrito or core.

Drill holes in a snowball and bowl it at penguins.

Sing Ebony And Ivory while counting your black and white toes.

Develop profound appreciation of your tiny hut by spending an instant outside it.

Spend months training an albatross to help you recreate that Monty Python sketch and still not find it funny.

Harness the intelligence of killer whales by dressing seals up as chess pieces and trying to get a game going.

Drift off to sleep on the wings of a prayer that this time you won't wake up.

Hold a fun Easter hunt for your fingertips.

Pen a fifteen-volume academic thesis on just how much you fucking hate snow.

Plan to write the world's first all-penguin recipe book, but then try penguin.

Grow a beard, shave it off, repeat ad infinitum.

Netflix and windchill with your walrus girlfriend.

Realize that keeping a stiff upper lip looks brave only when it's not frozen stiff.

Self-harm with the razor shards of your bitter tears.

Edit Chapter 62 of Ways Cold Burns.

Tell those fool Finns to abandon the picnic.

Pee the last rites in the snow.

353. Cherished Childhood Memories Of Donald Trump Jr.

The first time he was allowed to evict some poor people himself instead of just watching from the limo.

How warm and wanted he always felt hugging the locked door of Daddy's office.

When he was too little to shoot yet, killing his first elephant with a hand grenade.

Suing everyone who wouldn't eat lunch with him.

The day he learned that terrified employees are just friends that always want to play whatever game you like.

Perusing Eastern European Vogue to find new mommies.

Instructing the maids to polish his golden potty.

Daily visits to Uncle Yuri at the embassy.

Showing Dad how to sound out the hard words in The Fat Cat In The Hat.

Being voted the school's Sneery Sociopathic Little Fuck Most Likely To Succeed.

Playing with his Gunny The Gun stuffed toy from that nice man at the NRA.

Holding Eric while the old man beat him up.

Feeling proud to remember all the porn stars' real AND stage names.

Getting an extra million in his allowance whenever he made the weak cry.

First in the family to learn how to finish sentences.

Entrusted with the secret of where Pop keeps his hair.

Collecting humourous postcards from shithole countries.

Studying the wall chart with Daddy of which skintones we hate (all but orange).

Convincing Eric the attic's the coolest place to live.

That time he saw a book.

Making Barbie and Ken do stuff to avoid their camper being repossessed.

Grabbing the girls by the pussy, bragging about it and then being elected student body president.

354. Facts About Chimneysweeps

They were originally called chimney-Qtips.

The biggest turnon for a chimneysweep is the line, 'Talk clean to me,' but most can't ejaculate unless they're being chomped by bats.

Chimneysweeps are quite happy to be referred to as potheads.

Retired chimneysweeps often find work cleaning the pipes of Russian oligarchs, and that's not a euphemism.

The French won't date clean freaks like chimneysweeps.

Apprentice chimneysweeps practice on barbecues.

'Shove a brush up it!' is a line that always kills at the Chimneysweeps Annual Convention.

It's a myth that the Victorians sent children up chimneys to clean them. In fact, sweeps of that period were employed to remove the children that often hid in chimneys to disturb homeowners' sleep with their dreadful nocturnal poetry.

Lameness is rife in the industry due to the crippling scourge of sootfoot.

Extreme chimneysweeping is cleaning a chimney while the fire is still burning, soaked in kerosene.

The most common nickname for a sweep is SwabBob Graypants.

There's a radical movement of Japanese chimneysweeps who believe that chimneys should be swept from the top down. Many believe this is a simply a way to generate business for cabals of illicit Yakuza fabric cleaners.

A group of chimneysweeps is an 'infestation'.

355. Signs You're Obsessed With Security

The locks on your doors are worth more than your house.

There's a panic cupboard in your panic room.

You refuse to wear any garment that isn't mostly Kevlar.

Your Scrabble repertoire consists almost exclusively of 'perimeter'.

You demand city officials show you on the books where it says you can't vaporize a squirrel.

Via self-hypnosis and deep focusing techniques, you have rerouted optical processes and neural pathways in the cortex such that your eyes now serve as highly sensitive motion detectors as you sleep.

After pawning your heirlooms to fund extensive home Weinsteinproofing, you sell a kidney to upgrade the counter-Spacey panelling.

Birds frolic carefree in your yard, safe in the knowledge that cats will flee the sniper fire from the guard towers, plus your attack dog's name is Bourne.

You routinely piss yourself struggling with the padlock on your fly.

You sleep on the lawn at least three times a week when you forget the fifty-digit security code.

Your canary can detect any wavelength on the gas spectrum, all known neurotoxins and whether someone is lying, and wouldn't sing under torture.

So impregnable is your house that the only way you'd know of nuclear Armageddon is if Christmas cards fail to arrive.

Your mailbox says There's No-One Here.

Your favourite joke is the Secret Service.

356. Proper Flasher Etiquette

'Ta-daaaa!' is probably superfluous.

Add a little glamour by the careful application of sparklers.

Don't manually prod those in line at the park fountain.

Use the correct fork to waggle your balls.

Doff your hat when flashing royalty.

Mind that your gentleman is dry before whirling him helicopter-style.

Sporting just a trenchcoat and a 'stache that won't clash, add a dash of panache to the flash with a sash.

A standing-room-only bus means something else.

Heed the old maxim that the proudest oft lack cause.

Help your victims preserve the precious moment for all eternity by presenting them with a charming caricature of their expression.

If you happen to get flashed yourself, compliment him on his technique but don't shake his hand.

357. How To Compensate When You Don't Have A Dog

With only years of intense yoga training, you'll be able to hump your own leg.

Throw a stick until you just can't be bothered to fetch it.

Refuse to take your heart medicine unless someone wraps it in a piece of cheese.

Wear yourself out chasing your own ass and fall asleep on a pile of shoes.

When people try to point out a dog on TV, gaze bewilderedly at their finger.

Arrive at work with your hair in a tangle since you drive with your head out the window.

Stare intently at your food and slobber till you give yourself some.

Put wheels on a fern and take it for a walk.

Whimper and run in your sleep.

Deprived of the live performances, you'll need to mail-order bestial auto-analingus DVDs from Malaysia.

Cause school-run chaos by leaping excitedly into the back of the car and waiting impatiently for one of the children to drive.

End your baths by bolting out and racing through the house panicking, shaking water everywhere.

Leap up on guests till they yell, 'Down! Get DOWN, damn it!'

Paw at your boss until she gives you a raise.

When you leave the house, head straight for the hydrants.

358. You Might Not Be Cut Out For Life As An International Playboy If...

What you play is mostly Pokémon Go.

Your idea of a threesome is all Back To The Future movies back-to-back.

You ask the Ferrari dealer if you can get one with wood panelling.

You think you're a lady-killer in your Scooby-Doo underoos.

You feel at home on international runways, driving the baggage cart.

Your tailor is Mr. Walter Mart.

When someone offers you a hit of coke, you ask for diet.

You're hugely disappointed when you find out your supermodel girlfriend can't even fly, let alone shoot lasers out her eyes.

The only hot club you want into is Mickey Mouse.

When you really want to impress a lady, you let her order the Taco Supreme.

Your private jet has a ballpit.

You complain incessantly that the casinos of St. Tropez and Monaco never offer high-stakes Yahtzee.

You have a diamond pinky ring. You won't say where.

You race horses, to the trough.

Miley Cyrus is always calling you. A stalker.

You bought a ball team. Hat.

359. Soap Operas That Never Made It Past The Pilot

Very Much Ado About Precious Little

Many Generations Of Doing Business Honestly

Valley Of Communicable Diseases

Mogadishu 40627

One Life To Live Over And Over Every Day Formulaically Forever

Random Occurrences Unrelated To Previous Plot Development Because, Like Many Of The Characters, The Writers Have Amnesia

Keeping Out Of Other Peoples' Business Avenue

A More Addictive Habit For Bored Housewives Home Alone On Opioids

Lake Tedious

Miami Beach Nuns

Aging Actresses Who Made Their Fortunes In The Non-Digital Era And Now Fear HDTV More Than The Death They Look Like

Monogamy Road

Well-Behaved Teen Town

STD Hospital

Little Whorehouse On The Prairie

The Brittle And The Bulbous

The Vapid And The Gassy

The Young And The Feckless

360. Best Excuses For Speeding

My speedometer is calibrated in parsecs per fortnight and I struggle with the conversion.

Saw the flashing lights, thought disco was back, panicked.

Sorry, I believed I was in a parallel dimension where you can drive as fast as you want and cops aren't jerks.

Had to do a meth speedball to counteract the whiskey so I wouldn't be driving drunk.

Speed is defined relative to time and what is time, really, other than a fallacious human construct to help us make sense of an infinite, impersonal universe?

Tried to outrun the Red Hot Chili Peppers song on the radio.

Upset up by getting canned for being too eager to give head to strangers in uniform.

After years of impotence, I achieved a spontaneous erection and raced to get home before Sharknado ends so I didn't waste it.

Wife's in labour and I'm trying to find her.

Car backfired, took it for a starter's pistol.

It's those Duke boys you really wanna go after. They're fixin' to bust Uncle Jesse outta jail for queerin' Boss Hogg's land deal with them slickers from the city.

Just saw the inspiring motivational film The Fast And The Furious.

Medication for Restless Accelerator Leg Syndrome wore off.

Engine was on fire and I was trying to blow it out.

Had to get to the crackhouse before it closes.

The airflow at 90 is the only way to cool this McDonald's apple pie.

Oh. Sure. Typical cop. You see a wealthy, young, white man driving erratically way over the limit in an insanely fast car and you jump to the conclusion that he's speeding.

361. Signs Your Toddler Will Be A Diva

Won't return to her room till someone around here learns proper dust-ruffle fluffing.

Launches gargantuan crimson furies when she spies an Unlucky Charm.

Marks the peasants' houses with a P.

Storms out of dinners when grace takes too long.

Favourite game is Shoo My Lackeys.

For Show And Tell, demonstrates her obvious breeding.

Will only let you bathe her good side.

Demands a second Barbie playhouse so the servants have somewhere to live.

Tries to trade Gran's seeing-eye dog for one that will fit in a purse.

You spent months trawling the Internet for a vendor of satin diapers.

Won't agree to a playdate with any kid that has fewer than a thousand followers.

Your reflexes are so honed from dodging juice boxes you can pluck flies from the air.

You find yourself working nine jobs so you can trade in the family stationwagon for a pink Rolls.

Refuses to leave her panic suite when Katy Perry and Moana fail to turn up at her birthday party.

Won't set foot off the school bus until the red carpet and receiving line are in place.

362. How To Be Fired As A Walmart Greeter

Lick your lips when giving directions to the incontinence products.

Adopt the greeting, 'Whatchu lookin' at?'

Demonstrate an incomplete grasp of your welcoming role as you drive away shoppers with rocks, singing self-laudatory folk songs about how, thanks to your intrepid heroics in the face of superior forces, the entrance held.

Ask shoppers for help with the cleanup in Aisle 40.

Thoughtfully suggest that the best way to relax while shopping is to drag their butts like dogs through the rug department.

Change your nametag to Bouncer.

Address men as Pffft and their wives as Holdmeback.

Welcome shoppers with a slap on the back so hearty their eyeballs shoot all the way to Linens.

Provide encouraging thumbs-up prostate exams.

Run a contest to see who can nail the most babes in Vitamins.

Start a little collection, in the trunk of your car, of the shrieking kids.

Wearing a Kevin Spacey mask, root about in their trousers with such unbridled abandon you take gold in the groping Olympics.

Ask if they're with the bride or the groom.

Tousle the hair of the little ones so vigorously you cause scalp wounds.

Hail each shopper in the offensive stereotypical accent their appearance might suggest.

Insist the Jehovah's Witnesses come on in.

Have them sign the 'Guestsheet', which is clearly your scrotum.

Frantically direct shoppers to other stores in other towns.

Add adventure to the greeting experience by dressing as a shelf of Pop Tarts and leaping out at customers with scalding jam.

363. Signs Your Kid Will Grow Up To Be A Proctologist

The dressup box contains nothing but latex gloves.

When he draws Winnie The Pooh and Tigger, they are always bent over a table.

Fails spelling tests but nails 'peristalsis'.

Neither staff nor kids want to see his hemorrhoid collection, so he's excused from Show And Tell.

He's not afraid of THAT dark.

When girls walk by, his friends think they misheard when he says, 'Look up the ass on THAT!'

Holds unusually strong views on lube for a preschooler.

Forever getting his arm stuck in a Slinky.

Refers to the garden hose as the colonic cleanse device.

Sobs when his diarrhea clears up.

Favourite toy is the Roto-Rooter.

Whilst the other children are playing fun games, going on adventures and making friends, yours is more entertained by sniffing his fingers.

Feels dogs have the best greeting protocol.

When he secretly hides tubes of KY, it is your most earnest hope that he's masturbating to hardcore pornography.

Feels the best part of Christmas is reaching into the stocking.

Within two blocks of your home, there is a much higher incidence of PTSD than the global average, and other than the one Iraq war veteran, it's all down to playing Doctor with your kid.

When you buy him a telescope for Christmas, he is visibly disappointed that it isn't the bendy kind with the light on the end.

Started by peering into antholes.

364. Disturbing Things About Cows

Cows consider making eye contact to be a sign of aggression, and failing to make eye contact.

Cows' greatest heartbreak is that, being hooved, they can't play the accordion.

The collective term for a group of cows is a bloodbath.

Cows kill more people than sharks; that is to say, each cow kills more people than all sharks.

The word 'hobo' is derived from 'hobovine', denoting strays who wander away from the herd.

They're so vicious because they're bitterly trying to live down the word coward.

A standard manhole cover can fit easily in each nostril.

Cowbells were originally invented so that farmers could determine in which trees their herd were hiding.

Cows not only damage the ozone layer with their farts, but, by striking their razor-sharp hooves together, can quickly become docile grass-powered flamethrowers.

Cows have four stomachs, one for digestion and three for airship aviation.

Savvy farmers have learned to keep feed costs down by giving cows access to a rich supplementary diet of lambs, dogwalkers and feral children.

The barn is the scene of nightly horny games of Truth Or Dairy.

When you're 'pasture prime', you're ready for slaughter.

The intestines of every cow alive, stretched end to end, would be really gross.

365. Unpopular Circus Acts

Puffin Tamer

The Human Rhombus

The Barnacled Lady

The World's Largest Pygmy

Siamese Twin Acrobats

Human Ballcannon

Wall Of Near-Certain Horrific Injury But Very Little Chance Of Actual Death

Low-Wire Act

Sedated Cheetahs Of The Serengeti

Chainsaw Swallowing

Sodden Sawdust Of Mystery

Enraged Lion Dunk Tank

Manufactured by Amazon.ca
Bolton, ON

13575323R00303